WILCOMB E. WASHBURN received his B.A. from Dartmouth College and his PhD. from Harvard University. He has taught at the College of William and Mary at Williamsburg and the American and George Washington Universities. Since 1965 he has been Chairman of the Department of American Studies at the Smithsonian Institution.

PUBLISHED FOR THE
Institute of Early American History and Culture
AT WILLIAMSBURG, VIRGINIA

SIR WILLIAM BERKELEY

From the portrait at Berkeley Castle by Sir Peter Lely

THE GOVERNOR
and
THE REBEL

❖❖❖

*A History of Bacon's Rebellion
in Virginia*

❖❖❖

by WILCOMB E. WASHBURN

W · W · NORTON & COMPANY
New York · London

Books That Live
The Norton imprint on a book means that in the publisher's
estimation it is a book not for a single season but for the years.
W. W. Norton & Company, Inc.

Library of Congress Cataloging in Publication Data

Washburn, Wilcomb E.
  The Governor and the rebel.

  (The Norton library)
  Includes bibliographical references.
  1. Bacon's Rebellion, 1676. I. Title.
  F229.W28   1972   975.5'02   72-4626
  ISBN 0-393-00645-X

W. W. Norton & Company, Inc., 500 Fifth Avenue, New York, NY 10110
W. W. Norton & Company Ltd, 10 Coptic Street, London WC1A 1PU

PRINTED IN THE UNITED STATES OF AMERICA

7 8 9 0

To Harry, Sidsell, Lélia, and John

"How miserable that man is that Governes a People wher six parts of seaven at least are Poore Endebted Discontented and Armed." (Governor Sir William Berkeley to [Thomas Ludwell], July 1, 1676, Longleat, LXXVII, fol. 145.)

❖❖❖

    "Sedition
Had now the face of piety, which (once Receiv'd as just) can hardly be repell'd." (Sir William Berkeley, *The Lost Lady* [1638], Act I, speech of physician.)

PREFACE

✧✧✧

EVERY MORNING during the chilly London winter of 1953-1954 I boarded a No. 11 bus at King's Road, Chelsea, and got off half an hour later at Fleet Street and Chancery Lane. A few strides placed me in the reading room of the Public Record Office. There white-coated attendants brought dusty Colonial Office volumes to my seat, and I immersed myself for six or seven hours in another century and another continent. It may come as a surprise to some that most of the documents concerning Virginia's seventeenth-century history are in English archives, yet this is the case.

I had not come to England to study Virginia history, let alone Bacon's Rebellion. I had come to study the legal and moral justifications for dispossessing the American Indians, my Ph.D. dissertation topic at Harvard University. The search for material had led me to the declarations of Nathaniel Bacon, Gent., of Curles Neck, Virginia, formerly of Friston Hall, Suffolk, who had audaciously led a rebellion against his cousin by marriage, the royal governor of Virginia, Sir William Berkeley. Bacon's views on the legal right of the Indians to occupy the King's Virginia domain (or rather his belief that they had no such right) puzzled me. Should a democratic champion of the oppressed, as we all supposed Bacon to be, limit his benevolence to whites only? Possibly. Was not Andrew Jackson a friend of the "little man" as long as he was white and not red? I was not completely satisfied, however, that justice should draw such a strict color line. Nor was I satisfied that existing accounts of Bacon's Rebellion accurately reflected the source material I was studying. I therefore began a detailed examination, footnote by footnote, of all references to the event in the works of the leading authority on the subject. I found that I could not agree with the interpretations this scholar had drawn from the documents he had cited. I thereupon resolved to get to the bottom of what now seemed to me a mystery.

First I began to search for more documents (for, providentially, the historian of the seventeenth century is blessed with relatively few). I was especially hopeful of finding Berkeley's own defense of his actions in putting down the revolt, a defense he told one correspondent he was carrying with him to England when he made his final journey "home" in April 1677. As the English spring came on I shifted my base of operations from London to Oxford, but not before I had noted, in one of the early reports of the Historical Manuscripts Commission of Great Britain, a reference to a number of Virginia letters, some concerning Sir William Berkeley, among the papers of Henry Coventry at Longleat, the estate of the Marquis of Bath, in Wiltshire, in the West Country of England. Through the courtesy of Lord Bath I was allowed to visit Longleat, one of England's most exquisite country houses, to look for this material. The fascination of the search was enhanced by the privilege of working in the top-floor library known as "Bishop Ken's" since the time it served as a refuge for that strong-willed seventeenth-century divine. The task was made easy and congenial by the kindness and skill of the librarian, Miss Dorothy Coates.

Sometime after the agent of the Historical Manuscripts Commission submitted his report on the Longleat manuscripts, the

PREFACE

loose documents were bound in handsome volumes under the
supervision of J. E. Jackson, the rector of nearby Leigh-Dela-
mere. As I opened a volume of Coventry's colonial papers,
collected during the course of his duties as one of Charles II's
Principal Secretaries of State, a seventeenth-century copy of a
letter from Bacon to Berkeley appeared. Turning the pages of
the volume further, unknown letters in Berkeley's hand lay
revealed. That volume and one other were filled with material
on the rebellion, material never before used in any account of it.
Indeed, I saw that the Coventry Papers contained more docu-
ments on the rebellion than existed in the Public Record Office,
traditionally regarded as the most important source for a study of
that unsuccessful uprising.

My belief that the accepted interpretation of Bacon's Rebellion
was incorrect, although formed before I discovered the material
at Longleat, was confirmed by the papers there. Because of the
significance of the new material and novelty of my interpretation
I decided to petition for a change in my dissertation topic from
the Indian study to Bacon's Rebellion. The change was effected
with the approval and help of Samuel Eliot Morison, my thesis
advisor, whose wisdom, kindness, and practical advice, have been
an inspiration and guide to me from the time of my entering the
Harvard Graduate School of Arts and Sciences in 1948. I spent
the year following my return from England putting the thesis
in scholarly form, and in June 1955 received my doctor's degree.
Louis Hartz, Professor of Government, and Chairman of the
Committee on Higher Degrees in the History of American
Civilization, in which field I received my degree, was the second
reader. I am deeply grateful for his continuing aid and encourage-
ment.

The manuscript underwent numerous and significant revisions
after its submission as a doctoral dissertation. I would like par-
ticularly to thank Lester J. Cappon, James Morton Smith, and
Lawrence W. Towner of the Institute of Early American His-
tory and Culture for long hours spent in the reading and revision

of the manuscript. I would like to thank also Wesley Frank Craven of Princeton University, Richard L. Morton of the College of William and Mary, Jane D. Carson and John M. Hemphill of the Research Department of Colonial Williamsburg, Inc., the late James Kimbrough Owen of Louisiana State University, Eleanor G. Pearre of the *William and Mary Quarterly*, my father Harold E. Washburn of Dartmouth College, my wife Lélia Kanavarioti Washburn, and my brother John N. Washburn, for their helpful advice and criticisms.

I owe a debt to numerous libraries (and their staffs) at home and abroad: to the British Museum, Public Record Office, and Institute of Historical Research, London; the Bodleian Library, Oxford; the Pepysian Library of Magdalene College, Cambridge; the Library of Congress, Washington; the Henry E. Huntington Library, San Marino, California; the Virginia State Library and Virginia Historical Society, Richmond; the Alderman Library of the University of Virginia, Charlottesville; the Library of the College of William and Mary and the Archives of Colonial Williamsburg, Inc., Williamsburg; the Duke University Library, Durham, North Carolina; the North Carolina State Archives, Raleigh; the New York Public Library and New-York Historical Society, New York City; the Massachusetts Historical Society and Archives of the Commonwealth of Massachusetts, Boston; the Harvard College Library, Cambridge; and the Dartmouth College Library, Hanover, New Hampshire. I am particularly grateful to Dartmouth College for the award of a James B. Reynolds Scholarship which enabled me to do research in England during the year 1953-1954.

Needless to say I am deeply thankful to the Marquis of Bath for permission to quote from the Coventry Papers at Longleat. Rules for transcribing the documents quoted in this book are, in general, those outlined in Section 32 of the *Harvard Guide to American History* (Cambridge, 1954), in the discussion of the "Expanded Method." Abbreviations, under this procedure, are expanded, and certain other changes are made, but, in general,

[x]

complete fidelity to the original language is maintained. Dates are given as found in the original manuscripts except that when the date falls in the period January 1 to March 24 the year is given in the "New Style," *i.e.*, that of today.

Wilcòmb E. Washburn

Williamsburg, Virginia
July, 1957

NOTE TO THE PAPERBACK EDITION

In the ten years since this book was published, I have eagerly examined all criticism (and praise) directed at it. Like the Governor who emerges as its protagonist, I have challenged critics to prove wherein I have failed to do justice to the participants in the event. Nothing I have read or heard since inclines me to change a word of it, and it is therefore issued as it appeared ten years ago. Dissent from my thesis there has been, but I have been heartened to find it increasingly accepted by scholars and textbook writers in place of the view which it challenged.

For the paperback edition, new maps have been prepared by The University of North Carolina Press.

W.E.W.

Smithsonian Institution
Washington, D. C.
March, 1967

Contents

[xiii]

Contents

Illustrations

[xv]

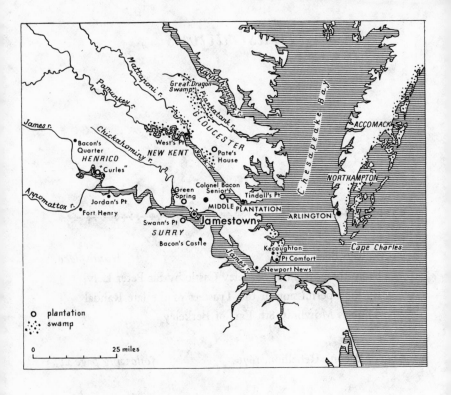

The Area of Bacon's Rebellion, 1676

The Governor and the Rebel

A HISTORY OF BACON'S REBELLION
IN VIRGINIA

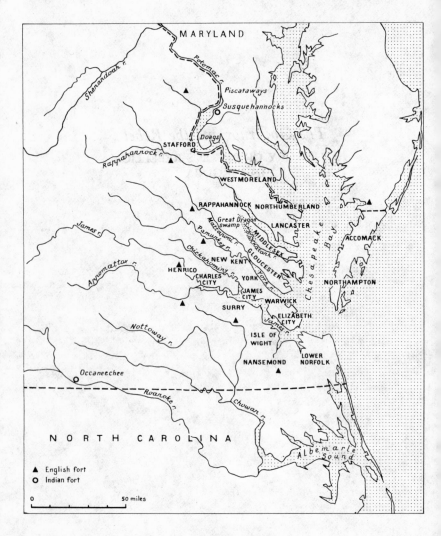

MARYLAND

Shenandoah r.

Potomac r.

Piscataways

○ Susquehannocks

Doegs

STAFFORD ▲

Rappahannock r.

WESTMORELAND

RAPPAHANNOCK ▲

NORTHUMBERLAND

Great Dragon swamp

Mattaponi r.

Pamunkey r.

LANCASTER

MIDDLESEX

Piankatank r.

James r.

Chickahominy r.

NEW KENT

GLOUCESTER

ACCOMACK

HENRICO ▲

Appomattox r.

CHARLES CITY

YORK

York r.

JAMES CITY

NORTHAMPTON

WARWICK

▲

SURRY

▲

James r.

ELIZABETH CITY

Nottoway r.

ISLE OF WIGHT

LOWER NORFOLK

NANSEMOND ▲

○ Occaneechee

Chesapeake Bay

Roanoke r.

Chowan r.

NORTH CAROLINA

Albemarle Sound

▲ English fort
○ Indian fort

0 _____ 50 miles

Virginia, 1676

Chapter 1

THE RISE OF A DEMOCRATIC MYTH

✦✦

THROUGHOUT THE nineteenth and twentieth centuries the rebellion of Nathaniel Bacon in Virginia in 1676 has been presented as a valiant but premature attempt to overthrow an oppressive royal government in order to establish a just and democratic society. Most accounts of the rebellion written in the last century and a half, whether "historical" or "fictional"—and there are dozens of each type—have held to this view. In them Bacon is the torchbearer of revolutionary democracy, while the royal governor, Sir William Berkeley, plays the despotic villain. Yet how strange would this view have seemed to persons living in the seventeenth and eighteenth centuries! In both of those centuries accounts of the rebellion tended to defend Berkeley and to denounce Bacon.

Can the explanation of the phenomenon be found in the facts of the rebellion? Only to a minor extent, for favorable and unfavorable facts about the two antagonists have been available, in roughly equivalent proportions, from the time of its occurrence to the present day. The explanation must lie elsewhere.

The key that unlocks the "meaning" of Bacon's Rebellion is to be found in the American Revolution. The "Spirit of 1776" lent an appearance of legitimacy and respectability to all revolts against British authority. Bacon's Rebellion, seen as a democratic movement, was one of its results. Within a few years of the Revolution the democratic interpretation of the earlier rebellion became orthodox. When the justice of the colonial relationship with the mother country was accepted, however, Bacon's Rebellion was excluded from historical respectability.

The first historians of Bacon's Rebellion were the participants in it. Needless to say the two principal actors, Berkeley and Bacon, vociferously defended themselves. Their foremost lieutenants, Philip Ludwell for Berkeley, and Giles Bland for Bacon, as well as the two leaders' wives, similarly supported their masters. Although their writings provide us with some of our most important evidence it is reasonable in a historiographical study to disregard their interpretations of the rebellion.[1]

It is valid, on the other hand, to deal with their contemporaries who were less directly interested in the outcome. Most important was William Sherwood, a lawyer, whose long narrative of the events of the rebellion and letters on Bacon's activities are discussed throughout this work.[2] Sherwood became Governor Berkeley's great enemy following the rebellion. His contemporary account of it, however, fully justified Berkeley and condemned Bacon and his men.

The other important account by a contemporary not an active participant in the affair is "The History of Bacon's and Ingram's Rebellion," or Burwell Manuscript, written, in all probability, by John Cotton, of Queen's Creek. Cotton's wife wrote a brief description of the fighting also.[3] Neither of the two Cottons saw the rebellion as a democratic revolt of the people against an oppressive governor, but as the tragi-comic work of a clever rogue who played on the fears and hopes of the people to satisfy his fickle will.

The reports of the commissioners sent by King Charles II to investigate the causes of the rebellion are less significant historically than they might have been for two reasons. First, the commissioners arrived after the rebellion was put down, and hence all their information was based on the testimony of persons trying to vindicate their conduct. The hearsay evidence obtained is suspect for another reason: immediately on their arrival the commissioners began feuding with Governor Berkeley over the extent of their authority and his. Their reports of the rebellion were inevitably colored by their post-rebellion conflict with Sir William. Despite their condemnation of the governor, however, they did not exonerate Bacon, nor did they see his movement as an effort at political reform.

Sometime after the rebellion Mrs. Aphra Behn wrote a play called "The Widow Ranter, or, The History of Bacon in Virginia." It was found among her manuscripts after her death in 1689 and was performed in the following year. Apparently based on little more than a newsletter account of the rebellion, the play is a wildly imaginative creation which deserves no historical consideration. The dramatic opposition between the cowardly Council and Deputy Governor and the dashing Bacon and his lieutenants gives coherence to the story. The climax occurs when Bacon advances against the Indians, kills the Indian King and rescues the Indian Queen with whom he is in love, unwittingly kills her, and then, to make a thorough job of it, kills himself.[4] It is possible that the democratic ferment preceding the "Glorious Revolution" of 1688 inspired Mrs. Behn as the American Revolution did later American writers. The play is less a historical drama, however, than an imaginative exercise.

Almost as dubious as a legitimate history is "The Beginning, Progress, and Conclusion of Bacon's Rebellion" written in 1705 by "T. M." for the edification of Robert Harley, His Majesty's Principal Secretary of State, afterwards Earl of Oxford. The author, who was undoubtedly Thomas Mathew, a rich planter of northern Virginia, was himself largely responsible for the Indian troubles which led to the rebellion.[5] In addition Mathew, a burgess in the assembly of June 1676, aided Bacon (probably through fear) to such an extent that he was excepted from Governor Berkeley's post-rebellion pardon to the rebels. Writing thirty years after the event, Mathew fell into frequent errors of fact. His suggestion that Bacon was motivated in part by a desire to reform abuses in the government is challenged by numerous other participants writing at the time of the events themselves.[6]

In the same year that Mathew wrote his account Robert Beverley published his *History and Present State of Virginia*, in which he dealt extensively with Bacon's Rebellion. Beverley, the son of one of Berkeley's right-hand men, was a small child of three in 1676. Although not an eyewitness he was the first to deal with the rebellion as a conscious historian, and he made a particularly thorough analysis of its causes.[7] In Beverley's account Bacon emerges as an Indian-hating demagogue, and Berkeley as an honest but unfortunate governor. Beverley, who like his father had long fought tyrannical governors, could find no similarity between Berkeley's rule and that of his successors.[8]

Writing at about the same time, John Oldmixon, an English historian, published an interpretation of the uprising much less perceptive than Beverley's, but equally condemnatory of Bacon's actions and laudatory of Berkeley's. Oldmixon wrote his history from the accounts of others, primarily from Beverley's and from a manuscript history by William Byrd II, son of one of Bacon's active supporters. There is no suggestion in Oldmixon that Bacon aimed at political reform. As for Berkeley, Oldmixon wrote that "Those who liv'd on the Spot, have a great Respect for his Memory, and they who are the best Judges of his Merit, always speak of him as a wise and a just Governour." [9]

In 1731 the "Maryland Muse," Ebenezer Cooke, wrote a satire on Bacon's Rebellion based largely on the Burwell Manuscript. The "Champion" of the People, Nathaniel Bacon, is described as

> A Man respected by the Mob,
> As a fit Fool to do their Jobb;
> Who, Sword in Hand, would rescue Cattle,
> And give the *Indians* bloody Battle ....[10]

Lawrence C. Wroth, in editing Cooke's poem, gives us a twentieth-century view when he writes that Cooke "sneered at and satirized his [Bacon's] aspirations, displaying hard indifference to the dignity of human personality and thorough ignorance of the deeper meaning of the rebellion that Bacon bravely led." [11]

Sir William Keith, one-time governor of Pennsylvania, published in London, in 1738, the first part of his *History of the British Plantations in America*. Part I, the only section Keith actually brought out, dealt with Virginia and was little more than a rehandling of earlier accounts. Keith found it "not easy to conceive how any general Insurrection or Rebellion could be fomented in *Virginia* against so good a Governor as Sir *William Berkeley....*" Bacon is seen as a "giddy-headed Youth" who charmed "the unthinking Multitude" into supporting his schemes against the Indians.[12]

In 1747 Dr. William Douglass began publishing his *Summary, Historical and Political, of the First Planting, Progressive Improvements, and Present State of the British Settlements in North-America* (Boston, 1747-1752). Douglass dealt with Bacon's Rebellion in a chapter on the English wars with the Indians. The occasion of the rebellion he saw as the result of "some mutual murders" which happened between the English and the Indians in the "out-settlements." Bacon, "a hot-headed young gentleman of the council, because, as he thought, the assembly was too dilatory in fitting out against the Indians; in contempt of the government, and without a proper commission, inlists soldiers of his own accord, and occasioned an intestine civil mutiny of the white people against the government...." Soldiers were sent from England to quell the disturbance, but Bacon dying before their arrival, the commotions ceased. "Bacon's body," wrote the doctor, "could not be found to be exposed to infamy." [13]

In 1757 there appeared *An Account of the European Settlements in America* usually attributed to Edmund Burke, the famous friend of the colonies, but which was probably the joint work of Edmund and William Burke. Edmund Burke called himself merely the reviser of his kinsman's work. Burke's *Account* is a rapid survey of the most significant occurrences in the various colonies and two pages are given to "a sort of rebellion" which arose in Virginia, following the Restoration, "from mismanagement in the government, from the decay of their trade, and from exorbitant grants inconsiderately made [by the King], which included the settled property of many people." These grievances raised a general discontent among the planters which was exploited by "a young gentleman" named Bacon. "This man, by a specious, or perhaps a real, though ill-judged, regard for the public good, finding the governor slow in his preparations against the Indians, who were at that time ravaging the frontiers of the province, took up arms, without any commission, to act against the enemy." Bacon's actions are related without the suggestion that his principal purpose was either reform or revolution. There is, however, a perceptible shift in emphasis away from the Indian causes of the rebellion to the economic and political grievances that existed at the time.[14]

In 1764 appeared the forty-first volume of the Modern Part of the *Universal History*, written anonymously by various hands, and containing a "Sequel" to the earlier history of Virginia which had appeared in Volume 39 (1763).[15] Traditional causes of dissatisfaction in Virginia prior to the rebellion are given: high prices of imported goods, grants of land to noblemen, excessive taxes, and Indian raids. Although Bacon is not pictured as a democratic hero or Berkeley as an oppressive governor, both are seen as representing conflicting parties in England to whom they made their appeals. "Their interest at court and in the parliament admitting of no comparison, Berkeley received encouragement to persist in making no concessions to the rebels, and orders were given for the equipment of a squadron of men of war...."[16] The author's concern with Whig-Tory political divisions in eighteenth-century England appears throughout the rest of his discussion of Bacon's Rebellion and Virginia's later history.

"Bacon's cause," he observes, "had at this time many advocates among the people of *England*, and even in the parliament itself; so that the court party, though they disliked the principles of it, behaved with lenity towards its authors, who were by far the greatest number of the colonists." [17]

In 1769 Edward Bancroft, an American living in England, published his *Remarks on the Review of the Controversy between Great Britain and her Colonies*. Bancroft's book was a polemic against certain pamphlets upholding the right of Parliament to tax the American colonies without their consent. In support of his position that the American colonies were distinct political bodies outside the Realm of England and not subject to the authority of Parliament, Bancroft made an extensive review of colonial history in the seventeenth and eighteenth centuries. In the course of his argument against the Navigation Acts enacted following the Restoration of Charles II, Bancroft asserted that these acts of Parliament

were the principal, if not only Cause, of that general insurrection in *Virginia*, which soon after followed under Colonel *Bacon;* for when Sir *William Berkley*, the Governor of that Province, was compelled to fly from the Place of his usual Residence, and retire to *Accomack*, instead of that friendly Reception which he had promised himself from the known Attachment of the Inhabitants to him, even they began to make Terms for a Redress of those Grievances they suffered by Acts of the Parliament of *England;* and when, after *Bacon's* Death, this Insurrection subsided, the Province sent Agents to *England*, to remonstrate 'against Taxes and Impositions being laid on the Colony, by any Authority but that of the General Assembly.' This Remonstrance produced a Declaration from King *Charles* the Second, under the Privy Seal, and dated the 19th of *April*, 1676, affirming, that *'Taxes ought not to be laid upon the Proprietors and Inhabitants of the Colony, but by the common Consent of the General Assembly;* except such Impositions as the Parliament should lay on the Commodities imported into *England* from the Colony.' [18]

Bancroft incorrectly placed the Virginia protest after the rebellion instead of before, and did not know, or mention, that the King's declaration of April 19 was never put into effect.[19]

On May 19, 1774, a letter from "E. B." to the London *Morning Chronicle* was reprinted in Rind's *Virginia Gazette*. The writer, obviously Edward Bancroft and not Edmund Burke as the Virginia editor thought, repeated his arguments of 1769, though neglecting to mention any other cause of the rebellion than the Navigation Acts. The Indian troubles and all other causes are overlooked. On the verge of a new revolution it was perhaps natural that the justification for the American Revolution should be sought in Nathaniel Bacon's abortive enterprise one hundred years earlier. It only remained for a successful revolution in 1776 to make the leader of the rebellion of 1676 seem a premature George Washington.

Neither colonial independence nor honor to rebels was to be won without a fight, however. The English Tory George Chalmers, in his *Political Annals of the Present United Colonies, from their Settlement to the Peace of 1763* (1780), and in his *Introduction to the History of the Revolt of the American Colonies* (1782), denounced "this inconsiderate insurrection" [20] of Bacon, and defended the loyalist party not only against the rebels but also against the royal commissioners who went to Virginia to investigate the causes of the affair but who spent most of their time criticizing Governor Berkeley for his post-rebellion activities. Chalmers considered the "real designs" of the rebels "impossible to discover." [21] But he suspected they "wished probably to enjoy the pleasures of present power...." [22] Chalmers was one of the first to base his account of colonial affairs on a study of the actual documentary sources in the British Public Record Office; indeed his zeal was so great that he made off with some of the original documents.[23]

Independence won, the former colonists began to interpret their past with American eyes. As revolutionary passions subsided, however, party divisions arose. By the turn of the century conservative Federalists battled Jeffersonian Republicans. Emerging triumphant, both in the field of contemporary politics and in the interpretation of past politics, were the Jeffersonians. From the conflict were born, after some travail, the images of Bacon the democratic hero and Berkeley the tyrannical royalist.

The process began in 1804 with the publication of the previously mentioned narrative of Thomas Mathew, which was filled with colorful descriptions of the leading personalities and their disagreements. Written in 1705 by one of those involved with Bacon, it found its way into the London book market where it was bought by Rufus King, the United States Minister to Great Britain, in 1801. On December 20, 1803, King presented it to President Thomas Jefferson who made a copy of it in his own hand and returned it to King on March 10, 1804. "I had an opportunity too of communicating it to a person who was just putting into the press a history of Virginia, but still in a situation to be corrected." [24] Jefferson's reference is undoubtedly to John Daly Burk, whose *History of Virginia* appeared in 1804-1805.[25] It was probably Burk who sent the narrative to the editor of the Richmond *Enquirer* where it was printed on September 1, 5, and 8, 1804. The enthusiastic letter accompanying the text, mistakenly believed by some to have been written by Jefferson,[26] baldly stated that "If this little book speaks the truth, Nathaniel Bacon will be no longer regarded as a rebel, but as a patriot. His name will be rescued from the infamy which has adhered to it for more than a century; the stigma of corruption, cruelty, and treachery, will be fixed on the administration by which he was condemned; and one more case will be added to those which prove, that insurrections proceed oftener from the misconduct of those in power, than from the factious and turbulent temper of the People." [27] The letter writer's interpretation goes far beyond his material. Thomas Mathew was as far from asserting that Bacon was right as he was from claiming that Berkeley was wrong.

A *caveat* against undue enthusiasm for the newly emerging democratic hero was entered in the same year in Chief Justice

John Marshall's *Compendious View of the Colonies Planted by the English on the Continent of North America, from their Settlement to the Commencement of that War which Terminated in their Independence*. This was the first volume of Marshall's *Life of George Washington*. Staunch Federalist that he was, Marshall saw little nobility in Bacon's violent attempt to overthrow the settled government of Virginia. He did not deny the existence of popular grievances against the low price of tobacco, the restraints placed on trade by the Navigation Acts, the large grants of land made by the King to his favorites, and the great tax burdens caused by the hostility of the Indians.[28] But he found little in the grievances to cause, still less to justify, rebellion. "Treading the path by which ambition marches to power," commented the great jurist, Bacon "harangued the people on their grievances, increased their irritation against the causes of their disgust, and ascribed the evils with which they thought themselves oppressed to those who governed them, while he professed no other object than their good."[29] Marshall admitted his inability to comprehend fully the real motives of the rebels. Some historians, he noted, felt that Bacon's design was merely "to gratify the common resentments against the Indians"; others that he intended "to seize the government." "Whatever may have been his object," Marshall concluded, "the insurrection produced much misery, and no good to Virginia."[30]

Marshall's Bacon was no match for Burk's. The new democratic Bacon was successfully launched by Burk, in his *History of Virginia from its first Settlement to the Commencement of the Revolution*, among a people who had repudiated Federalism in the election of 1800. The second volume, which dealt extensively with Bacon's Rebellion, was published in Petersburg, Virginia, in 1805. Born in Ireland in 1775, Burk soon revealed his radical temper. In 1796, shortly after being expelled from the University of Dublin for his republicanism and deism, he fled Ireland to avoid arrest and prosecution on a charge of sedition. In America, his burning love of liberty found expression in various newspapers which he edited, and in several patriotic plays which he wrote, including one entitled "Bunker Hill." Succeeding Philip Freneau as editor of the New York *Time Piece* in 1798, Burk was soon arrested for "seditious and libellous" utterances against President John Adams. The case was dismissed on Burk's promise to leave the country, a promise he violated by going into hiding under an assumed name. Following the election of 1800, Burk came into the open again, and solicited Jefferson for a position in the government. No suitable place could be found, however, and Burk moved to Petersburg, Virginia, where he devoted his talents to the law and to the writing of his *History of Virginia*.[31]

Burk's researches, like those of Chalmers twenty years earlier, were marked by detailed investigation of primary source material. How relatively unimportant such research can be in comparison with the conceptual scheme applied to it is shown by the total variance that marks the views of the two men. To Burk the Indian threat against which the rebellious colonists took arms was principally a pretext under which, on the "imposing plea of self-preservation, they could give utterance and effect to their resentments" against political oppression, resentments "long nourished in secret or manifesting themselves in partial riots and insurrections.... All ranks and classes of society," in Burk's eye, "were equally affected with the public grievances and oppressions, and impatiently longed for an occasion, by one great violent effort, to burst their chains and assert their independence...." When Indian depredations presented the opportunity, "the people immediately flew to arms, and although no previous concert or correspondence had taken place, the popular movement was rapid, general, and consentaneous."[32]

Berkeley, as the King's lieutenant, had to take the blame for the discontent even though most of the popular grievances were beyond his power to remedy. To make Berkeley *look* like the villain, however, was more difficult for, by Burk's own admission, the governor's "nice principles of honor had ever been without reproach." [33] It was in the post-rebellion period of hangings and confiscation of property that Burk found the opportunity to condemn Berkeley's character and administration, charging him with "avarice" and the shedding of "innocent blood" at this time. "It may be urged," he conceded, "that these charges are utterly irreconcilable with the character for nice honor and severe virtue, which has been unanimously ascribed to sir W. Berkeley. I cannot help it." [34]

Burk's democratic interpretation of Bacon's Rebellion was not to go unchallenged despite the growing power of Republicanism in the new nation. A particularly significant objection came from a Virginian who had been caught in the fierce party strife of the early years of the Republic and who, like Governor Berkeley before him, had been forced from the government under accusations of corruption and disloyalty. Edmund Randolph, Secretary of State in George Washington's cabinet, was, in 1795, accused of treasonable relations with the government of France. Randolph's alleged misconduct involved the charge of soliciting a French bribe in order to offset British machinations in the West during the Whiskey Rebellion. Though not actually tried or convicted in court, his reputation was virtually ruined by the charge and he was forced to retire from public life. In the last years of his life, prior to his death in 1813, he worked on his "History of Virginia."

Randolph's comments on Bacon appear to be a direct answer to Burk's transformation of the ardent young seventeenth-century demagogue into a democratic hero. Although a Republican, Randolph was an opponent of the revolutionary democracy so dear to the heart of Burk, and his comments on Bacon show it. [35] In his history he noted that Bacon's Rebellion "has lately received an historical gloss, the object of which is to metamorphose it into one of those daring efforts, which gross misrule sometimes suggests, if it may not strictly vindicate. But the whole force of precedent having been already obtained in the successful resistance of the American colonies to Great Britain, we ought not to sanction a new case, in which tyranny is less palpable or less clearly meditated. Let the transaction therefore be seen in its real character." Randolph then discussed the causes of dissatisfaction in the colony to show "upon what a fund of inflammable material such a penetrating demagogue, as Bacon could now operate." In speaking of the "bloodshed and revenge" which accompanied the suppression of the rebellion, actions for which Burk took Governor Berkeley to task, Randolph asks:

But is rebellion unseen amidst these facts? A legitimate government existed. It was honest in the measures of general defence. Bacon branded them as being inadequate; remonstrated; and finding remonstrance ineffectual, he took up arms to prescribe and enforce a wiser conduct; pretending that the ordinary, constitutional modes of redress or punishment would come too late; but at the same time criminating the governor with that deliberate wickedness, which sometimes justifies a revolution. In a country like ours, where the will of the people justly predominates, let us not lend a sanction to any perversion of that will, by approving a resort to arms, until all, which ought to be endured, shall have been endured, and redress be sought in every legal, constitutional and reasonable shape. Our own revolution was not without its clouds, hardships and impoverishment; and who can assert, that the price of another will not be dearer? [36]

Randolph continued his musings on revolution with a warning, drawn from the French Revolution, against the dangers of political excess. Bacon's Rebellion, like the French Revolution, was an event on which observers could agree on the facts, but divide on the interpretation.[37]

In his editing of *The Statutes at Large . . . of Virginia*, William Waller Hening, like Burk aided in his researches by Thomas Jefferson, provided additional support for the idea of Bacon as a liberal reformer working against the oppression of Governor Berkeley. The second volume of Hening's *Statutes*, containing the laws passed during Bacon's Rebellion, was issued in 1810. It was apparently Hening's assumption that the laws of the assembly of June 1676 were passed under Bacon's "influence" that led him to print them with the running head "Bacon's Laws" and with several laudatory footnotes concerning the rebel's noble attempt to reform the colony.[38]

Historians throughout the remainder of the century and until this day have tended to give credence to whatever interpretation of the rebellion is most consistent with their own philosophy of history. Since most American historians of the past one hundred and fifty years have held republican, anti-monarchical sentiments, Bacon has usually been presented as a fighter against oppression in behalf of the suffering "People." This view has been propagated even more consistently by the "creative artists" who have woven the tale of the rebellion into their fictional outpourings. Credit for the first "fictional" portrayal of Bacon as the forerunner of George Washington and the rebellion as a premature struggle for independence must go to Alexander Caruthers for his book *The Cavaliers of Virginia* (1835).[39]

The only historian of the middle nineteenth century to give Bacon's Rebellion fresh, scholarly treatment was George Bancroft. Bancroft was an ardent believer in the virtue of democratic government which, in its ideal form, he saw evolving in nineteenth-century America. It was not hard for him, therefore, "in the midst of contradictory testimony on the character of the insurgents," to decide that Bacon was truly representative of the progressive forces in Virginia and to conclude that the acts of the June Assembly "manifest the principles of Bacon; and were they not principles of justice, freedom, and humanity?"[40]

Historians following Bancroft echoed the same tune. The "democratic reformer" interpretation of Bacon became unassailably orthodox in the world's greatest "democratic reform" nation.

So acceptable, indeed, had the heroic conception of Bacon become by the end of the century that physical tributes to his memory began to appear in Virginia. On November 14, 1901, a memorial window to Nathaniel Bacon was unveiled in the powder magazine at Williamsburg. The memorial address by

Robert S. Bright saw Bacon as "the author, and George Washington, the finisher" of that faith in "the Divine right of the people" first established by Oliver Cromwell. Bacon's "only blemish," his use of the wives of several loyalist leaders as a screen behind which to construct siege lines in front of Jamestown in September 1676, is disposed of with Southern gallantry. Since the ladies of the Association for the Preservation of Virginia Antiquities had decided to erect the memorial to Bacon, Bright suggested, discussion of the "unchivalrous charge" was unnecessary. "Had their verdict not swept this charge away," he admitted, "it would still be hard to reconcile it with the otherwise conceded chivalry of the soldier and gentleman." [41]

Fifteen years later an even more impressive memorial was erected behind the Speaker's chair in the Virginia House of Delegates in the Capitol at Richmond. The plaque commemorates Bacon as "A great Patriot Leader of the Virginia People who died while defending their rights, October 26, 1676. Victrix Causa deis placuit, sed victa Catoni." [42]

Although Mrs. Mary Newton Stanard published her *Story of Bacon's Rebellion* in 1907, no extensive new research in the sources was done until Thomas Jefferson Wertenbaker brought out his *Virginia under the Stuarts* (1914). Wertenbaker made the most thorough examination to that time of the documents in the Public Record Office in London and emerged, if anything, an even stronger proponent of the "democratic reform" theory than his post-Revolutionary predecessors. Wertenbaker renewed his assault on Governor Berkeley and enhanced the status of Bacon still further in his *Torchbearer of the Revolution: The Story of Bacon's Rebellion and Its Leader* (1940). Here he presents a fully elaborated picture of "oppressed yeomen" versus the "corrupt grandees," of Bacon acting as "a champion of the weak" against "the archenemy of colonial democracy," Governor Berkeley.[43] Professor Wertenbaker's belief in Bacon's Rebellion as a democratic reform movement remains unshaken to this day.[44]

In 1949 Wesley Frank Craven, in his *The Southern Colonies in the Seventeenth Century, 1607-1689*, questioned the heights to which Bacon had been raised and insisted that his rebellion be treated as a "complex problem" for which there was "no simple answer." Craven emphasized the importance of the Indian troubles which led to the rebellion, an aspect of the affair which had been increasingly ignored as historians built up the conception of Bacon the reformer. Similarly Craven asked embarrassing questions about some of the so-called "Bacon's Laws" which seemed directed not so much at Governor Berkeley as at Bacon himself. Treating the subject briefly, Craven had little chance to do more than raise doubts concerning the democratic interpretation of the revolt.

What was the issue in Virginia in 1676? Political reform? Or Indian policy? Was the rebellion a democratic reform movement against an oppressive royal government? Or was it the result of a disagreement on how to protect the colony against the Indian danger? Earlier writers emphasized the Indian question. Later writers saw it as a fight for democracy. In the following chapters the evidence will be reviewed and a conclusion drawn.

Chapter 2

BACKGROUND TO REBELLION

❖❖❖

THE TWO figures who dominated Virginia history in the latter half of the seventeenth century—Governor Sir William Berkeley and Nathaniel Bacon, Jr.—were, interestingly enough, cousins by marriage.[1] The two present a striking contrast. Sir William was nearly seventy years old, a veteran of the English civil wars and of Virginia's Indian wars, a favorite of the King, a playwright, scholar, and "Darling of the People" of Virginia.[2] He had been appointed governor of the colony in 1641, six years before Bacon was born, and governed almost continuously after that date except during the period of the English Commonwealth, 1652-1659, when he was forced from office by a Parliamentary fleet sent from England. So well thought of was he by the people, however, that the house of burgesses and council joined together before the restoration of Charles II in 1660 to invite him to become governor again. His willingness to sacrifice his own interest to promote that of the colony and his concern with the people's grievances were demonstrated time and again, and called forth frequent eulogies from grateful assemblies.

Berkeley's cousin, Nathaniel Bacon, Jr., was a young man in

his twenties when he came to Virginia in the summer of 1674. His father, Thomas Bacon, a well-to-do Suffolk gentleman, had withdrawn him from Cambridge University after two and a half years' residence for having "broken into some extravagancies." His tutor, John Ray, described him as a young gentleman of "very good parts, and a quick wit," but "impatient of labour, and indeed his temper will not admit long study." [3] When he married Elizabeth Duke, daughter of Sir Edward Duke of Benhall, that gentleman was so deeply angered that he disinherited his daughter and never spoke to her again. Extravagant and improvident, Bacon "could not contain himself within bounds" despite a very "genteel competency." After he had become involved in a scheme to defraud a neighboring youth of a part of his inheritance, Bacon's father decided that the best place for his ne'er-do-well son would be the New World. He gave him £1,800 and put him on a tobacco ship for Virginia. [4]

Bacon was welcomed warmly to Virginia not only by William Berkeley, but by another cousin, Nathaniel Bacon, Sr., one of His Majesty's councilors of state in Virginia. [5] When the adventurous youth desired to establish himself on the frontier, Berkeley smoothed the way. Bacon bought about 1,230 acres of land along the James River from Thomas Ballard: a main plantation at "Curles," about twenty miles below the falls where he took up residence, and an outer plantation at the falls, run by an overseer. [6] The governor granted his request for a commission to trade with the Indians, and Bacon was soon engaged in that occupation as well as in planting. [7]

Bacon attributed his urge to live away from the settled areas to the fact that he had "always bin delighted in solitude and mistique imployments," [8] and it seems true that powerful psychological forces encouraged him in his decision to live on the frontier. He was described as being "indifferent tall but slender, blackhair'd and of an ominous, pensive, melancholly Aspect, of a pestilent and prevalent Logical discourse tending to atheisme in most companyes, not given to much talke, or to make suddain replyes, of a most imperious and dangerous hidden Pride of heart, despising the wisest of his neighbours for their Ignorance, and very ambitious and arrogant." [9] Perhaps the earlier failures and disgrace he had suffered as a student, suitor, and gentleman, had forced him to flee the society of his social equals and to search for respect among the solitary, self-reliant men of the frontier who knew nothing of his past. [10]

Governor Berkeley gave him the extraordinary honor of an appointment to the council of state on March 3, 1675. Yet the melancholy young man seemed to care little for political life. He attended only three meetings before embarking on his rebellion a year and a half later. [11] There is no evidence to show that he was at all interested in political reform in this period, although he is frequently credited with such an attitude.

When Bacon arrived in the colony the local Indians had ceased to be an important threat to the settlers. Earlier the Virginia Indians had been numerically superior to the whites and in 1622 had nearly wiped out the colony. During 1644-1646, under the leadership of Opechancanough, they tried and failed once again, and that defeat marked the end of their existence as independent and powerful "foreign" nations. Renouncing their independent status by the peace treaty of 1646, the local Indians accepted the overlordship of the English King. In effect the treaty formalized a relationship which would have been required of them eventually because of the rapid expansion of the English population. In 1640 there were 8,000 English inhabitants of Virginia; in 1670, 40,000. [12] The Indians tributary to the colony, who at the coming of the English had probably totalled 10,000, could muster in 1670 only 725 bowmen (perhaps three or four thousand men, women, and children in all) in nineteen different tribes, the strongest numbering but ninety bowmen. [13] Three of the most important tribes were the Pamunkey, Appomattox, and Chickahominy. The subject Indians at this time held their land as a grant from the colony, and if they committed an offense against the English, whose settlements often extended beyond their towns into the wilderness, they were triable in the colony's courts.[14] As Governor Berkeley wrote in 1671: "The Indians, our neighbours, are absolutely subjected, so that there is no fear of them."[15]

The very increase in the power of the English over the Indians, however, brought new problems. Fear of the Indians had acted as a restraint on white expansion in the early period when the Indians outnumbered the whites. Now, having little to be afraid of from such an insignificant minority, the English began to encroach on their lands with increasing frequency. Governor Berkeley and the council, motivated by concepts of honor and policy, attempted to restrain the whites. But the violations continued.[16] The locus of significant power in Virginia was not in the governor but in the individual Englishman, made a superman by his possession of firearms. Neither the Indian in front of him nor the government behind him had the power to curb his desires except in a limited fashion: this was one of the benefits —to the frontiersman—of living under English law. The government could neither effectively restrain him nor protect the Indian. As a result the reckless expansion went on, in the manner of a chain reaction, into the lands of tribes which were not tributary to the English. It was at this point, as the "foreign" tribes struck back, that the conditioned contempt of the settlers towards the Indians was discarded for the original, primal fear. The resulting confusion is what we know as "Bacon's Rebellion."

The spark that ignited the train of powder leading to Bacon's Rebellion occurred in July 1675 in the Potomac River valley, the last great tidewater area of Virginia to be settled, and the frontier region farthest from Jamestown, the capital. One of the wealthy planters of the vicinity, Thomas Mathew, had obtained certain goods from the Doeg Indians in Maryland. They charged that Mathew never paid them, and to obtain satisfaction, a Doeg war party crossed the river and attempted to steal some of Mathew's hogs. The party was intercepted and pursued by the English. Some of the Indians were killed, and the hogs recovered. The surviving Indians reported the affair to their superiors. For revenge a war party was sent out which killed Mathew's herdsman, named Hen, at an outer plantation.[17]

On learning of the Indian attack, the local militia captains George Brent and George Mason, with thirty Virginians, set out to look for the murderers. Crossing the Potomac into Maryland at the break of dawn they divided forces at a fork in the path. Brent's men soon arrived at a cabin which they surrounded. Brent called upon the Indians to come out to parley. A Doeg chieftain "came Trembling forth," was grabbed by the hair by Brent and charged with the murder of Hen. When the chief denied all knowledge of it and "Slipt loos," as the chronicler relates it, he was shot. A fight ensued between the remaining Doegs and Brent's men. Ten Indians were killed and the chief's son captured. A few Doegs escaped. Meanwhile, Mason had surrounded another cabin occupied by Indians. Frightened by the shooting nearby caused by Brent's men, these Indians came pouring out. Mason's men picked off fourteen of them. In the midst of the "fight" one of the Indians got near enough to Mason to shout "Susquehanaugh friends." Mason, realizing his mistake, quickly called out to his men: "For the Lords sake Shoot no more, these are our friends the Susquehanoughs."[18]

This unfortunate episode started a fatal sequence of events. The Maryland authorities protested to Governor Berkeley against the invasion of their territory in time of peace and the killing of innocent Indians. Nothing seems to have been done, however, to compensate the Indians or punish the Virginians, and there followed an increasing number of Indian depredations on outlying Virginia and Maryland settlements.

On August 31, 1675, Governor Berkeley commissioned Colonel John Washington and Major Isaac Allerton to "call together the severall Malittia *officers*" of the regiments between the Rappahannock and the Potomac rivers and make "a full and thorough inquisition" of the true causes of the various murders

and raids, "and by what Nation or Nations of Indians donne."
After the investigation was completed Washington and Allerton
were to demand satisfaction and, "if they find cause," to raise
men and attack the Indians adjudged guilty of the assaults.[19]

Washington and Allerton conducted no investigation of the
incidents. Instead they wrote the Maryland authorities saying
that they had been directed to summon the *militia* of the counties
between the Rappahannock and the Potomac in order to conduct
the investigation ordered by Berkeley. They asked the Mary-
landers to send representatives to consult with them, and desired
to be informed by letter "what number of men you will be
pleased to Order to Our asistance." [20] The Marylanders re-
sponded by dispatching 250 horse and dragoons under Major
Thomas Truman. The force was directed to rendezvous with
Washington on September 23.[21]

While Governor Berkeley's directives were being ignored in
the north, his authority was being flouted in the west. In Henrico
County Nathaniel Bacon, Jr., seized some friendly Appomattox
Indians allegedly for stealing corn, although the corn was neither
his nor his neighbors'. On September 14 Berkeley rebuked the
young planter for his "rash heady action" pointing out that his
unauthorized act of law enforcement could only excite the nerv-
ous settlers and further alienate the friendly Indians.[22]

On Sunday, September 26, the Marylanders and Virginians
arrived at the fort of the Susquehannock Indians. The Susque-
hannocks, along with the Doegs, were assumed by the English
to be responsible for the frontier troubles. At the invitation of
Truman, the Maryland commander, five of the Susquehannock
chiefs came out to parley.[23] They asked to know the reason for
the hostile army. One thousand white men were drawn up
around a fort containing one hundred Indian braves, and their
women and children.[24] Truman informed them that the English
had come to demand satisfaction for the outrages committed in
Maryland and Virginia. The chiefs denied responsibility, blam-

ing instead the Senecas, one of the fierce Iroquois tribes constantly threatening them from the north.[25]

After Truman had finished, Washington and Allerton accused the chiefs of the murders committed on the Virginia side of the Potomac. They alleged that some of the raiders on the Virginia side had been seen returning to the Susquehannock fort, which lay on the Maryland side.[26] The Susquehannock chiefs positively denied it. One of them, realizing that his life was in danger, brought forth a silver medal given by the former governor of Maryland as a pledge of protection and friendship for as long as the sun and moon should endure.[27] But to no avail.

The chiefs were led away and murdered. The Marylanders claimed Colonel Washington and the Virginians committed the assault.[28] The Virginians charged Major Truman and the Marylanders with responsibility.[29] Truman was impeached by the lower house of the general assembly of Maryland, found guilty, but punished merely by a small fine. The upper house of the assembly declared that the punishment would neither satisfy the heathen "nor have it made appeare to the world how much the wickedness of that action is detested and disowned by. us." The lower house, however, refused to reconsider its penalty saying that "the Unanimous Consent of the Virginians and the generall Impetuosity of the Whole feild" forced Truman to act as he did "to prevent a mutiny of the whole Army." The upper house did not press the matter but pointedly denied the validity of the excuse, observing that "at the Said Trumans Tryall [it] did to[o] plainely appeare that his first Commands for the killing of those Indians were not obeyed and that he had some difficulty to get his men To obey him therein and that after they were put to death not a man would owne to have had a hand in it . . . ."[30]

Governor Berkeley was outraged by the breach of faith. "If they had killed my Grandfather and Grandmother, my father and Mother and all my friends," he exclaimed, "yet if they had come to treat of Peace, they ought to have gone in Peace."[31] An investigation was ordered to see if any of the Virginians were implicated in the murders. The results seemed to clear them of responsibility.[32]

Actual responsibility for the murders must rest with the Maryland commander on the scene. But as the highest civil and military officer in Virginia, Berkeley was formally responsible for whatever happened to the colony. Ideally he should have called Washington and Allerton to account for their failure to conduct any investigation before calling out the militia. But he had to rely on their independent judgment and to accept their decision to march against the Susquehannocks without an investigation. The power of local officials and even ordinary planters in Virginia was not comprehended in England at the time, nor has it been fully understood since. Berkeley could lead, encourage, and inspire, but he could not direct or even oppose when the mass of the people demanded a particular course of action. Hence his initial plan for a careful investigation and his later courageous denunciation of the murders won him popularity neither with the people nor with the English government.[33]

The enraged Susquehannocks successfully withstood the ensuing siege of their fort. Finally, on the verge of starvation, they "bouldly, undiscovered," slipped out of the fort one night with all their women and children, killing ten sleeping English guards on the way. The dispirited Virginia and Maryland troops picked over the plunder left in the fort and went home.[34]

Whoever may have committed the previous "outrages," the Susquehannocks were now definitely responsible. In a daring raid in January 1676 they killed thirty-six persons near the falls of the Rappahannock and Potomac rivers, and then disappeared into the forests west of the settlements. Governor Berkeley, on news of the raid, ordered Sir Henry Chicheley to raise a force to pursue them. Before it could march, however, he caused it to be disbanded.[35] Probably he realized that Chicheley would never be able to find the Susquehannocks.[36] The problem facing the English was to locate the Indians and force them into a fight. As one of the commissioners later sent to investigate the causes of the rebellion wrote, Virginia lacked no men to fight if the Indians showed themselves, but if they would not, "who can find them in their Coverts?" [37]

It is thought by some that Berkeley recalled Chicheley because of a peace proposal made by the Susquehannocks.[38] Following the raid the Susquehannocks sent Governor Berkeley a remonstrance drawn up by an English interpreter asking why the Virginians, heretofore friends, had become such violent enemies as to pursue them even into another province. They complained not only that their chiefs, sent out to treat for peace, were murdered, but that the act was countenanced by the governor. Seeing no other way of obtaining satisfaction, they declared they had killed ten of the common English for each one of their chiefs, a ratio they thought justified by the disproportion in rank. If the Virginians would provide compensation for the damages caused by the attack on them and withhold aid from the Marylanders, they promised to renew their ancient league of friendship. Otherwise they would fight the war to the last man.[39]

The contemporary who reports the Susquehannock peace proposal tells us that the English rejected it as derogatory "both to honour and intress." [40] It was probably politically impossible to concede the justice of the Susquehannock cause especially if, to provide the desired reparation, it meant taxing the frontiersmen who had suffered from their ravages.

After recalling Chicheley, Berkeley gave orders that planters living in exposed locations should draw together until there were ten men in each occupied house. This measure may have preserved the frontiersmen but it could not satisfy them because, they complained, it gave the Indians "both Opertunites, and Encouragement to Committt . . . many Outrages. . . ." [41]

Berkeley had more than the Susquehannocks and the frontiersmen to worry about, however. His great fear was of a general Indian combination against all the whites from New England to Virginia. In the summer of 1675 King Philip's War had broken out in New England. Early in 1676 traders brought news of the great battles that had been fought there during the winter. The reports were terrifying, the Virginians hearing of burned towns, deserted settlements, and continuing Indian victories.[42] Berkeley suspected that the New England troubles were influencing Virginia's, and feared that Virginia's tributary Indians might be enticed to join with the colony's Indian enemies in a plot to destroy all the English settlements.[43] Should the tributary Indians defect, the colony would suffer a staggering blow, for these Indians served both as intelligence agents and as an outer defense for the English plantations.[44]

Berkeley's policy was to preserve the friendship and loyalty of the subject Indians while giving the white settlers assurance against their possible hostility. To achieve this end the governor attempted to make the tributary Indians incapable of doing harm to the English, while at the same time preventing the English from harming them. The difficulty of carrying out such a policy in the face of the prejudice of the whites against all Indians in general and the unauthorized administration of "justice" by self-appointed vigilantes, was obvious. Yet Berkeley stuck to this policy until forced by the overwhelming pressure of events to alter it.

To effect the first objective, Berkeley relieved the subject Indians of their powder and ammunition.[45] To deal with the second problem, and all others related to the Indian troubles, Berkeley summoned the assembly, which convened on March 7, 1676.[46] This was the last meeting of the so-called "Long Assembly" which later historians have designated as "corrupt" and totally subservient to Sir William. The March assembly declared war upon

all such Indians who are notoriously knowne or shalbe discovered to have committed the murthers, rapins and depredations aforesaid, their fautors ayders and abetters, and against all other suspected Indians who shall refuse to deliver us such suffitient hostages, or other security for their fidelity and good affection to the English as shalbe required, and that shall refuse to be ayding and assisting us in discovering, persueing, and distroying those our enemies....[47]

The act also made detailed provision for defense against Indian attack. Considering that "wee are to warr with an enemy whose retirements are not easily discovered to us, soe that a Flying army may not be soe usefull at present," it provided for the raising of five hundred men (a quarter of them to be horsemen) from the most secure counties. These men were to be placed at the "heads" (i.e., falls) of the rivers and in certain forts. The horsemen in each garrison were to range continually between the garrisons, and the foot soldiers were to be sent into action at the discretion of the garrison commanders for the defense of the neighboring plantations. A clearly defined chain of command was set up. Individual commanders were named for the garrisons. Other commanders were appointed for the counties adjacent to the forts with orders to make exact lists of the remaining forces of their counties and to be ready at any time to march to the relief of the forts. The assembly restricted the right of uncontrolled action by local commanders—which had so often brought more trouble than it cured, as in the case of the Mason-Brent and Washington-Allerton expeditions—and gave control of operations other than local security to the governor or to some regional commander whom he should appoint. Local commanders, on discovery of any Indian fort or habitation, were required immediately to notify the governor and await his orders before attempting an attack.[48]

In another act the assembly decreed the death penalty for anyone selling arms or ammunition to any Indians, friendly or enemy. Oaths were to be taken by authorized traders not to furnish them arms and ammunition. Provisions were made, however, to supply "the neighbouring Indians (that are in amity with us and will come in and noe other) with such goods and merchandizes as Indians usually deale for (except powder, shott and armes...)."[49] Because "sade experience" had shown that the regular traders had sold powder, shot, and guns to the Indians in violation of earlier laws, and might continue to do so even under the provisions of the new law, the act excluded all the regular traders from the allowed trade and authorized commissions to be issued by the county courts for the purpose.[50] The reason assigned for this trade was that "wee are sencible that such Indians as are amongst us in peace, if they be not supplyed with matchcoates, hoes and axes to tend their corne and fence their ground, must of necessity perish of Famine or live on rapine." [51] The regular traders, not unnaturally, resented their exclusion from the Indian trade. Nathaniel Bacon, Jr., angrily accused the governor of excluding "others" from trading with the Indians while giving the right to certain of his "favorites." As a regular trader who had just built a trading house, Bacon was directly affected by the prohibition.[52]

Some of the frontiersmen charged that although Berkeley publicly prohibited trading with the Indians, "he privately gave commicion to trade to some of his friends, who accordingly did sell store of powder and shott etc. to the Indians then in arms against us." [53] The commissioners sent to investigate the causes of the rebellion made a thorough investigation of these charges but found no evidence of any such trade.[54]

Although historians have asserted that Berkeley continued to control the Indian trade at this time and to draw profits from it, their evidence is based on the unproven and discredited charges of Bacon and his followers. The only valid evidence on the subject is the statute enacted by the March Assembly which specifically relieved the governor of control of the Indian trade that was allowed, and put it in the hands of the county courts. It is quite possible that Berkeley himself asked the assembly to take control of the Indian trade out of his hands. This would be in keeping with his action, on first entering the government in 1642, of releasing to the use of the public many of the perquisites of his office "that he might keep his Reputation cleere from all hazards of Calumny." [55]

Just as the charge that Berkeley refused to take a firm line against the Indians for fear of losing his Indian profits is false, so is the charge that Bacon precipitated the rebellion for the sake of retaining *his* fur profits. Robert Beverley, the historian and son of one of Berkeley's loyal supporters, noted that many had charged that the rebellion was caused by "the Instigation of Two or Three Traders only, who aim'd at a Monopoly of the *Indian* Trade...."[56] The two or three traders referred, no doubt, to Bacon and his trading partner William Byrd. Beverley rejected the charge as much too simple an explanation of the causes of the rebellion. One can see how the story might have arisen, however. Bacon and Byrd, both of whom were cousins of Frances Culpepper, Lady Berkeley,[57] had been granted licences by the governor. In return for the privilege, they promised him eight hundred pounds of beaver for the first year and six hundred a year thereafter.[58] The profitable trade of the two was suddenly cut off, however, by the act of the assembly of March 1676, by which all regular traders lost their trading privileges. A few weeks after passage of the act Bacon led a group of frontiersmen on an unauthorized expedition against the friendly Occaneechee Indians, an event which is discussed in the next chapter. According to some of Bacon's men the "great designe" of the expedition was to get the £1,000 store of beaver possessed by the Occaneechees.[59] Since Bacon's activities against the Indians throughout 1676 consisted entirely of killing and plundering friendly Indians, it is easy to see why many believe that his attacks on the natives were motivated by the desire to regain his fur trade profits, even though it had to be by illegal and violent means. While there is reason to believe that Bacon might never have engaged in rebellion had his trading privilege not been revoked by the March act, there is not enough evidence to substantiate such a belief, and the nature of Bacon's character strongly suggests that his actions were not determined by the profit motive.

In the tense days of March 1676 the wildest rumors found

ready acceptance. Even the assembly, in a formal address to the King asking for arms and ammunition, reported that "to our griefe wee finde by certain intelligence, within these few dayes" that the colony's Indian enemies were offering vast sums of their wealth to hire other nations of Indians, two or three hundred miles distant, to fall upon them, and that they were gathering on the James River some fifty or sixty miles from the plantations.[60] This rumor, apparently groundless, may have been the final link in the chain of circumstances that turned the people's grumbling into open disobedience.[61]

Fear of attack from without increased the fear of disloyalty from within. A profound disquiet fell upon the legislators who felt unable "to ghuesse where the Storme will fall, for that all Indians as well our neer Neighbours as those more remote ... [give] us dayly Suspitions that it is not any private grudge, but a generall Combination, of all from New-England hither...." The assembly concluded that there was "an absolute necessity, not only of fortifieing all our frontiers more strongly; but of keeping Severall, considerable parties both of Horse and foot still in motion to confront them where soever they shall attaque us. Which cannot be done without a vast expence." The assembly informed the King that it could not support the cost of such measures in "our present low condition," and would therefore use the arms on hand "to defend and keep our ground untill we can procure a new Supply." The new supply they begged from the King.[62]

On April 1 Berkeley discussed the tense situation in a letter to Thomas Ludwell, secretary of the colony, then in England. The problem of the Indian war, he wrote, was complicated because some individuals "would faine perswade the People that al their High Taxes wil bring them no benefit." Berkeley hoped that "we shal easily repel the Ennimie if some seditious sperits amangst ourselves hinder not our proceedings who for pretext of their Villiny spread amongst the People the intollerablenesse of this most necessary charge of the Warr. I thanke God the Assembly

has given me nothing this last three years els that would have
been a pretext also." [63]

What made the Indian alarms and high taxes more difficult to
bear was the economic distress that hung over the colony. There
was genuine distress, genuine poverty. Historians disagree on the
cause of the poverty—in particular, whether the English Navi-
gation Acts should be blamed—but there is little doubt as to its
existence, or as to Governor Berkeley's honest attempts to relieve
it.[64] One indisputable cause of the colony's economic misfor-
tunes was bad weather in 1676 that nearly ruined the tobacco
crop, the very life of the colony. "If wee make ¼ Cropps this
year," wrote Philip Ludwell in the summer of 1676, "Ile swear
it must be by miracle, haveing the Dryest year, added to the
maddest that ever I think the world saw . . . ." [65] Thomas Mathew
similarly commented that the summer of 1676 was "so dry as
stinted the Indian Corn and Tobacco etc. Which the People
Ascribed to the *Pawawings, i.e.* the Sorceries of the Indians. . . ." [66]
Added to the other troubles which dogged the colony after the
Restoration—declining tobacco prices, increasingly restricted
English market, growing competition from Maryland and Caro-
lina, increasing prices for English manufactured goods, heavy
losses in the naval wars with the Dutch, hailstorms, floods, hurri-
canes, and epidemics—the curse of a dry year was a final calamity
to a desperately poor people. All contemporary sources speak
of the great mass of people as living in severe economic straits.

Unlike their brothers in England, however, the Virginia plant-
ers were not of a temper simply to deplore their condition and
hope for better times. Years of freedom from restraint, years
of familiarity with firearms, had developed in the New World
colonists an unwillingness to accept their fate passively. To
govern such desperate men by paper decrees not backed by royal
troops was not feasible. "How miserable that man is," wrote
Governor Berkeley just before active civil conflict broke out,
"that Governes a People wher six parts of seaven at least are
Poore Endebted Discontented and Armed." [67] In 1646 the forty-

year old Berkeley had captured the aged Opechancanough in a daring cavalry raid on the chief's headquarters. In 1676 youth and vigor were on the side of the governor's enemy.[68]

During April the people had not reached the stage of rebellion. Their complaints were many and bitter, however, and were centered on the acts of the March Assembly providing for the defense of the colony. Most objected to being taxed to pay for the defense measures, and some implied that it was all a plot to enrich certain "favorites." They asserted that the Indians could go right around the forts and attack in the interior of the country. Of course they were right if fixed fortifications were the only defense. But the act provided for more than immobile garrisons for the forts: one quarter of the five hundred men raised were to be horsemen. The act specifically directed "that the horsemen in every garrison be commanded to range Continually betweene the garrisons till they meete if possible, that a constant intelligence be maintained betweene them, And the foote to be in motion at the discretion of the commanders, for secureing the adjacent plantations." [69] Even "The humble Appeal of the Volunteers to all well minded and charitable people" against the forts and against the Indians admitted that patrols did range the areas between the forts. The "Appeal" merely asserted that the forts are "soe scantly mann'd as they cannot draw out any competent force either to oppose or range or number sufficient to relieve one another in their Patroles...." [70]

In terms of the overall defense of the colony forts were sound; they had proved effective in 1645-1646 and again in 1678-1680.[71] The frontiersmen's complaints, however, were understandable. Forts have never been capable of preventing infiltration behind them. The frontiersman, with his own home and family to consider, could not see the larger picture. He wanted complete safety immediately and considered the goal attainable only by rushing out and exterminating all Indians.

Berkeley had ordered the militia officers to prosecute the war as they thought fit.[72] Many of the colonists, however, in addition to grumbling at the taxes necessary to build the forts and to support the five hundred men raised by the March Assembly,[73] continued to feel insecure and afraid. Rumors of devastation and imminent attack swept through the colony. There are frequent general references in documents of the period to a death toll of hundreds, but the validity of such estimates is subject to doubt. The commissioners asserted in their post-rebellion "Narrative" that at this time the murders, rapins, and outrages became "more Barbarous, fierce and frequent." If this were so, it must have been a terrible period in Virginia's history, for the commissioners reported that in the year preceding the meeting of the March Assembly three hundred persons were killed.[74] However, the largest number of killings *specifically* reported is thirty-six, representing those murdered by the Susquehannocks in January following their escape from the fort. There are occasional specific references in the documents of the period to one, two, eight, or fifteen persons being killed by the Indians during 1675 and 1676, but the total number of reports of individual deaths at particular points in space and time amounts to only a small proportion of the number *generally* reported killed.

Moreover there is evidence to suggest that rumor entered into many reports of casualties. Governor Berkeley wrote that "al April and May [1676] we lost not one man out of any Plantation...."[75] And Thomas Mathew recalled that

In these frightfull times...no Man Stirrd out of Door unarm'd, Indians were (ever and anon) espied, Three, 4, 5, or 6 in a Party Lurking throughout the Whole Land, yet (what was remarkable) I rarely heard of any Houses Burnt, tho' abundance was forsaken, nor ever, of any Corn or Tobacco cut up, or other Injury done, besides Murders, Except the killing a very few Cattle and Swine.[76]

In their excited condition the planters turned their eyes to the most convenient targets for their wrath: the several villages of subject Indians within the colony. Here were ideal sacrificial victims: the color of their skin exactly matched that of the frontier marauders, they fitted nicely into the role of "traitors in our midst" if not by overt acts, by secret intention, and there were few of them. The policy of Governor Berkeley and the council, as has been pointed out, was to preserve these small groups of Indians as spies, buffers, and allies against the real enemy. Frontier theory, however, required that the neighboring Indians bear the burden of guilt for frontier troubles. When the settlers heard that Colonels William Cole and Nathaniel Bacon, Sr., had publicly told the inhabitants of New Kent County that the Pamunkey and Appomattox Indians were "our friends, and that we ought to defend them with our blood," they concluded that the government was as traitorously inclined as the Pamunkeys and Appomattox themselves. Yet no evidence was ever produced to show that the local tributary Indians committed a single act of hostility against the English, or even that they had expressed any intention of committing such an act. The best proofs of Indian "guilt" the frontiersmen could find were their own "apprehensions" that the country was in danger of being destroyed by Indians.[77]

Driven from their plantations by fear, many of the frontiersmen gathered in armed groups in the more settled and secure areas of the country. A group from Charles City County, terrified by reports that hostile forces were gathering on the upper James River for an attack, called for volunteers to go out against the Indians. At the same time they presented a petition to Governor Berkeley requesting that they be allowed to choose officers to lead them against the enemy they imagined rapidly approaching the plantations.[78] Berkeley seems to have been doubtful both of their information and of their intentions. He told the petitioners that regular forces were coming up to defend the frontier, tried unsuccessfully to make them aware of their duty to the lawfully constituted officers of government, and finally he "gave us back the petition, [and] bid a pox take us. . . ."[79]

The seven men who signed the post-rebellion document purporting to contain the "Grievances" of Charles City County asserted that Berkeley, after this incident, "by proclamation under great pennalty prohibited the like petitioning for the future." [80] However, the investigation into the affair ordered by the commissioners failed to bring forth a bit of evidence to support this malicious rumor, and the writers of the grievance were forced to admit that the authority for their charge was merely that "wee did heare" that such an order was issued.[81] Nevertheless the rumor was dignified by inclusion in the commissioners' "Narrative" and accepted as truth by the Lords of Trade and Plantations.[82]

The fears of the frontiersmen, though groundless in this particular and exaggerated in general, were nevertheless real, and they were too great to be allayed by reason or ridicule. A blood sacrifice was required. The frontiersmen's need was for a high priest to tell them the cause of God's wrath and what sacrifices they must make to appease Him. Nathaniel Bacon was fated to be the appointed vessel.

Bacon's assumption of the role of high priest seems to have been partly fortuitous and partly planned. He was drinking one day with James Crewes, Henry Isham, and William Byrd, three planters who lived near the falls of James River, "making the Sadnesse of the times their discourse, and the Fear they all lived in, because of the Susquahanocks who had settled a little above the Falls of James River, and comitted many murders upon them, among whom Bacon's overseer happen'd to be one. . . ." In the course of the meeting, Bacon's companions persuaded him to visit the volunteer soldiers gathered at Jordan's Point near the junction of the Appomattox and James rivers, and to take a quantity of rum to give the men to drink, "which they did, and (as Crews etc. had before laid the Plot with the Soldiers) they all at once in field shouted and cry'd out, a Bacon! a Bacon! w'ch taking Fire with his ambition and Spirit of Faction and Popularity, easily prevail'd on him to Resolve to head them. . . ." [83]

Bacon's unauthorized acceptance of command caused Governor Berkeley to dispatch several letters warning him against becoming a mutineer, and finally to send for him under a safe conduct guarantee.[84] Although Bacon answered these letters protesting his abhorrence of the name of mutineer and his readiness to wait on the governor, he continued to justify his proceedings and to find excuses for not coming to Jamestown.[85] He did, however, hint that if the governor would "please in some measure to entrust mee with the Countrys safety by your Honors Commission for *volunteers*," he would agree to accept the distinction made by the March Assembly between friendly and enemy Indians. He intimated that he would, in such a case, follow Berkeley's orders "whatever my sence and opinion bee of the neighbour Indians...."[86]

What Bacon's "sence and opinion" of the neighboring Indians was, is revealed in "The humble Appeal of the Volunteers to all well minded and charitable people." The "Appeal" first denounces the system of defense by forts as useless against Indian infiltration. The need for a moving force then is affirmed, but an army is rejected as too expensive. Next the rhetorical question: If the present tax levy is too difficult to bear, how can a bigger one for an army be raised? The "Volunteers'" patriotic solution is to offer themselves as "both actours and paymasters of this necessary defensive warr." Finally the probable motive for their generous selflessness: a vigorous assertion of the guilt of the friendly neighboring Indians and a denial of their right to any land in the King's territory. Briefly summarized, the "Appeal" asserts that the government's action against the *foreign* Indians is both ineffective and costly and that the true solution is to let the petitioners serve as unpaid volunteers against the friendly *local* Indians.[87]

The frontiersmen's legal argument, identical with that used by Bacon in his letters and later in his "Manifesto," suggests how irresistible a movement for violence can become when justified by a theory—however specious—of its own. The "Volunteers" ask

Whether or no wee ought not to judge his Majesty's title prerogative good here, and his claime better then that of ... all Indians whatsoever, and whether since his Majesty hath been possessed of this part of America, wee have not been invaded, and his Territories claimed, and his subjects barbarously murdered, his Lands depopulated and usurped by those barbarous Enemies, whose outrages, wrongs and violences offered to our Soveraigne and his subjects have been soe cunningly mixt among the severall Nations or familyes of Indians that it hath been very difficult for us, to distinguish how, or from which of those said Nations, the said wrongs did proceed.[88]

Needless to say, Bacon did not get his commission. Berkeley could see no reason why the regularly commissioned officers of the militia and government could not handle the situation, and he continued to remain suspicious of Bacon's intentions toward the neighboring Indians. Bacon was, nevertheless, the uncommissioned "General of the Volunteers." The frontiersmen had taken him to heart, not only because of his belief that all Indians should be extirpated, but because he let it be known that he would bear all the costs of the campaign. "It is hardly to be beleeved," wrote Berkeley, "how this promise and undertaking tooke with the country ... so that like a trayne of powder as it were in a moment it enfected not only Virginia but Maryland...."[89] Forty years later Governor Alexander Spotswood asserted that had Berkeley had £1,000 of public money on hand at the beginning of Bacon's Rebellion the outbreak could have been prevented. Instead, the rebel Bacon, not the King's governor, was able to promise the people what they wanted at no expense to them.[90]

The first action of Bacon and his volunteers was to "terrify" and "threaten" the Pamunkeys so much "that they fled for security." The volunteers' "coveting the good Land" on which they were settled was undoubtedly a strong inducement to

[37]

the enterprise.[91] The assault further undermined the governor's policy of maintaining stability on the frontier by just treatment of the friendly neighboring Indians. Because of the attacks on the Pamunkey and other tributary Indians, wrote Philip Ludwell, "wee have not now that wee Know of 100 Freind Indians on all our Borders, but at least 1500 enemies more than wee needed to have had...."[92]

The men of the American frontier were never careful to distinguish between guilt or innocence so far as Indians were concerned, especially when the white man's interest was involved. New Englanders, at this very same time, under the impact of King Philip's War, were treating the friendly "praying Indians" in much the same fashion Virginians were dealing with their Indian neighbors. As in Virginia, only a few men were to be found willing to defend the friendly Indians from the unjust charges and violence offered them. Nor is the phenomenon limited in time any more than it is in space. Bacon would have been at home among the "Paxton Boys" in Pennsylvania in 1763, and with Colonel Chivington's soldiers in Colorado in 1864.

It is difficult to estimate intentions but the evidence of the actual deeds of Bacon and his men in 1676 indicates that a legitimate defense of the frontier was, if anything, only an incidental consideration in their minds. For Bacon and his men did not kill a single enemy Indian but contented themselves with frightening away, killing, or enslaving most of the friendly neighboring Indians, and taking their beaver and land as spoils.

Bacon proved an able leader of the frontiersmen. That personal greed led him to this role is unlikely. It is more probable that he enjoyed playing the role of admired "leader." What he lacked in military experience he made up in a clever understanding of mob psychology. He filled the air with appeals, petitions, and justifications to the people, government, and King. He dredged up all possible grievances, attributing their cause to the "unworthy Favourites and juggling Parasites" in the government.[93] His primary aim and his justification were always, however, the necessity for "defense" and "revenge" against the barbarous Indians. The appeals associated with his side also deal almost solely with this issue.[94] By understanding what he and his followers meant by "defense" and "revenge" we can better judge the justice of Bacon's "cause."

By the King.
A PROCLAMATION
For the Suppressing a Rebellion lately raised within the
Plantation of Virginia.

CHARLES R.

Hereas Nathaniel Bacon the Younger, of the Plantation of Virginia, and others his Adherents and Complices (being Persons of mean and desperate Fortunes) have lately in a Traiterous and Rebellious manner levyed War within the said Plantation, against the Kings most Excellent Majesty, and more particularly being Assembled in a Warlike manner to the number of about Five hundred Persons, did in the Moneth of June last past, Inviron & Besiege the Governor and Assembly of the said Plantation (then met together about the Publique affairs of the same Plantation) and did by Menaces and Threats of present Death compel the said Governor and Assembly to pass divers pretended Acts: To the end therefore that the said Nathaniel Bacon and his Complices may suffer such punishment as for their Treason and Rebellion they have justly deserved: His Majesty doth (by this His Royal Proclamation) Publish and Declare, That the said Nathaniel Bacon, and all and every such Persons and Person, being His Majesties Subjects within the said Plantation, as have taken Arms under, willingly joyned with, or assisted, or shall hereafter take Arms under, willingly joyn with, or assist the said Nathaniel Bacon, in raising or carrying on the War (by him as aforesaid levyed) are and shall be guilty of the crime of High Treason. And His Majesty doth hereby strictly Charge and Command all His Lo-

Opening lines of Charles II's controversial
proclamation of pardon of October, 1676

Chapter 3

THE OCCANEECHEE CAMPAIGN
MAY, 1676

****

D ESPITE THE laws and orders of the March Assembly many
Virginians continued to feel insecure. The "continuall
Allarmes" over King Philip's War in New England put
all the people "in an uprore." The tax of sixty pounds of tobacco
per poll, levied to support the Virginia agents' fight against the
King's grants of the colony to some of his favorites, continued
to make "al those that thought they were not concerned in it
apt to mutiny." The added cost of building the forts and raising
the troops authorized by the March Assembly was resented, and
soon rumors arose that everyone would be required to pay 1,000
pounds of tobacco for the purpose. Two busybodies, Mrs.
Thomas Grindon and Mrs. Anthony Haviland, spread malicious
falsehoods concerning Berkeley's intentions, and the governor
complained that "twas presently through the whole country that
I was a greater frend to the Indians then to the English." [1] Bacon,
taking advantage of the discontent, talked of solving Virginia's
problems in his own way. [2]

On May 3 Governor Berkeley, unsuccessful in his attempts
to persuade Bacon to let the regularly constituted militia cap-
tains handle the situation and angered by Bacon's refusal to

appear before him, gathered together about three hundred well armed gentlemen and rode out to Henrico County "to call Mr. Bacon to accompt." [3] By the time he arrived in Henrico County, Bacon—still protesting his loyalty—had plunged off into the wilderness with two hundred men in search of "a more agreeable destiny then you are pleased to designe mee." [4] The governor contented himself with issuing two proclamations on May 10. The first declared Bacon a rebel and relieved him of his seat on the Council. However, because many might have been "seduc'd and delud'd by his spetious pretences," Berkeley granted a pardon to all who would go home, remain quiet, and resume their obedience by the end of May or three days after their return from the Indian march. Bacon and two others were excepted but were promised a "faire and legal triall." [5]

Berkeley's second proclamation should be read carefully by those who assume that he was by nature tyrannical, grasping, and stubborn. In this proclamation the governor dissolved the "Long Assembly" and ordered elections for a new assembly which was instructed to redress all grievances and provide for the security of the country against the Indians. Berkeley announced that the council would serve "att their owne personall Charges for the ease of the Country" and hoped that the elected burgesses would do the same. Then he issued a challenge:

And because the Country may perhaps conceave some defect to bee in the present Government, I doe will and require that att the election of the said Burgesses all and every person and persons there present have liberty to present freely to their said Burgesses all such Just Complaints as they or any of them have against mee as Governor for any Act of Injustice by mee done or any reward bribe or present by mee accepted or taken from any person whatsoever and that the same bee by the said Burgesses presented to the Assembly and there duely examined and redressed. And supposeing I whome am head of the Assembly may bee their greatest grevance I will most gladly Joyne with them in a petition to his most Sacred Majesty to appoint a new Governor of Virginia And thereby to ease and discharge mee from the great care and trouble thereof in my old age.[6]

While Berkeley awaited the return of Bacon, news came to him that the Queen of Pamunkey had tortured an English interpreter and then turned him loose with instructions to tell the governor "shee did intend to visett him shortely." The governor was, in addition, "much moved to heare that the people should so basely Abuse him in thear murmering that it is through his love to the Beavor that he doth not take a speedye course and destroy the Indeans. . . ." [7] On top of these reports came one from Colonel Thomas Goodrich that the tributary Indians had turned against the English.[8] In his reply of May 15 Berkeley expressed horror over "the death of those poore innocents these barbarous Villaines have killed" and declared that "I beleive all the Indians, our neighbours are engaged with the Susquahannoes and therefore I desire you to spare none that has the name of an Indian for they are now all our Enemies." Berkeley dashed off another letter on the same day to Colonel William Claiborne in which he ordered him "to take all Indians for Enemies that have left their plantations." [9]

Berkeley's policy of protecting the subject Indians had thus failed. Had he been willing to compromise his rigorous defense of the rights of the Indian minority a month earlier he might have headed off the rebellion. The cost would have been the lives and property of the subject Indians, and the honor of the English nation, a price which the people of Virginia were willing to pay. Governor Berkeley was willing to pay the price also, but he refused to do so until he received what seemed to be conclusive proof that the subject Indians were guilty of attacks on the colonists. When it became apparent, a few weeks later, that the reports he had received were false, he quickly returned to his former views.[10]

While Berkeley and his horsemen waited in Henrico, Bacon won his first great "victory" against "the Indians." That is to say, in the words of the commissioners sent to investigate the causes of the rebellion, he "fell upon the Indians and killed some of them who were our best Friends of Indians and had fought against the Susquahanocks enemyes to the English." [11] Contemporary reports of the battle agree that in May 1676 Bacon and his men marched southwest from the James River to the Roanoke River, near the present border between Virginia and North Carolina. On an island in the Roanoke River near the present Clarksville, Virginia, lived the Occaneechee tribe in a well-constructed fort.[12] Near them were encamped a band of Susquehannocks who had drifted down from the north following the English attack on their fort. The Susquehannocks had tried to get the Occaneechees to help them against the colonists, but the Occaneechees refused and sent runners to the English to inform them of the Susquehannocks' whereabouts.[13]

Bacon's men arrived at the Occaneechee fort exhausted and almost without provisions. They were, it seems, brought over to the island in the Indians' canoes and given food, shelter, and entertainment.[14] Bacon asked about the Susquehannocks and was told that they had entrenched themselves in two forts five and ten miles away. When the young Englishman expressed a desire to attack the nearest fort, the Occaneechees offered to do the job for him, and Bacon agreed.[15] With the aid of certain Manakin and other Indians who were prisoners *within* the Susquehannock camp, the Occaneechees made the attack by themselves with complete success. The prisoners and the Manakins were brought back to the island. Some or all of the prisoners were presented to Bacon, tortured, and killed.[16]

From this point accounts of the expedition vary.

William Sherwood asserted that Bacon picked a quarrel with the Occaneechees to get their £1,000 store of beaver "for itt is most true, that the great designe (which is confessed by some that was with him) was to gett the beaver...." Sherwood also reported that Bacon felt he had to "do something" against the Indians or else lose popular support. Consequently he set guards on the Indian fort containing the fur and would not permit any of the Occaneechees to pass in or out. He also seized those Indians who were outside the fort. The Indians within, perceiving this, fired, and the fight was on. Bacon's men succeeded in slaughtering most of the Indians and then withdrew.[17]

Philip Ludwell's account of the fight is similar. He reported that on the Occaneechees' return, Bacon demanded the plunder and the six Manakins who, with some Annalecktons, had aided the Occaneechees from within the Susquehannock camp. To this demand, Persicles, the Occaneechee chief, replied that he thought it but reasonable that his own men have the plunder and that the Manakins should go free. When Bacon persisted, Persicles began to temporize. This tactic so alarmed the Manakins that one of them fired a gun and killed an Englishman, at which the English fell on the Occaneechees and destroyed most of them, including Persicles, "who had the Character by all that knew him of a very Brave man and ever true to the English." [18]

One of Bacon's soldiers also wrote an account of the fight. He justified the attack on the Occaneechees by saying that Persicles refused to give the English the provisions they needed, and that he lined one side of the river "thick with men soe that we could neither well attack them, nor depart thee Iland without some danger." Persicles was sent for, and the English conferred with him, but "being yet more and more dissatisfyed, we ordered our men to surround the Fort with all expedition, and if they could to enter it. . . ." The English were unable to seize the fort since it was protected by some of the Indians, but they were able to "hinder the rest from entering the Fort which were very many still crowding in and to demand satisfaction of their King, But he cunningly threw all the blame upon the Manakins, and Annalecktons whom he said were so many he could not Rule them but pretended to perswade them, which he presuming to doe, making faire pretences of lying in guard with us all night or what els would be thought convenient Provided wee would withdraw." Bacon and his men, however, refused to leave. Suddenly, a shot rang out from across the river, killing one of Bacon's men. Immediately the English poured a lethal fire into the Indians within the fort, and "fell upon the men woemen and children without[,] disarmed and destroid them all. . . ." The fight lasted through the night and into the next day when Persicles was killed. Finally, fearing rising water and shortage of provisions, Bacon's men crossed the river and returned home.[19]

A close reading of the account by Bacon's man raises certain puzzling questions. If Bacon was demanding only more food for his men, or a guarantee against attack, why all the talk about Persicles "cunningly" throwing "the blame" on the Manakins and Annalecktons "whom he said were so many he could not Rule them but pretended to perswade them"? Persuade them to what purpose? Certainly these rescued warriors did not have any food they could be forced to give to the frontiersmen, nor does it seem that they were numerous enough to challenge the English. If Bacon's aim was security against Indian attack, why did he not treat Persicles' offer of guarantees with more interest? Bacon's man asserted that the Indians manned their forts and lined the river "soe that we could neither well attack them, nor depart the Iland without some danger." But there was no act of violence, or even talk of violence, on the part of the Indians, until the fatal shot fired from across the river. This was long after Bacon had ordered his men to surround the fort "and if they could to enter it," after the Indians outside the forts had been seized, and after Persicles' offer of hostages and other pleadings had been rejected. The implication is, as Ludwell wrote, that Bacon's men wanted to persuade Persicles to give them the Manakins and Annalecktons for slaves. They perhaps also desired to get the store of beaver and win a great "Indian victory."

Bacon, in a letter to England in June 1676 did not bother to justify the attack morally, but wrote frankly that "we fell upon a town of the Indians, consisting of 3 forts strongly mann'd beginning our fight after midnight close at their port holes."[20] A contemporary Indian account, received by Major General

Abraham Wood at Fort Henry, reported that "twoe Kings of the Ockanechees with some of their great men were drawne in upon a treaty supprized and killed by them." [21] Governor Berkeley averred that "Bacon himselfe confesd to me and my Councel that he could not have forced his way by day [onto the Occaneechees' island] if they had had intelligence of their intentions." [22]

Later historians have almost without exception found nothing unjustified in Bacon's Occaneechee expedition despite the questionable consistency of the account by Bacon's follower and the frequent assertion by contemporaries of the disgraceful character of the episode. In general it is considered a "heroic victory over the Indians." [23] Yet the fact that Bacon's men reached the loopholes of the Indians' fort before the defenders were able to man them has suggested to one historian that the first hostile moves should be attributed to Bacon. As Professor Abernethy has written: "This feat is almost unparalleled in the history of frontier warfare, and since native warriors were never lacking in alertness, it can indicate but one thing: that the attack was made upon an unsuspecting foe." [24]

What was the result of Bacon's Occaneechee campaign? Thirty enemy Susquehannocks had been destroyed by the friendly Occaneechee, Manakin, and Annaleckton Indians. Bacon had not had a hand in the battle. He had destroyed not one of the Indians defined as an enemy by the March Assembly. He had killed only friendly Indians. [25]

Bacon returned to Henrico to find Berkeley gone back to Jamestown to prepare for the coming meeting of the assembly. Despite Bacon's unauthorized Occaneechee campaign and his continued flouting of the governor's authority, [26] Berkeley was willing to forget the past for the sake of the peace of the country. Bacon insisted that he would not forgo his campaign against "all Indians in general, for that they were all Enemies; this I have allwaies said and do maintain," but he offered to come to some agreement with the governor, if it could be done without sacrificing his honor.[27] This could best be accomplished, Bacon thought, if he were allowed a hearing before King Charles. Governor Berkeley solemnly swore that he should have his wish.[28] The council, though recommending that the young man acknowledge his errors and beg his pardon directly from the governor, wrote Bacon conveying Berkeley's assurance. They hinted strongly that if he asked for a pardon the governor would give him "a full and absolute" one.[29]

On May 28 Bacon rejected the suggestion that he beg for his pardon from the governor, and ignored his original request for a hearing before the King. Although professing himself "one that respects your Honors authority and holds your person sacred," he renewed his demand on the governor for a commission.[30]

Hopes for a reconciliation were thus shattered. The next day Berkeley issued his "Declaration and Remonstrance," calling God to witness that he knew of no unjust, corrupt, or negligent act of which he had been guilty. He challenged Bacon to show a single precedent in the history of any nation where actions such as his had ever been approved. If Bacon could do so, Berkeley promised to mediate with the King for a pardon for him, "but I can shew him an hundred exemples where brave and greate men have been put to death for gaining victories against the command of their superiors." As for Bacon's "victory," "that very action wherein he so much boastes was Rashly foolishly and as I am informed Treacherously carried to the dishonor of the English nation Yet in it he lost more men then I did in three yeares warr...." Then Berkeley declared his policy: "I would have preservd those Indians that I knew were hourely at our mercy to have beene our spies and intelligence to find out the more bloudy Ennimies. But as soone as I had the least intelligence that they also were treacherous Ennimies I have given out commissions to destroy them al as the commissions themselves will speake itt." Three times, he noted, he had given Bacon pardons "which he has scornefully rejected." There was obviously nothing left but to proceed against him as a rebel.[31] The council, in a proclamation of the same day, declared him a rebel and called on all persons to assist the government against him.[32]

On June 1 the governor's proclamation was sent to England by William Sherwood, a lawyer in the colony, with the comment that Bacon's actions were "of most daingerous consequence in this time of warr with the Indians...." "This Country hath had thirty fower years experience of the valour, conduct, Justice, and Impartiall proceedinge of our honorable Governor who hath endeavoured the Generall good of the Country, by spending and laying out his estate amongst us," exclaimed Sherwood, "yett he and all authority and Magistracy are by the rabble contemned." [33]

When the sheriff attempted to read the governor's declaration and the council's proclamation at the election meeting in Henrico County, Bacon, with an armed guard, thrust him aside and prevented the reading. The people were not to be given the opportunity of being converted by Berkeley's eloquence.[34] Bacon, his prestige as a frontier hero enhanced by the Occaneechee "victory," was elected burgess along with his lieutenant James Crewes.[35]

The strain was beginning to tell on Berkeley. Riding over the country had exhausted the seventy-year-old governor, and dealing with Bacon must have filled him with sadness and loathing. As soon as he returned from Henrico he put his wife aboard a ship for England,[36] and on June 3 wrote to Secretary of State Coventry:

Sir I am so over wearied with riding into al parts of the country to stop this violent rebellion that I am not able to support my selfe at this age six months longer and therefore on my knees I beg his sacred majesty would send a more vigorous Governor. Sir if I out live this I shal ever be

> Your most obedient servant
> Will Berkeley [37]

Chapter 4

THE JUNE ASSEMBLY

❖-❖

IT IS customary to speak of the assembly of June 1676 as "Bacon's Assembly," and of the laws passed at the session as "Bacon's Laws." Some doubts have been raised as to the extent of Bacon's influence on the passage of the laws, but few have challenged the assumption that the assembly reflected his interest in reforming abuses that had developed under Berkeley's administration. The belief that Bacon pushed through democratic measures against the opposition of Governor Berkeley is, indeed, the cornerstone of the interpretation that Bacon's Rebellion was an attempt at political reform. Obviously the passage of reform laws must have been the primary aim of Bacon, if he was a reformer. However, as we shall see, he had no genuine interest in political reform and his name has been mistakenly associated with the June Assembly.

Very little is known about the composition of the assembly. It is true to say, however, that it was "much infected with Bacon's principles," [1] in the sense that the general unrest churned the more radical elements to the surface. Berkeley had encouraged this tendency by allowing, at the urging of the council, all freemen, not alone property holders, to vote. [2] The practice had been outlawed in 1670 because of tumults at election time and the need to bring Virginia's laws into conformity with the laws of England.[3] That Berkeley allowed all freemen to vote in the June election demonstrates both his good will and his inability to rule with unquestioned authority in Virginia. He had to make concessions to the real power in Virginia: the people.

The commissioners sent to investigate the causes of the rebellion reported in 1677 that "such was the Prevalency of Bacon's Party" that the people chose "instead of Freeholders, Free men that had but lately crept out of the condition of Servants . . . and such as were eminent abettors to Bacon, and for faction and ignorance fitt Representatives of those that chose them." [4] One of the assemblymen voted out of office at this time was George Jordan. Jordan wrote to Colonel Francis Moryson, then one of Virginia's agents in England and later one of the commissioners sent to Virginia, that "the giddy people . . . have hardly Chosen one fitt well byased man for the Countryes peace: nor any of frendship with the Honorable Governor by which unhapy Accident I am put with all the rest of our dear freinds . . . out of the house. . . ." [5]

Berkeley himself wrote later that "but eight of the Burgesses . . . were not of his [Bacon's] faction and at his devotion. . . ." [6] Isaac Allerton, a prominent figure in northern Virginia, noted that "the Southerne Counties sent Burgesses, proportionable to their factious and Rebellious humours and a considerable partie of the Burgesses, were of his [Bacon's] side apparently enough. . . ." [7] Colonel Edward Hill, in answering the post-rebellion grievances against him in May 1677, asserted that Thomas Blayton was "Bacon's great engin" in the June Assembly and that James Minge, also one of Hill's accusers and clerk of the assembly, was "another [of] Bacon's Great friends in formeing the lawes" in the June Assembly.[8]

These opinions would seem to support the conventional assumption that Bacon was the leader of a radical political reform movement which attempted to correct the abuses of Sir William Berkeley's government. However, nothing could be further from the truth. Least of all should one consider the reformers in the June Assembly as organized by Bacon or acknowledging his leadership. What is to be kept in mind is that Bacon's "cause" was not a scheme of political reform, but a crusade for extirpating the Indians.

Bacon and his henchman James Crewes had been elected burgesses from Henrico County. Bacon was hesitant to claim his seat because Berkeley's proclamation against him as a rebel still stood. The assembly met on June 5, 1676. On June 6 Bacon sailed down the river to Jamestown with fifty armed men, "thinking as we must suppose," wrote the governor, "to surprise me and the councel." [9] That night he slipped ashore for a secret conference with William Drummond and Richard Lawrence, two of his prominent supporters in town.[10] The following morning Berkeley ordered Captain Thomas Gardner, master of the merchant ship *Adam and Eve*, to seize Bacon and bring him before the general assembly "to Answere to such things as shall be Layd to his Charge. . . ." [11] Gardner successfully captured the young rebel in his sloop and brought him before the governor.[12] Hearing of his capture hundreds, possibly as many as two thousand Virginians, crowded into Jamestown determined to free him, although Bacon was unaware of their presence.[13]

On June 9, on his knees, in the presence of the house of burgesses, the young rebel handed to the governor a written confession acknowledging his misdeeds and promising to be a dutiful subject in the future.[14] Berkeley, after a short pause, "Answered 'God forgive you, I forgive you,' thrice repeating the same Words." [15] The house of burgesses then requested he be pardoned, the council recommended it, and Governor Berkeley pardoned him.[16] On June 10 he was restored to his seat on the council.[17]

Why the governor pardoned Bacon after having him in his power has mystified many. The home government condemned Berkeley for his leniency.[18] The governor answered the question saying that "we al thought we had Gained a great Poynt in making him acknowledge his fault on his knees before the Grand Assembly whilse he was Ignorant of the Numbers that were Armed and resolved to rescue him out of our hands. . . ." Berkeley believed that Bacon sincerely meant to keep his promise "til within two dayes after he heard what an incredible Number of the meanest of the People were every where Armed to assist him and his cause. . . ." [19]

According to Bacon, "one of the Burgesses proclaimed mee Generall to satisfy and disperse the people, who were so satisfied herein that they all retired peaceably, but hee [Berkeley] brok his word, and refused to signe my commission. . . ." [20] This statement seems to be close to the truth, though not too close. Certainly Governor Berkeley would not announce any such decision by a single unnamed burgess when he had a full council and a complete house of burgesses which could have made the announcement. Moreover the statement is ambiguous. "Generall" of what? Of volunteers? Of all the armed forces of the colony? It is probable that, after his release, he heard a garbled version of what some frightened burgess said to some of the frontiersmen during the confusion of his arrest, and used it to good advantage.

There is little doubt that Berkeley promised Bacon a commission, but there were two important qualifications. Philip Ludwell, deputy secretary of the colony, stated one in a letter of June 12, after Bacon had been pardoned and readmitted to the council. Ludwell wrote that the ex-rebel "is now speedily to have a Commission to Gett what volunteirs he Can, and march out against the Indians." [21] Ludwell's letter is significant because it was written immediately after the promise was given and before it was broken (according to Bacon) obliging him to leave Jamestown and collect enough men to obtain the commission by force. Ludwell, in a letter of June 28, after Bacon had forced his commission from the assembly, similarly remarked that Bacon had received the "Governors promise that on his Future Good behaviour he should have a Commission to Gett volunteers to Goe against the Indians, wherwith he Seemed well sattisfyed, but this lasted not long. . . ." [22]

That Berkeley promised to grant the fiery young twenty-nine-year-old a commission to lead volunteers, if only to drain his energies away from a more seditious course, is suggested by one of the orders of the assembly, probably drawn up early in the session. The order reads as follows:

Whereas This Grand Assembly is informed that over and above the Commanders and Soldiers by law of this present Session to be raised there may probably offer themselves divers gentlemen and Soldiers as Reformades, Volunteers or Privateers, who will for the Service of the Country against the Common Enimy first haveing granted to them lawfull Commissions from the Right Honorable the Governor and Captain Generall of *Virginia*, barely for the Reward of all lawfull plunder of Indian Enimies Captivated or other goods belonging to the said Indian enimies . . . march out and endeavor to kill and Captivate the Common enimie
Ordered that the Right Honorable the Governor be requested at his owne discretion, and with such Limitations as his honor shall think fitt, to grant Such Commissions for the beating of drums, and raiseing volunteers for Such Service as aforesaid. . . . And further that his honor be requested in all Such Commissions as he shall graunt, strictly to prohibit the falling upon or injureing in any sort any Indians, who are and continue in friendship with us. . . . [23]

Possibly the restrictions placed on volunteer commissions by the assembly made Bacon unwilling to accept such a commission and to demand a broader one. His known views on the "guilt" of all Indians make it seem unlikely that he would be willing to distinguish between friendly and enemy Indians. Bacon himself admitted that Berkeley had some excuse which served as the "occasion" for not giving him a commission. What it was, Bacon does not clearly state, but it does concern a disagreement between the two men over Indian policy. [24]

Although the pardon given to Bacon had pacified his Indian-hating followers, the situation remained tense. Philip Ludwell wrote on June 12 that "beyond al reason they Continue soe Insolent, that wee have all the reason in the world to suspect, their Designes are Ruinouse beyond what they yet pretend which a little tyme will now discover; wee have an Assembly, From the Greatest part whereof wee may expect all that men of that size Can doe For the peace and safety of the Countrey." [25] Ludwell drew a dismal picture of the "approaching Confflagration," noting that "The Indians are now our Least Care, though wee hardly know, (or deserve to Know) a freind Indian Round our Borders, Judge our Condition!"

In a postscript written the next day Ludwell reported the troubles caused by Giles Bland, Virginia's collector of customs, who had been ousted from his office by Berkeley for previous misdeeds. Bland, who had powerful friends in England, had refused to recognize the suspension, and Ludwell reported that he

refuses to have any of his papers recorded, yett sayes all the world (though he keeps them in his pockett) ought to be obliged to obey them, and within these 2 howers most malapertly, to the Governors face, thretned the Councell to Give an account of them in to England; I have a strong fancie I shall never see you more, such a mess of stuff I think was never seen or heard of from an Assembly, as wee have partly in open practiced and partly more in expectation, Farewell, Farewell till next ship, or world. [26]

Bacon waited in town for several days after being reinstated to the council on June 10, and then suddenly slipped off to Henrico County. [27] Until his departure, the burgesses, according to Philip Ludwell, "took little notice of him, being desirouse to Finish their Buisiness...." [28] A member of the assembly, Thomas Mathew, similarly reported that throughout the early period of committee work and hearings, the assembly was ignorant of what Bacon was doing until "One Morning early a Bruit ran about the Town, 'Bacon is fled, Bacon is fled,'...." [29]

Why should this June Assembly, packed as it was with men of

Bacon's "faction," pay so little attention to its "leader"? The answer can be understood only when it is realized first, that by Bacon's "faction" the writers of the period meant primarily those who applauded his aggressive attitude towards the Indians, and, second, that Governor Berkeley converted these followers of Bacon into his own supporters by shaming them into a more charitable position towards the Indians. One of Berkeley's first acts was to lecture the assembly on the injustice of the killing of the five Susquehannock chiefs. In a "Short abrupt Speech" with a "pathetic Emphasis" Berkeley denounced the brutal murders.[30] The evidence of Berkeley's success in converting the burgesses is seen not only in the assembly's order on volunteers for the Indian war,[31] but in the preamble to the act for conducting the war. This preamble states that

Whereas the many outrages, cruell murders, and violent incursions dayly committed perpetrated and made by the barbarous Indians . . . hath inevitably drawne us upon a necessity of declareing warr against them . . . but forasmuch as wee are not altogether satisfied that all Indians are combined against us, and are our enemies, and that wee are taught as well by the rules of our sacred religion, as those of humanitie, that we ought not to involve the innocent with the guiltie. *It is thought fit that it be enacted. . . .*

The act then defines as enemies those Indians who have abandoned or shall abandon their usual dwelling places without license from the governor or assembly, those who refuse to deliver their arms and ammunition and such hostages as might be required, and those who receive enemy Indians into their towns or fail to warn the English of their arrival.[32]

The burgesses also repudiated the charges of oppression, corruption, and treachery against the governor which occasionally accompanied the attacks on his Indian policy. When Berkeley dissolved the old assembly and called for new elections, he directed the people to hand in their grievances to their newly elected representatives for presentation to the grand assembly.[33]

But, although there were only eight of the burgesses not of Bacon's "faction and at his devotion," Berkeley noted, "this very Assembly after I had dared them to declare any fault I had ever committed in reference to the Goverment and shewed them my Petition to his sacred majesty to send in an abler Governor ... this Very factious Assembly I say absolv'd me from al crimes relating to the country and desird me not to sollicite his Majestie to remove me." [34]

The proof of Berkeley's statement is contained in an order of the June Assembly which states that

Whereas the Right Honourable Sir *William Berkeley* Knight our good Governour hath for many yeares most wisely, gratiously Lovingly and justly governed this whole Country, and still continues to governe the same with all possible prudence Justness and mercy, This house in a deep Sence of the premisses doth humbly intreate and request his honor that he will please still to continue our Governor. And this house doth further heartily declare that they cannot Consent or joyne with his Honor in petitioning the Kings Sacred Majestie for his honors remoovall from this Government, but on the Contrary in all humblenesse and due Submission earnestly petition his most Sacred Majesty that he will gratiously please still to continue Sir *William Berkeley* Knight our honorable Governor.[35]

The burgesses seem to have been, as Isaac Allerton put it, "mastered by some gentlemen of Reason." They went on to express their praise of Berkeley in a letter to the Virginia agents in London, but before it could be signed Bacon came roaring into Jamestown with six hundred men "and found other Imployment for them." [36]

Bacon returned on June 23. Berkeley attempted to organize a defense of the island on news of his approach, but the forces he could muster were so few and their morale so bad that he decided to take the "most politick way," dismissed the men, and returned to the state house to await his erratic cousin. Bacon soon arrived and drew up his troops in front of the state house.[37] The governor sent to know what he wanted. "God damne my Blood, I came for a commission, and a commission I will have before I goe," Bacon shouted. In a scene melodramatic but characteristic, Berkeley stormed out of the statehouse, denounced Bacon as a rebel before his men, and refused his demands. Baring his breast, the governor chided the hot-headed youth: " 'Here! Shoot me, foregod, fair Mark, Shoot,' often Rehearsing the same, without any other Words. . . ." [38]

Bacon first demanded a commission as general "of all volunteers against the Indians. . . ." [39] But when Berkeley finally agreed to such a commission, Bacon refused it. He demanded instead a commission as "General of all the forces in Virginia against the Indians." [40] Berkeley raged that he would rather have both his hands cut off than grant his new demand, turned on his heel and walked towards his private apartments a short distance away. The council followed him, "and after them Walked Mr. Bacon with outragious Postures of his Head, Arms, Body, and Leggs, often tossing his hand from his Sword to his Hat and after him came a Detachment of Fusileers. . . ." [41]

Bacon now declared he would no longer be put off saying he would fane know who dare oppose him, upon which the Governor went to him saying for prevention of the efusion of Christian Blood lett you and I decide this controversye by our swords, come along with me. Mr. Bacon answered that was not his business, he came for redress of the peoples grieveances; the Governor demanded what they were, he replyed two were already delivered, and the rest they would loudly proclaime. [42]

Meanwhile the burgesses had crowded to the windows of the assembly house to watch the play of wills. Suddenly Bacon's men cocked their pieces and aimed at the legislators shouting "We will have it [the commission], We will have itt." At the same time Bacon, passing from "dreadfull, new coyned oaths" to his favorite curse, swore "Dam my Bloud, I'le Kill Governr Councill Assembly and all. . . ." The terrified burgesses expected to share the fate of the governor and council. One burgess, unable to stand the strain, waved a handkerchief from the window saying, "You shall have it, You shall have itt" three or four times. This action pacified the mob, and eventually the burgesses and council persuaded the governor to give in to Bacon.[43] The governor, who had adamantly refused to be cowed personally by Bacon's threats, now complied with the pleas of the fearful assembly. The result may be seen in the Indian bill with its Berkeley beginning and Bacon ending.

The preamble to the bill, with its careful distinction between enemy and friendly Indians, has already been quoted.[44] How utterly at variance with Bacon's views the preamble was, Bacon's June letter to England revealed. In this letter he asserted that no one dared to destroy the Indians since "some of them" were protected by the governor, "tho we find them all alike, neither can we distinguish this fatall undistinguishable distinction of the Governor, who only for the gain sake has so bridled all people, that no man dare to destroy the Indians, even in the pursuit of murder untill I adventured to cutt the knott, which made the people in generall look upon mee as the countries friend." [45] Yet the man who wrote this letter was appointed by the assembly, in the final clause of the Indian act, to be "commander in chiefe of the force raised, and to be raised dureing this Indian warr." [46]

Though it is evident from the language of the act that the proviso making Bacon commander in chief was added to an already completed act, confirmation is provided in the copy of the acts of the assembly in the files of Secretary of State Henry Coventry. There the Indian act stands without the "Provided nevertheless" clause appointing Bacon commander. The latter clause is written separately at another place in the transcription of the acts with the note that it is to be added to the Indian act. We have the testimony of William Sherwood, moreover, that when Bacon complained against the raising of a thousand men at the charge of the counties, the burgesses replied that "what was 3 times read and passed ... could not be altered." [47]

After Bacon forced his commission, wrote Philip Ludwell, "other propositions and demands, very hard ones, Followed, which For expedition, as long as they concerned not life or limbe were Granted as fast as they came." [48] There is no evidence that any of these "propositions and demands" were in the nature of political grievances. None of the chroniclers of the event mention any political demands. The only reference to a discussion of political grievances comes in Thomas Mathew's recollection, thirty years after the event, of a half-hour harangue made by Bacon to the assembly. Mathew reported that an hour or so after the dramatic scene outside the state house on June 23,

Mr. Bacon came up to our Chamber and Desired a Commission from us to go against the Indians; Our Speaker sat Silent, When one Mr. Blayton a Neighbour to Mr. Bacon and Elected with him a Member of Assembly for the same County (Who therefore durst Speak to him,) made Answer, ' 'twas not in our Province, or Power, nor of any other, save the Kings Vicegerent our Governour'; he press'd hard nigh half an hours Harangue on the Preserving our Lives from the Indians, Inspecting the Publick Revenues, th' exorbitant Taxes and redressing the Grievances and Calamities of that Deplorable Country, Whereto having no other Answer, He went away Dissatisfied.[49]

Mathew's evidence indicates that, even if delivered at all, Bacon's talk was little more than a political harangue—and an unsuccessful one at that—to get the approval of the burgesses for his Indian design. But most probably Mathew confused the time and exact nature of the talk. William Sherwood, writing a few days after the event, reported that on Saturday, June 24, Bacon entered the house of burgesses with his guard to add several more demands to the ones he had made the previous day.[50] In his "Virginias Deploured Condition" the same statement is made.[51] Sherwood reported the events of both days in great detail, but made no mention of political demands or even of a political harangue.

Bacon's demands, as given by the commissioners, by Philip

Ludwell, by William Sherwood, and by Thomas Mathew, were as follows: (1) a commission to go against the Indians, (2) an act of pardon and indemnity, (3) a letter to the King justifying Bacon's action, (4) thirty blank commissions for subordinate officers, and later more, (5) an order against Captain Thomas Gardner for £70 for the sloop Bacon lost when Gardner captured him on June 7, (6) a prohibition against certain persons, who had been active in obeying the governor's commands, from holding public office, and (7) a demand that it should be discovered whether the governor had written the King desiring aid in suppressing the tumults and if so that it be publicly contradicted by the governor, council, and burgesses. The rebels' general protest against the act to raise a thousand men by taxation was satisfied by adding the proviso that Bacon might dispense with all or any part of the men to be raised if he felt he could carry on the war well enough by volunteers. All of Bacon's demands were concerned with carrying out his project against the Indians without interference. He made no demands for political reform.

It has been alleged that the acts of the June Assembly were formulated or at least pushed through by Bacon and his men. In his printing of the acts of the assembly Hening used as a running title the phrase "Bacon's Laws." [52] An examination of the acts, their passage, subsequent disallowance by the King, and later repassage, suggests that this view is incorrect.

The acts of the June Assembly follow. An asterisk before the act indicates that it was repassed in substantially the same form in the assembly of February 1677 following the rebellion. [53]

Act I. "An act for carrying on a warre against the barbarous Indians," which has already been discussed in this chapter.

Act II. "An act concerning Indian trade and traders," which repealed a similar act of March 1676, and tightened restrictions on trade with the Indians.

Act III. "An act concerning Indian lands deserted," which

provided that lands reserved to the Indians but deserted by them were to be sold to defray the cost of the war.

Act IV. "An act for suppressing of tumults, routs, etc.," which "impowered and strictly commanded" every officer and magistrate within the country to "suppress and punish" all "unlawfull assemblies, routs, riotts and tumults." The act was directed specifically at "certain ill disposed and disaffected people" who had "of late gathered and may again gather themselves together by beate of drumme, and otherwise in a most apparent rebellious manner, without any authoritie or legall commission, which may prove of very dangerous consequences. . . ." The governor was requested to suppress at the public charge any such unlawful assemblies and to inflict "condigne punishment upon the offenders."

* Act V. "An act for the regulateing of officers and offices," which provided that no person could hold the office of sheriff for more than one year successively, that no person could hold two of the offices of sheriff, clerk of court, surveyor, or escheator at the same time, and that no one who had not resided in the country for three years (Bacon had arrived in Virginia two years earlier) could hold any office within the country. Penalties were prescribed for abuses in the offices of clerk of court, sheriff, escheator, surveyor, and collector, and stricter regulation of the activities of public officers was ordered.

Act VI. "An act for chooseing of Vestries," which abolished the previous system whereby vestrymen themselves chose a member to fill a vacancy caused by death, and threw open the entire vestry to election by a majority of the freeholders and freemen of the parish.[54]

Act VII. "An act enabling freemen to vote for burgesses and preventing false returns of burgesses," which repealed the act of 1670 denying freemen not property owners or housekeepers the right to vote. Freemen were to be allowed to vote as formerly together with freeholders and housekeepers.[55]

* Act VIII. "An act for representatives to vote with the justices at Levie Courts, and makeing bye lawes," which attempted

to correct abuses committed by justices in laying the county levies by providing for representatives of the parishes to sit with them.

* Act IX. "An act for countie courts to appoint their collectors and disabling counsellours to vote in countie courts."

* Act X. "An act for limitting Sherriffs, etc. a time to demand the levies and for tenders to be made them," which gave debtors more time to pay their debts and allowed tax debts to be paid in tobacco.

* Act XI. An act to allow two justices of a county court to sign probates, etc., instead of requiring the governor to sign them.

* Act XII. An act which repealed an earlier act exempting councillors and ministers from paying levies. Additional salary was granted the councillors instead.

* Act XIII. "An act altering the encouragement for killing wolves," which repealed an act allowing 200 pounds of tobacco for each wolf killed. Instead, county courts were allowed to grant the reward at their discretion.

Act XIV. "An act for the further prevention of mischief from unrulie horses."

Act XV. "An act against exportation of corne."

Act XVI. "An act for the suppressing of ordinaries."

Act XVII. "An act limmitting the bounds of James Cittie."

* Act XVIII. "An act repealing lawes concerning Accomack and Northampton."

Act XIX. "An act of general pardon and oblivion," which pardoned all crimes, treasons, etc., committed between March 1 and June 25, 1676.

Act XX. "An act disabling Edward Hill and John Stith to beare office."

The last two acts, and the proviso to the first act, were forced by Bacon. Just how important Bacon's men regarded the other acts—most of which can be called "reform laws"—is shown by their reaction, on June 23, to the attempts to have the laws read. Almost immediately after Bacon entered Jamestown that day the assembly tried to have the laws read to his followers. As Philip Ludwell wrote: "the laws of this assembly being hastyly finished, were put out to be read to the people, supposeing they might have made some Converts, but they Rise up like a swarme of Bees and swear they will hear noe laws, nor have any but what they pleased, which, haveing Reason by their behaviour to take for Granted, the lawes were withdrawne. . . ." [56]

William Sherwood wrote about this attempted reading of the laws in almost identical terms. Sherwood noted that the assembly informed Bacon that the raising of the thousand men at the country's charge could not be altered, "of which Mr. Bacon was informed with this desier of the Governo'r that the proceedings of the Assembly might be redd att the head of Mr. Bacons Company for theire sattisfaction, and on their assureance that he should have a commission, [but] Mr. Bacon declared he would not be longer put off, he could not permitt any Laws to be read there. . . ." [57] In his longer account, "Virginias Deploured Condition," Sherwood was even more explicit. As Bacon was demanding his commission, his men shouting "Noe Levies, Noe Levies":

The Assembly acquainted him they had taken all possible care for carrying on the Indian Warr at the easiest charge that could be, that they had redressed all theire Complaints, and desiered that for sattisfaction of the people, what they had don might be publickly read, Mr. Bacon answered there should be noe Laws read there, that he Would not admit of any delays, that he came for a Commission, and would immediately have itt. . . ." [58]

The state of tension continued from Friday, June 23, until Sunday the 25th. While the house was preparing letters to the King justifying Bacon's actions, Bacon talked about punishing some of the councillors and obtaining from the governor, council, and burgesses oaths to honor what they had granted. But about noon news was received that the Indians had murdered eight Englishmen in the heart of the country. Berkeley, using Bacon's former argument, pleaded for the right of the members of the government to go out and protect their defenseless families.[59] Taken aback by this request, Bacon began to plan his next move.

On Sunday afternoon "the Lawes were Redd in the court house before the Governor councell and Burgesses after the usuall manner, and the assembly disolved. . . ." [60] The bills were signed into law by Governor Berkeley and Speaker Thomas Godwin.[61] In the evening Bacon let several people, including the governor, go out of town to see their families, and the next morning marched out against the Indians. Philip Ludwell and William Sherwood sat down soon after and wrote their letters to the secretaries of state in England. Ludwell commented "I doubt it will not be long ere wee hear of him again." [62]

What is significant about this story is the unconcern, indeed antagonism, displayed by Bacon and his men towards the political reforms of the so-called "Bacon's Assembly." It is customary to give Bacon and his followers the credit for the reform laws enacted. It is evident, however, that the bills were, for the most part, drawn up when Bacon was securing his release or when he was absent, not during the hectic week-end of June 23 to June 25. Indeed there is no evidence to indicate that Bacon had any interest whatsoever in the bills which had been drawn up, even those directed specifically against him. Neither is there evidence that his leadership was acknowledged by the men within the assembly who put through the reform bills.

The actions of Bacon and his supporters at Jamestown on June 23 indicate that they were very little concerned about anything but a commission authorizing Bacon to lead them as volunteers against all Indians in general. If they had been seriously aggrieved by the "oppression" they were allegedly suffering, they would certainly have shown more concern with proposals to remedy the situation. Instead of cheering the reform laws, however, they shouted them down. The events from June 23 to June 25 prove not that the rebellion was an attempt at political reform but that it was not.

So strong is the myth of "Bacon the Reformer" that just as his actions are ignored, so are his words. In a letter to England Bacon frankly asserted that the hopes of the people in the assembly were deceived, and that there was no hope of redress for their "grievances" except by an appeal to the King. He carefully avoids mention of any of the acts of the assembly and instead asks rhetorically whether "the Majesty of power and authority, the dignity of Judicature, those precious jewells of the peoples safety, have not been abus'd by jugling mountebanks." True, he goes on, the hopes of the people were in the assembly, but the "poor people" are debarred of fair election by being in debt to, and hence in awe of, the "great men"; there are lacking "men of ability and courage" to "stand up in the peoples behalfe and oppose the oppressing party"; "artifices, promises, and arguments" are used to "bring over the minds of men in towns," committees are "packed," "badges of disfavour" are set upon those who "speak freely or dissent." In brief the assembly has failed because the leading men have "quash'd and aw'd the sincere intentions of the rest." As a result, Bacon explained, agents must be sent to England to explain the situation to the King.[63]

Giles Bland, Bacon's accomplice in rebellion, expressed similar disgust with "Bacon's Assembly" in his letter of July 8, two weeks after the burgesses had finished their work. Bland repeated Bacon's charge that efforts to secure redress in Virginia had failed and that it was therefore necessary to appeal to the crown.[64]

The letters of both Bacon and Bland seem to have been designed to raise suspicions in England about Berkeley's justice and competence. Hence they are couched in vague generalities without specific disapproval of any of the acts passed by the June Assembly or recommendations for measures which should have been taken. They suggest that the rebel leadership felt itself now isolated not only from the governor and council but from the burgesses as well. That they indicate more than a propaganda concern with the need for reforms is doubtful.

In another letter sent back at the same time Bacon discussed the whole story of the June Assembly and his appointment to command the forces raised against the Indians without once mentioning the political reform laws. The people looked upon him as their friend, he wrote, because of his resolution to wipe out all the Indians. He asked how any man "could perceive in my manner, Estate, or manner of living, how any indirect end, as levelling or rebellion, could make me desirous to exchange my fortune for worse; altho by the Governor and some other of his creatures, such terms were putt upon mee...." [65] Moreover, in another document sent to England by the rebel leader at this time the desire to reform the laws was flatly denied. Entitled "The Virginians Plea for Opposing the Indians without the Governor's Order," it denounced Berkeley only for his failure to assert "his majesties Right in this his Collony" against all Indians whatsoever. The "Plea" protested that

though wee cannot deny but that wee have vented our discontents ... in Complaints of other grievances also, too great to bee wholly smothered, especially those that tended to protect and cherish the enemy, and hinder our opposing them ... yet wee doe againe declare, That our taking upp Armes so disorderly ... was purely intended ... to preserve our very being, and not ... to free and releive ourselves by the sword from [any] pressures in Governement (much lesse to alter it) as some would charge [us] unjustly with. ... [66]

Just as no evidence exists to show that Bacon's aim was reform, so no evidence exists to prove that Governor Berkeley's "intent was to frustrate this aim of reform." [67] Berkeley's guilt in the affair is usually seen in his message to the opening session of the June Assembly not to meddle with anything until provisions for defense against the Indians were made.[68] The same historians who criticize the governor for dilatoriness in meeting the Indian threat in March denounce him for too great haste in meeting it in June.

In point of fact the June Assembly, in passing the reform acts, had acted as many an assembly before it had done. Berkeley's assembly of November 1645, to cite one example, passed more significant reform legislation than the assembly of June 1676.

Yet no one has ever tried to prove that a democratic revolution occurred at that time. The purpose of assemblies was reform! To show that Bacon did not force through democratic reforms does not make it necessary to prove that someone else did. If it were necessary to postulate a "hero-leader," the most logical candidate would be Berkeley himself. Francis Moryson, later one of the commissioners sent to investigate grievances against Berkeley, wrote in his 1662 revisal of the laws of Virginia that Berkeley was "the only Author . . . of the most and best of them." [69] Moreover, the assembly of February 1677, supposedly "but an instrument of oppression in the Governor's hands," [70] passed most of the same reform acts previously enacted by the June Assembly, "packt" though it was for Bacon. Are the same acts to be attributed to Bacon's influence in one assembly, and to Berkeley's the next? [71]

Hening's republican bias led him to conclude that the re-enactment of these laws in February 1677 furnished "a conclusive proof that very great abuses had crept into the government, which those in authority were unwilling to acknowledge; nor had they the magnanimity to give *Bacon* credit for the good he had done." [72] An example of equally confused thinking is the statement of Armistead Gordon that "because they contained within them the very essence of freedom, their rude appeal did but emphasize their meaning and their truth; and by degrees, and from year to year, they were reintroduced one after another into later Assemblies and re-enacted, until they had been once more re-established. . . ." [73]

Our forefathers believed in the inevitable triumph of freedom over oppression. Since Bacon represented the forces of "freedom" in Virginia in 1676, he had to be given credit for the democratic laws passed then. And since Berkeley represented the inevitably decaying force of authoritarian government, the fact that the laws were passed under his administration had to be an indication of his inability to resist the democratic tide. Such assumptions have prevented a true understanding of what actually happened in June 1676.

Chapter 5

VIRGINIA UNDER BACON
JULY–AUGUST, 1676

❖❖❖

W ITH the departure of Bacon on June 26 Jamestown settled down to an uneasy peace and tried to assess the consequences of his hectic visit. Governor Berkeley must have been nearly in a state of shock. The old man had risen to new heights of physical courage to meet the challenge Bacon offered, but the rebel had nevertheless won an overwhelming victory. Exhausted and disgusted, Berkeley seems to have washed his hands of matters of state and retired to his plantation at Green Spring. There he no doubt spent much time watching the sun-baked fields bring forth new and more governable forms of life. He seems to have decided not to contest the legality of the forced commissions or those acts extorted by Bacon. After all, he may have reasoned, the people forced me, the council, and the burgesses to accept Bacon's plan for fighting the Indian war. Let Bacon, then, fight it as he sees fit. I tried my best to see that the war was conducted honorably and intelligently, but no one would follow me. I have done my duty. The King will eventually call Bacon to account. In the meantime I will tend to my vineyards and tobacco and let Bacon worry about the security of the colony.

Berkeley's lackadaisical attitude is evident in his letter of July 1 to Thomas Ludwell. "Every thing here is now deplorable," wrote the King's governor, "and three Young men that have not beene two Yeares in the Country absolutely Governe it: Mr. Bacon, Mr. Bland, and Mr. Ingram. . . ." [1] For a month after the assembly was dissolved nothing was done to denounce the legality of Bacon's commission or the acts of the assembly. Instead, orders were issued recruiting men and supplies for Bacon on their authority.[2] Magistrates who doubted the legality of Bacon's activities were "threatened with plundering and pulling down their house. . . ." [3]

In preparation for his campaign against the Indians Bacon sent out parties to scour the forests and swamps in every place where Indians might be hiding.[4] He then appointed a rendezvous at the falls of James River and was about to set out against the natives when called upon to meet a potential threat to his rear.[5] The threat stemmed from a petition sent Berkeley from Gloucester County against the depredations of Bacon's soldiers. Bacon's men had confiscated horses, arms, and ammunition of citizens there leaving them exposed to Indian attack. The Gloucester petition asked if Bacon's commission was good, and begged for protection from the Indians.

The question roused Berkeley from his lethargy. The proud governor replied that Bacon's action in obtaining his commission was no better than "if a Theife should take my purse and make me owne I gave itt him freely." He promised protection against the Indians and went to Gloucester to raise forces against them.[6] The attempt to raise troops, however, failed. Many of the recruits suspected that they were designed to be used against Bacon rather than against the Indians and refused to be drafted.[7] Whether their suspicion was justified or not is difficult to say. Isaac Allerton, who attempted to recruit troops in Gloucester, reported that "we are accused of the raysing forces against him, though wee never designed anything but against the Indians and to have power to Ballance his, att the End of the Indian warr if

God gave us success, butt in this wee were so unhappy that few of the vulgar would follow us, saying wee would fight Bacon." [8] The Gloucester yeomen refused not because of hatred of Berkeley or positive approval of Bacon, but because they felt that it was somehow unjust to declare themselves against Bacon (which they then felt they would be doing by enlisting under Berkeley) while "he was now advanceing against the common enimy, who had in a most barberous manner murthered som hundreds of our deare Breatheren and Countrey Men...." [9]

Bacon, when he heard of this attempt to raise troops in Gloucester, countermarched and arrived at Middle Plantation (Williamsburg) on July 29, 1676. [10] Berkeley, sensing his impossible position in the face of his failure to recruit troops in Gloucester, retired across Chesapeake Bay to the safety of Accomack County on the Eastern Shore of Virginia, "which place I understood continued Loyal (and indeed halfe of it was so)." Berkeley urged Sir Henry Chicheley, his deputy governor, to accompany him to Accomack but Chicheley, delaying several days, was captured and held twenty weeks by Bacon, although "no cause ever yet [was] assigned why he was a prisoner." Only four gentlemen accompanied Berkeley to Accomack, but, he reported, forty gentlemen of the best quality in Virginia later came over to him, many with their wives and children, leaving their estates to be plundered by Bacon's soldiers. [11] Berkeley's headquarters on the Eastern Shore was at Arlington, the plantation of Major General John Custis.

The next day, July 30, Bacon issued his famous "Declaration of the People" to which he appended his name and "the eloquent phrase": [12] "General, by the consent of the people." Lyon G. Tyler saw a "tremendous significance in the words with which he signed the paper.... Here was democracy proclaimed a hundred years in advance of Thomas Jefferson." [13] Most writers have based their assumption of the democratic character of the "Declaration" on the belief that it was the product of Bacon's Middle Plantation conference of August 3 and 4. In reality the

"Declaration" was written by Bacon before the meeting and without the known consent of anyone but himself.[14]

The "Declaration" was in the form of an indictment. The first charge was that Berkeley "upon specious pretences of publique works raised greate unjust taxes upon the Commonality." The second was for rendering justice "contemptible" by advancing favorites to high places. The governor was then accused of monopolizing the beaver trade and "haveing in that unjust gaine betrayed and sold his Majesty's Country and the lives of his loyall subjects, to the barbarous heathen." He was further charged with protecting and favoring the Indians and never preventing their invasions and outrages. His countermanding of Chicheley's orders to go against the Indians in January 1676, his opposition to the enforced decision of the assembly to place control of the war in Bacon's hands, and his having "forged a Commission," presumably the Gloucester petition, to embroil the country in a civil war, are all cited as accusations of the people against him.[15]

Berkeley and a number of loyalists were commanded in the "Declaration" to surrender themselves within four days or be declared traitors to the people and suffer confiscation of their estates. Bacon further declared "That in whatsoever place howse or shipp any of the said persons shall reside be hid or protected wee doe declare the Owners Masters or Inhabitants of the said places to be Confederates and Traitors to the people and the Estates of them as also of the aforesaid persons to be confiscated." [16]

Bacon seems also at this time to have issued his melodramatic "Manifesto" which begins: "If vertue be a sin, if Piety be giult." His policy of extermination is frankly stated in this document:

Another main article of our Giult is our open and manifest aversion of all, not onely the Foreign but the protected and Darling Indians, this wee are informed is Rebellion of a deep dye For that both the Governour and Councell are by Colonell Coales [William Cole] Assertion bound to defend the Queen [of

Pamunkey] and the Appamatocks with their blood. Now . . . we doe declare and can prove that they have bin for these Many years enemies to the King and Country, Robbers and Theeves and Invaders of his Majesty's Right and our Interest and Estates, but yet have by persons in Authority bin defended and protected even against His Majesty's loyall Subjects. . . .

Another main article of our Giult is our Design not only to ruin and extirpate all Indians in Generall but all Manner of Trade and Commerce with them. . . .

Another Article of our Giult is To Assert all those neighbour Indians as well as others to be outlawed, wholly unqualifyed for the benefitt and Protection of the law. . . Now since the Indians cannot according to the tenure and forme of any law to us known be prosecuted, Seised or Complained against . . . would it not be very giulty to say They have bin unjustly defended and protected these many years.[17]

On August 1 Bacon dispatched Giles Bland and Captain William Carver with three hundred men to take the ships in James River. Three were captured, including that of Captain Thomas Larrimore. Larrimore was at first imprisoned, but pretending to support the rebels, he was allowed to continue as master of the ship under Bland's watchful eye. The rebels fitted the ships with ordnance taken from the fort at Jamestown. They then attempted to seize Captain Christopher Evelin's ship to prevent intelligence of the recent events from reaching England and to capture Governor Berkeley, who was rumored to be aboard. Evelin, getting advanced information, escaped.[18]

While Bacon made preparations to carry the war to Berkeley in Accomack with his newly acquired "navy," he also called a convention at Captain Otho Thorpe's house at Middle Plantation to give the rebellious temper of the fickle people more solid form. Many gentlemen, with the threat of confiscation of property hanging over them, responded to Bacon's call. Then, according to the commissioners, "After a long debate, pro and con, a mischievous writing was drawne up and produced by Bacon, unto which (the doors of the house being fast lock'd on them) many by threats, Force and Feare were feigne to subscribe." [19]

The author of the Burwell manuscript gives a slightly different account of the assembly. He reported that the entire convention agreed not to help Berkeley in any way against Bacon. But as the clerk of the assembly was putting the resolution in writing, Bacon added two more conditions: that the signers should agree to rise in arms against Berkeley if he should, with armed forces, attempt to resist Bacon, and that they should likewise resist even troops sent from England until the country's cause could be reported to the King. These two provisions "did marvellously startle the people" who agreed to accept the earlier resolutions but not the added conditions. Bacon thereupon argued with great skill, urging among other things that Berkeley would have his revenge on the signers as much for signing part of the oath as all of it. "In the urging of which he used such specious and subtill pretences ... which he manidged solely against a grate many of those counted the wisest men in the Countrey, with so much art and sophisticall dixterety, that at length there was litle said, by any, against the same. ..." The argument was clinched when a gunner from the fort on York River arrived with the news that the fort was in danger of Indian attack. When asked by Bacon how such a strong interior bastion could be in danger, the gunner replied that Governor Berkeley had stripped it of its guns and put them on his ship. Bacon, of course, knew how to capitalize on this bit of news, "which he managed with so much cuning and subtillety, that the peoples minds became quickly flexable, and apt to receve any impression, or simillitude, that his Arguments should represent to there ill desarneing judgments; in so much that the Oath became now more smooth, and glib, to be swollowed, even by those who had the gratest repugnancy against it. ..." [20]

The greater part of the opposition was thus won over, but in a final master stroke Bacon allowed to some an oral condition that if there was anything in the oath that might taint their allegiance, then they should stand absolved of every part of the oath. Since the provision was not written into the oath, the author of the Burwell manuscript could not see "what benifit could posible accrew" to those who were indulged the condition more than to those who were not "since both subscribed the ingagement as it stood in the letter, not as it was in the meaneing of the subscriber." "It is trew," remarked this writer, that "before God and there owne consciences, it might be pleadable, but not at the Bar of humane proseedings, with out a favourable interpretation put upon it, by those who were to be the judges." [21]

The formal results of the conference at Middle Plantation were issued in a series of declarations. On August 3 a declaration signed first by Colonel Thomas Swann, one of Berkeley's councilors, and sixty-nine others, accused Governor Berkeley of fomenting civil war by opposing Bacon's efforts against the Indians. All swore they would aid Bacon in resisting even the King's authority until Bacon's case could be known in England. [22]

The following day, August 4, Thomas Swann again led the list of twenty-nine signers who noted that Berkeley had removed the ammunition from the Tindall's Point fort on York River, and that "certaine persons in Contempt of the authority of Nathaniel Bacon Esquire" were in open hostility in Westmoreland County while others had refused to surrender the fort at the falls of Rappahannock River. The signers advised Bacon to call an assembly, set up a government to take care of civil affairs, and then to prosecute the Indian war and those who attempted to prevent him. [23]

An order was directed on August 5 to Colonel John Washington in Westmoreland County to administer Bacon's oath to every freeholder and freeman. If any person refused, his name was to be sent back. [24] Bacon's oath required the swearer to promise to oppose whatever force might be sent from England until Bacon could acquaint the King with the state of the country and receive his answer. It also required the taker to swear that what Governor Berkeley and the council had done was illegal, that Bacon's commission was legally obtained and lawful, that the taker would reveal what he heard said against Bacon, and that he would keep Bacon's secrets.[25]

On August 11 a letter signed by Thomas Swann, Thomas Beale, Thomas Ballard, and James Bray, all members of Berkeley's council, directed the sheriff of Westmoreland County to summon all "housekeepers and Freemen" to meet for the election of burgesses. Those elected were to appear in Jamestown September 4, 1676, indeed "are required not to faile to appeare precisely on the day appointed."[26]

Having finished his eminently successful Middle Plantation conference and sent his navy against Berkeley in Accomack, Bacon headed out to execute "his favourite scheme of extirpating the Indians."[27] He first went to the falls of the James River perhaps hoping to do something—at long last—against the Susquehannock enemy. But, instead, he reversed his course and marched north. Probably, like Berkeley before him, he despaired of finding the Susquehannocks in their mountain refuges. Near the upper reaches of the Pamunkey River he joined forces with troops from the Potomac and Rappahannock areas under Colonel Giles Brent. The army immediately plunged into the Great Dragon Swamp in an attempt to locate the Pamunkey Indians, who had been long suspected—falsely—of harboring evil intentions against the English.[28]

The Pamunkeys, like terrified children seeking to escape the blows of a drunken father, had fled into the swamps when threatened with destruction by the frontiersmen the previous spring, and there they had stayed. After tramping around in a fruitless search for his prey, Bacon drew up his impatient and hungry men and delivered a rousing speech. In it he vowed to continue his search for the Pamunkeys and to perform the service the country expected from him, and he had promised to execute, against the heathen. If he should fail, he told his followers, his adversaries would "insult and reflect on mee; that my Defence of the country is but Pretended and not Reall and (as they already say) I have other Designs and make this but my Pretense and cloke." Bacon insisted on his devotion to the cause of eradicating the Indians and, after allowing those who had grown discouraged to return home, he continued his search for the Pamunkeys. As the commissioners later observed, Bacon had to show results since his high pretenses had raised public hopes.[29]

Luck was with him. He finally found the Pamunkey encampment. This was his only problem and only accomplishment. For the Queen of Pamunkey, hearing of his approach, had left all her goods behind "to decline all occasion of offending the English," as the commissioners put it, and had given orders to her Indians "that if they found the English coming upon them that they should neither fire a gun nor draw an arrow upon them." When Bacon's men attacked, the Indians obediently "did not at all oppose, but fled, being followed by Bacon and his Forces killing and taking them Prisoners, and looking for the Plunder of the Field...." Forty-five captives were taken and much plunder. The Queen of Pamunkey, terrified, wandered about the forest for fourteen days before she dared to come in.[30]

This was Bacon's second and last great "Indian victory." He made much of his success, and it is understandable that later historians should treat it in the same manner. Yet the commissioners commented that "By the Queenes own account there were onely 8 of her Indians kill'd, saying she would not tell a Lye to mention more than indeed were. Though Bacon brag'd of many more to please and deceive the People, with a mighty Conquest." [31] Once again, all Bacon's victims were friendly Indians. He still had not come to grips with the Susquehannocks.

Chapter 6

BERKELEY REGAINS CONTROL
IN VIRGINIA
AUGUST, 1676–JANUARY, 1677

❖❖❖

WHILE Bacon pursued the Pamunkeys, Giles Bland, with two or three hundred men in Captain Thomas Larrimore's captured ship and two others, crossed Chesapeake Bay to take Berkeley and his friends dead or alive, Bland swearing "a thousand God dame him he would doe." [1] On their way across the rebels seized another vessel, of ninety tons, which had just arrived from England, so they appeared on the Eastern Shore with four sail. "So formidable an appearance, upon a coast that had not one vessel to defend it, struck the Governour with consternation, and he gave himself over for lost," according to one source. [2] Captain William Carver, Bland's associate and a man whom Berkeley described as an "able Stoute seamen [*sic*] and soldier," came off Larrimore's ship with 160 men "under pretence of treating with me." Berkeley told him to begone within eight hours, but the "contrary wind gave him a pretence to stay longer for an opertunity to corrupt or cease [seize] my Gaurd that wacthead [watched] his motions." [3]

About midnight a letter came to Berkeley from Captain Larrimore, stating that there were only forty Baconians aboard his vessel and that he would help the governor recapture it. [4]

[77]

Since it was reported that Larrimore had entered voluntarily into Bacon's service, Berkeley feared a trap. Colonel Philip Ludwell, however, pointed out that the governor had no choice. He must trust Larrimore or resign himself to surrender. Furthermore, Ludwell trusted Larrimore and therefore asked to be allowed to make the attempt, which Berkeley authorized.[5] With twenty-six men and Larrimore's cooperation, Ludwell within six hours [6] seized the ship and made Bland and the men on board prisoners.[7] Meanwhile, Carver, on shore, seeing Ludwell's rowboats going to the ship and "suspecting the Cause," made after them in a small boat. By the time he was within musket shot of the ship Ludwell's men had seized it. They let Carver approach until he was within pistol shot and then commanded him on board, "which he ascended like a chased Bore [boar]," relates Berkeley, "and would have stabd his lieutenant if he had not been prevented by our men."[8]

The capture of Bland and Carver and all of Bacon's fleet was the turning point in the war. As Berkeley wrote:

This great and miraculous mercy put al the soldiers into our hands who having not Victuals for eight howers surrendred themselves and Armes tooke the Oaths of allegeance and Supremacy but Kept them so as the Parliament soldiers used to doe in England. However this action gave the Loyal party a great reputation in the country and now the feare of me made many declare for the King who never after durst goe backe to Bacon.[9]

Berkeley immediately resolved to take the offensive. After Larrimore's ship and ship's company were sworn into the King's service,[10] two hundred men were raised and transported across Chesapeake Bay in the captain's ship and six or seven sloops. There, on the "mainland," Berkeley enlisted one hundred additional men and set sail for Jamestown.[11]

There has been much speculation concerning Berkeley's method of raising troops for his counterattack against Bacon. All the troops authorized by the assembly had been put under Bacon's command. It is probable, however, that the young "general" continued to rely primarily upon volunteers. When he turned his army against Berkeley in Gloucester, the governor had been forced to retire to the Eastern Shore with only a handful of his most loyal supporters. There he set about the herculean task of regaining control of the mainland. To succeed he would have to create an army and navy from nothing while in exile in a remote offshore position, supply and pay that force, and conduct the most difficult of all military operations, an amphibious assault.

Berkeley's method of raising troops was a rough and ready one. According to the commissioners' post-rebellion information most of Berkeley's men were "intent onely upon plunder or compell'd and hired into his service...." [12] Two Baconians who came over from the Eastern Shore just in advance of Berkeley's invasion fleet reported that the governor had promised the soldiers that they would be rewarded with the estates of those who had taken Bacon's oath, that they would be freed for twenty-one years from all impositions except church dues, and that they would receive twelve pence a day. Berkeley was also reported to have authorized the freeing of servants whose masters were fighting under Bacon or had taken his oath. The author of the Burwell Manuscript, who recorded these reports, did not know whether they were true or false, but noted that they "produced the efects of truth in peoples mindes." However, since the governor's proclamation on arriving at Jamestown granted a free and ample pardon to all who would return to their obedience, excepting only Richard Lawrence and William Drummond, ringleaders with Bacon in the rebellion, the Burwell author concluded that "what those two men (before mentioned) had sworn to, was probably a mere pack of untruths." [13]

Nevertheless, Berkeley had to find pay for his troops somehow, and he probably did it the same way he acquired his navy: by taking it from the rebels. On August 8, 1676, he issued a proclamation in Accomack and Northampton counties for the purpose.

It authorized the sharing of booty taken from rebels later condemned.[14]

Berkeley arrived off Jamestown with three hundred men on September 7, 1676.[15] The capital was garrisoned by five hundred rebels [16] under the command of Colonel Thomas Hansford.[17] Berkeley's own numbers, the governor asserted, were "trebled in the opinion of the Ennimie." [18] A proclamation was immediately issued offering pardon to all the common soldiers who would lay down their arms and to all the officers except Bacon, Drummond, and Lawrence. Berkeley noted that "thoughe they would not lay downe their Armes Yet the same night we arrived at James-Towne they al fled to Bacon." [19] The consternation the proclamation caused among the Baconians is ably recounted by the author of the Burwell Manuscript. He noted that

his Honours Proclamation was acceptable to most in Towne; while others againe would not trust to it, feareing to meet with som after-claps of revenge: Which diverseity of opinions put them all into a ressalution of diserting the place, as not Tenable ... which that night, in the darke, they put in execution, every one shifting for him selfe with no ordnary feare, in the gratest hast posible, for fere of being sent after. . . .[20]

Berkeley entered the town the next day, September 8, about noon, giving thanks to God for his safe arrival "(which he forgot not to perform upon his knees, at his first footeing the shore)." [21] The governor immediately reorganized the defenses of Jamestown and reconstituted his naval force. Captain Thomas Gardner, captor of Bacon in June, was made "Vice Admirall of the Fleete now riding at James Citty" and authorized to seek out and destroy Bacon's forces.[22]

Many of Bacon's men now deserted him so that, to supplement his numbers, the rebel leader proclaimed liberty to servants and Negroes of loyalists willing to join him.[23] Then, with six hundred men plus others who had fled from Jamestown,[24] and "a Thousand of his usual execrable oaths he would put us al to the sword,"

Bacon came down from his inland camp and besieged the liberated capital.[25] The rebel leader arrived to find the town skilfully fortified by a very strong and high palisade from James River to the "back river" and guarded by a force commanded by the governor in person. Bacon, on his horse, boldly reconnoitered the position. He immediately saw the impossibility of forcing such a defense and resolved to draw the governor from behind his lines. He dismounted and led his troops close to the palisade where he "bid defiance to the Governour, and fired upon the garrison; but the Governour, resolved to hazard nothing, kept himself secure, and submitted to the insult."[26] Berkeley had ordered that not a gun should be fired against Bacon or his party on pain of death, not wishing to spill blood if he could help it, and especially not wishing to be the beginner of it.[27] The governor hoped that lack of provisions would force the rebels to retire, but they supplied themselves liberally from Berkeley's estate at Green Spring three miles away and from the estates of other loyalists.[28]

Having failed to entice the loyalists out, Bacon decided to construct a deep ditch along the entire length of the palisade, lining it with the trunks and branches of trees.[29] It was at the building of these works that Bacon resorted to the one act for which most historians condemn him. This was the seizure of the wives of the loyalist leaders, Mrs. Nathaniel Bacon, Sr., Mrs. James Bray, Mrs. Thomas Ballard, Mrs. John Page, and others, whom he placed upon the ramparts while he dug his position.[30]

Bacon demonstrated his cleverness in other ways. He carefully showed off his Pamunkey captives during the course of his march to Jamestown, and when before the capital he placed them on the ramparts as visible evidence of his "success" as an Indian fighter.[31] The commissioners reported that the sight of these Pamunkeys on the march caused onlookers to praise God and Bacon for protecting them from the Indians.[32] No doubt the sight of the Pamunkeys on the ramparts also caused Berkeley's troops to doubt the justice of their fight against someone who was obviously fighting "the Indians."

Bacon continued his psychological pressure against Berkeley's troops by sending out a small party to "insult" the garrison. The party marched up to the palisade, fired upon the town, and returned without loss. The loyalists now became restless and displeased at their inaction, and some "began to suspect the Governour's courage," and to insist that he attack the rebels. Finding himself thus "obliged to keep the garrison in temper," Berkeley decided to make a sally with a considerable part of his force.[33]

The attack took place on September 15 and failed miserably. Berkeley's troops "(like scholers goeing to schoole) went out with hevie harts, but returned hom with light heeles."[34] The rebels' fire was so heavy that the front line soon broke, causing those behind to turn and flee back within the palisade.[35]

Berkeley's men now became dispirited, kept within their fortifications, and made no further effort to venture out. Still, Bacon saw that he could never become master of Jamestown until he could break through the palisade. He therefore procured some cannon and bombarded the town, but with little effect. Berkeley's men might have maintained their position almost indefinitely, but they failed him.[36] Success would have come, Berkeley wrote, "if our officers and soldiers had had Courage or loyalty but there was a want of both in both for the common soldiers mutinied and the officers did not doe their whole Duty to surpresse them but some of them as I afterwards found did al they could to foment the mutiny." When their fears became too much for them the officers came to Berkeley and urged him to abandon Jamestown. "I represented to them," wrote Berkeley, "the reputation we should loose and not only that but many hundreds that were now declaring for us which we found afterwards to be true desiring them with al passionate Earnestnesse to keepe the Towne but three dayes that Bacons men sufferd more than we did and were as like to mutiny as ours."[37]

The officers, however, went so far as to sign a statement urging the abandonment of Jamestown. Upon this, Berkeley reluctantly pulled out.[38] Bacon entered the town on September 19, and that night burned it to the ground.[39] Why Bacon burned Jamestown is in dispute but the most accepted view is that he did it for fear that Berkeley might fill his men with new courage to take it again. Bacon showed his understanding of the psychology of terror by waiting until night to burn the capital so that it might appear more dreadful in the dark, both to the rebels and to Berkeley's men in their ships on the James River.[40]

The next episode in this strange war was the transmogrification of a thousand newly-converted Berkeley troops back into Bacon supporters. While Bacon was in Jamestown, he received word that Colonel Giles Brent, his former adherent in the northern counties, had gone over to the governor's party and was marching south with a thousand men. Bacon roused his men and, "with abundance of cherefullness disburthening them selves of all impediments to expedition, order, and good decipling, excepting there Oathes, and Wenches," they went forth to battle. No battle was necessary, however, because Brent's men deserted him *en masse* when they heard that Bacon had burned Jamestown.[41]

One cannot read of these incredible reverses of military fortune without concluding that the people in general cared little for the political aspects of the struggle. No soldiers fighting for a "cause" would have shown themselves so timorous. One can say that the desertion of the capital by Berkeley's men shows the unpopularity of Berkeley's cause only if one makes the same statement regarding the desertion of the capital by Bacon's men just previously. Examples of "base desertion" can be multiplied many times from the history of the conflict, drawing illustrations from both sides. Such desertions indicate that the mass of Virginians on both sides fought with only the vaguest idea of a cause. More compelling motives may have been the orders of a forceful authority, the desire for plunder, the belief that they were on the winning side, or the love of battle.

After his retirement from Jamestown Berkeley proceeded to

re-establish his headquarters on the Eastern Shore. On his way down the James River he received welcome reinforcement in the form of a merchant ship, the *Young Prince*, Robert Morris commanding, which had just arrived from England. Berkeley boarded the ship at Newport News on September 26. On September 30 he gave orders to Morris and to Captain Nicholas Prinne, master of the *Richard and Elizabeth* of London, who arrived soon after Morris, and throughout the winter these ships worked in conjunction with loyal ground forces in the lower James River area.[42]

Bacon, meanwhile, after retiring from Jamestown to Gloucester County, drew up another oath of fidelity charging that Berkeley had deserted the country while he had marched out against the Indians and obtained "soe great a victory, as hath in a manner finished all the disaster and almost Resettled the country in a happy Peace...."[43] For trying to oppose him Bacon declared Berkeley a traitor. Bacon's oath of fidelity was "imposed on the People," according to the commissioners,[44] although the Rev. James Wadding, for one, had the courage to refuse it. Wadding was imprisoned for his audacity.[45]

Bacon also prepared an "Appeal" to the people of Accomack County on the Eastern Shore of Virginia, calling on them to seize that "abominable Jugler" Sir William Berkeley and the other "ring-leaders" and turn them over to his side. The "Appeal" invited the people of Accomack to send discreet persons within fifteen days to make satisfaction for the losses the Baconians had sustained by their "piracies." The demands were both too stiff and too bombastic, and Bacon lacked the means to enforce them. The "Appeal" had no known effect.[46]

Bacon now began to be troubled by the conduct of his troops, who looted and plundered the plantations where they were quartered. Colonel Edward Hill complained that

my house was plundered of all I had, my sheep all destroyed, wheat, barley, oates and Indian graine, to the quantity of seven, or eight hundred bushels, and to compleat their jollity draw

Grantham immediately had the guns dismounted and
a barrel of brandy for the three hundred soldiers,
to return to administer the oath of obedience to them
 them their pardon. Grantham then went over to the
 of the York and marched a few miles to Colonel John
 house, which served as the chief garrison and maga-
 rebels. There he found four hundred English and
 arms. These clamored that Grantham had betrayed
 ausing the surrender of West Point "and thereupon
 for shooting mee, and others for cutting me in peeces."
 had to talk fast, promising them all pardon and free-
the Negroes and the English servants, considerably ex-
he powers granted him by Berkeley. His ruse succeeded
 ollected about five hundred muskets and fowling pieces,
 f powder, a thousand weight of bullets and shot, three
 ns, and "several Chests of Merchants Goods and some
 ll of which he loaded in his sloop.⁶¹
 of the men he persuaded to disperse to their homes, but
 Negroes and twenty English refused to deliver their arms.
 en were naive enough, however, to accept a ride in a
 rantham was towing to a garrison down the river to
 hey wished to go. When they were all safely under the
 of his great guns, he had them disarmed and the Negroes
 servants eventually delivered to their masters. Ingram
 er leaders whom Grantham had in his own sloop he de-
 to the governor, "telling him I had promised them pardon,
 he immediately confirmed." Next Grantham persuaded
 ee hundred men he had left at West Point with the barrel
 dy to march down to Tindall's Point (now Gloucester
 where he gave them the oath of obedience, and received
 rms, drums, and colors. The soldiers drank both His
 y's health and the Governor's in brandy "with three
 s in the Governors sight," and were then dispersed by
 ham.⁶²

my brandy, Butts of wyne, and syder by payles full, and to
every health instead of burning theire powder, burnt my writ-
ings, bills, bonds, accounts to the true vallue of forty thousand
pounds of tobacco and to finish theire barbarism, take my wife
bigg with child prisoner, beat her with my Cane, tare her child-
bed linen out of her hands, and with her ledd away my Children
where they must live on corne and water and lye on the ground,
had it not been for the charity of good people. . . .⁴⁷

Bacon attempted to enforce a more strict discipline over his
crew, "finding that his Soldiers Insolences growing soe great and
intolerable to the People (of whom they made noe due dis-
tinction) and finding their actings to reflect on himself. . . ."⁴⁸
However, his efforts met with little success.

Suddenly, the rebel cause was dealt a mortal blow. On October
26, 1676, probably at the house of Major Thomas Pate in
Gloucester County, Bacon died of the "Bloody Flux" and
"Lousey Disease; so that the swarmes of Vermyn that bred in
his Body he could not destroy but by throwing his shirts into
the Fire as often as he shifted himself." ⁴⁹ His grave, if he had
one, has never been located. Governor Berkeley, seeing the just
hand of Providence, remarked that

his usual oath was which he swore at least a Thousand times a
day was God damme my Blood and god so infected his blood
that it bred lice in an incredible number so that for twenty dayes
he never washt his shirts but burned them. To this God added
the Bloody flux and an honest minister wrote this Epitaph on him

Bacon is Dead I am sorry at my hart
That lice and flux should take the hangmans part.⁵⁰

One Joseph Ingram now took command of the rebels. Or, as
the witty author of the Burwell manuscript put it, "The Lion
had no sooner made his exitt, but the Ape (by indubitable right)
steps upon the stage." "The Countrey had," this author went
on, "for som time, bin guided by a company of knaves, now it
was to try how it would behave it selfe under a foole." ⁵¹

Governor Berkeley, hearing of Bacon's death, seized the opportunity to attack the rebels. Through the agency of ship captains Morris and Prinne and the loyalist ground forces in the James River area Berkeley began to drive the Baconians from the lower counties. The journal of Morris' ship, the *Young Prince*, gives us a day-by-day account of the numerous raids, battles, sea-fights, and skirmishes that went on. The fighting was severe. We read of fifteen men killed in one encounter, thirteen prisoners taken in another. Positions shifted rapidly as raids and counterraids were made. One rebel garrison occupied Arthur Allen's brick house, still standing in Surry County, and now known as "Bacon's Castle." The rebels were forced to abandon the house, however, as the loyalists advanced farther and farther up the James.[52]

At the same time Berkeley began to choke off rebel power in the York River. On November 9 he ordered Captain Larrimore to sail his ship the *Loyall Rebecca* "soe neer to Wests Point that you may Comand all sloopes and boates that passes the River ... that thereby the Rebell Ingram and his Complices hath not the Oppertunity to passe and Repasse Yorke River."[53] Taking advantage of his growing control of Virginia's waters, Berkeley organized a series of small-scale amphibious and overland assaults on the scattered garrisons of the rebel army. Robert Beverley did outstanding service in these attacks. Since the rebel "garrisons" were scattered about the country at the abandoned plantations of the loyalists, where the rebel soldiers spent their time completing the ruin of the owners' property, the loyalist leaders went at their task with some relish.

One of the first rebel bands surprised was that of Colonel Thomas Hansford, who was reportedly captured while paying "his oblations in the Temple of Venus."[54] Beverley did the job "with courage and admirable conduct, never to be forgotten," according to Governor Berkeley, and brought the rebel leader to the governor on November 13.[55] Hansford asked to be shot like a soldier, not hanged like a dog, but was told that he was

not condemned for being a soldie
in arms, against the King, whose
death. To the end he affirmed tha
that "he had never taken up arms
the Indians, who had murthered so
ford, previously noted for his aba
the face of Berkeley's proclamation
"the first Native Martyr to Ame
because he was the first native-bor
scaffold.[57]

Beverley surprised another band
in the store of William Howard.[58] A
was Howard's son-in-law, who was i
were the rebels removed from the ho
of the store went too. But "Howard
measure, to see that go out of his sto
he intended to deliver out by the Ell,

The arrival in York River on Novemb
Grantham, master of the ship *Concord
significance. Grantham's ship mounted
formidable weapon into the hands of t
country in rebellion, Grantham sent a c
"who (upon the receipt of my Letter)
Grantham then played a very valuable
down Virginia's rivers, contacting the
an intermediary between them and the
Grantham's ship that Berkeley made an ag
leader Ingram for a "Cessation of Arms
arrived" while Grantham was held hosta
agreement "was broke by the Rebells in th
ever.[60]

The governor thereupon sent Grantha
rebels. Grantham stayed a week "till I m
their Errors; And upon the Second of Janu
and some of the Cheife Officers made a Sur

to me....
broke ou
promising
and to gi
south bar
West's b
zine of t
Negroes
them in
some we
Granth a
dom for
ceeding
and he
a chest
great g
Plate,"

Most
eighty
These
sloop
which
mercy
and th
and ot
livere
which
the th
of br
Point
their
Maje
Shou
Gran

The author of the Burwell manuscript considered Grantham's exploit in persuading Ingram to surrender not inexplicable:

What Arguments Grantham made use of, to ring the Sword out of Ingrams hand, to me is not visable, more then what he tould me of; which I thinke was not Mercuriall enough, against an ordnary Sophester. But to speake the truth, it may be imagin'd that Grantham (at this time) could not bring more reasons to Convince Ingram, then Ingram had in his owne head to Convince him selfe; and so did onely awate som favourable overtures (and such as Grantham might, it is possible, now make) to bring him over to the tother side.[63]

The capture of West Point, the loss of the central magazine, and the defection of their new general proved a death blow to the rebels' "cause." Some of the smaller garrisons, hearing of the turn in fortune, scattered to their homes without the stimulus of a little brandy. They simply walked or rode back to their plantations, muskets in hand, hoping that by deserting the rebel forces before they were captured they might escape responsibility for what they had already done.

On January 11, 1677, Berkeley, as captain general of Virginia, sat with other high military officers of the colony in a court martial on board Captain John Martin's ship at Tindall's Point in York River.[64] Thomas Hall, whom Berkeley described as "a Clerk of a County but more useful to the rebels than 40 army men," confessed himself guilty of rebellion against the King. Various writings under his hand proved the point. The court unanimously recommended death. Sentence of death by hanging was accordingly passed. Berkeley reported that he "dyed very penitent confessing his rebellion against his King and his ingratitude to me." On January 12 the same court passed sentence of death on three other rebels.[65]

The rebellion was not yet over, however, as the King's governor and captain general well knew. There were still garrisons scattered about the country and many of the leaders remained at large. The mopping up of these centers proved easy because the people in general were tired of being plundered by the rebels, and they had no conception that the rebels were fighting for any justifiable "cause." Furthermore the rebel soldiers, who seem to have been equally unaware that they were fighting for some democratic end, silently drifted away when they saw the tide turn, and left their leaders high and dry.

William Drummond, designated by Berkeley as "a Scotchman that we all suppose was the originall cause of the whole rebellion," [66] was taken in New Kent County on January 14, and the next or the following day presented to Governor Berkeley, who had come ashore at Colonel Nathaniel Bacon Senior's ruined plantation at King's Creek.[67] Drummond was sent aboard a ship in irons to await trial.[68] Some of the rebel leaders who had offended less than Drummond were pardoned on the spot. Captain Robert Boodle, for example, came aboard Berkeley's ship on January 17, submitted, and promised that the soldiers under his command would also lay down their arms. Berkeley granted him and his men their pardon.[69]

Berkeley now began his victorious progress inland. In his coach he traveled the five miles from Colonel Bacon's to Colonel James Bray's house. There, on January 20, William Drummond was tried and executed.[70] The following day the governor wrote Major Beverley, who was pursuing rebels in another part of the colony, that Drummond had been hanged and that James Crewes, "Bacon's parasyte," had been captured. In a few days he hoped to take Richard Lawrence, Thomas Whaley, and Anthony Arnold, "the chiefe remaining villians." "I here finde the people cheerfully come in to my service," wrote Berkeley, "and am disarming the rogues, and would have you take the same course where you are, and secure [i.e., seize] those magistrate's tobaccoes, who were swearers of the people to Bacon's execrable and treasonable oathes...." That night Berkeley moved to Major John Page's house at Middle Plantation,[71] and the following day returned to his devastated plantation at Green Spring.[72] With

Jamestown in ashes Berkeley's home became the headquarters for the loyalist forces and the government.[73] On January 24 a court martial there sentenced James Crewes and five other rebels to death for treason and rebellion against the King. One, Henry West, was found guilty but, because he had not been "so notorious as the rest," the court ordered him banished from the colony and his estate forfeited to the King except for £5 to pay his passage.[74]

As the governor was savoring the sweetness of his victory over the rebels, one thousand troops to put down the insurrection, and royal commissioners to investigate its causes, arrived from England. Berkeley's troubles were not yet over.

Chapter 7

THE ROYAL COMMISSION
OF INVESTIGATION

❖❖

IN ENGLAND news of the Indian troubles in Virginia had caused mild concern as early as April 1676, and when reports of political discontent began to be mixed with news of the Indian troubles the English authorities became seriously alarmed. The source of the reports of political discontent in the colony was Giles Bland, the King's collector of customs there. Bland was a hot-headed young man who owed his high post to his father-in-law Thomas Povey, a wealthy English merchant and official in Charles II's household. Bland had early gotten into trouble in Virginia because he falsely accused and insulted certain members of the governor's council. He was even censured by the assembly for a "public affront" to that body. During his various appearances before the General Court he outraged Governor Berkeley by his arrogant demeanor as well as by his false charges. As the King's collector of customs he was not responsible to the governor but to the commissioners of customs in England, and he used this independence to negate all attempts to curb his excesses.

In 1674 Bland was fined £500 by the General Court in connection with his affront to the assembly, but he was given two years to appeal to the Privy Council to have the fine remitted. When his petition for remission of the £500 fine was being considered by the King and the Lords of Trade and Plantations in the spring of 1676, Bland sent home a letter criticizing Berkeley for his inability to "Establish this Place in Peace, and securitie, not only from their [Indian] Enimies, but from the Pressures and discontents, which (they imagine at leaste) they receive from the Government...." Among these pressures Bland listed unequal taxes laid by the poll, arbitrary county levies, gifts from the assembly to the governor, and the high cost of assemblies because of frequent meetings and excessive salaries paid the burgesses. The Virginia agents in England, Francis Moryson, Thomas Ludwell, and Robert Smith, were called upon in June to answer Bland's charges. Their attempt to minimize the discontent backfired when news arrived of Bacon's continuing repudiation of the governor's authority.[1] Unfortunately, though Bacon and Bland were able to get their letters through to England during the summer and early fall, Berkeley had trouble getting his communications to the King because of the power of interception wielded by Customs Collector Bland.[2]

By September enough bad news had arrived to cause the King and his highest advisors deep concern about measures to put down the rebellion. The Virginia uprising was a matter of top priority not only because of the threat to the King's authority but because of the catastrophic effect it would have on his finances if allowed to continue. Virginia produced £100,000 revenue each year for the King.[3] This was an amount exactly equal to the subsidy Charles was then secretly receiving from the French King.[4] With the rebellion cutting off tobacco imports, the King, who needed financial independence to ward off the control of Parliament, was in real trouble. "Every day" during the latter stages of preparation for the expedition Charles pressed Antoine Courtin, the French ambassador, to hurry the payments of his subsidy from Louis XIV, a request which Louis met.[5]

As increasingly unfavorable reports arrived in the autumn of 1676 the Virginia agents, who in July had persuaded the King that no troops were necessary, now urged him to delay until a greater force than he had at first proposed could be assembled. The agents were frequently called upon, at this time, to answer questions concerning conditions in Virginia. In their attempts to explain why a country of so signal loyalty could have become so rebellious, the agents, lacking official word from Virginia, were forced to assume, as Bland charged, that real political grievances had arisen. The English government, similarly disturbed by the lack of any information from Virginia in answer to Bland's charges, grew suspicious and decided to send, in addition to troops to suppress the rebellion, commissioners to find out what caused it. An investigating commission had been first suggested by the Virginia agents themselves, so confident were they that no justifiable grievances could be charged against the Virginia government.

The commission incorporated the King's genuine fear that the distractions in the colony "have, in a great measure, been occasioned by divers Grievances which Our good subjects there have of late layn under; the particulars whereof are yet to us unknowne." King Charles therefore appointed three "Commissioners to enquire into and Report unto us all such greivances and pressures, which any of our Loving subjects, within the Plantation aforesaid, have suffer'd and layn under, or doe suffer and lye under, and more especialy such greivances, and all other causes, matters, and things which have occasioned the late Rebellion distraction, and disorders there...." He also directed the commissioners to collect their information and report with speed so that he might redress the people's grievances. The governor and all other officials of the colony were instructed to be helpful in aiding the commissioners in the execution of their commission.[6]

In private instructions to the commissioners, the King ordered them to be "assistant, to Our Lieutenant Governor or Commander in cheife there, with your Counsel and advice, whensoever hee shall demand it; and particularly in that affaire of renewing a Peace with the Neighboring Indians, in which wee doe particularly order him to demand your assistance." They were to inform themselves of all grievances, but particularly of the one which seemed most to disturb the people, the high salary paid to the members of the assembly, and in this matter they were also to be "assistant, with your advice, to Our Lieutenant Governor, in causing an immediate redress of it." All other complaints were to be reported to the King who would himself see that the guilty parties were punished.[7]

Francis Moryson, who had impressed the King with his presentation of Virginia conditions, was selected as one of the commissioners. Colonel Herbert Jeffreys, commander of the 1,130 troops finally ordered sent,[8] and Sir John Berry, commander of the naval force ordered to carry and escort them, were similarly appointed commissioners. In their roles as commissioners Moryson, Berry, and Jeffreys were clearly meant to act in subordination to Governor Berkeley or to whomever might be the King's highest representative in Virginia. The governor was ordered to demand their advice on the subject of the Indian peace, which he could presumably accept or reject at his pleasure, and he was directed to seek their advice in bringing about a lowering of the burgesses' salaries. In all other matters the commissioners' function was merely to collect the grievances and report them to the King for his action. Their authority as commissioners was in no way designed to override or interfere with the governor's prerogative as the King's highest representative in the colony.

Berry and Moryson left Portsmouth in the King's ship *Bristol* on November 19, 1676.[9] Two other ships of war, the *Rose* and *Dartmouth*, plus eight hired merchantmen carrying Colonel Jeffreys and the major part of the troops, left Deal harbor on December 3, after being held up for ten days by contrary winds.[10]

The commissioners went to Virginia with good will and with honest intentions of doing the King service. Their mission, however, would require patience, tact, and intelligence as well as good will and honesty. There was a dangerous overlapping of authority: the King's governor, the King's military commander, the King's naval commander, and the King's commission of investigation all had powers which were not sharply separated in their spheres of action. The officials who had drawn the commissions had been uncertain whether Berkeley was alive or dead, and strongly doubted that Virginia would be in loyal hands. Hence Jeffreys was not only commander of the King's powerful force of one thousand men, but empowered to succeed Berkeley as governor. The powers of the other commissioners were similarly based on the supposition that Bacon might be in control of Virginia and Berkeley exiled or dead.

With the lines of authority so tangled, it was essential that the personalities of the King's various representatives be such that differences of opinion might be healed by amicable give-and-take rather than widened by bitter insistence on individual points of view. The personalities of the King's representatives, however, left some doubt that this would be the case. Governor Sir William Berkeley was seventy years old, proud, quick-tempered, and deaf. Seven months before the commissioners arrived, he had written in despair: "I am not able to support my selfe at this age six months longer," and had begged the King to send a more vigorous governor.[11] His entire estate, the modest by-product of a lifetime of service to the colony, had in the following months been destroyed by the rebels. More important than his material loss, however, had been the psychological injury. The rebellion had been a personal insult to him, a repudiation of his universally accepted character as the best governor Virginia ever had. In the months following his plea to be relieved, he had, with immense physical and emotional exertions, successfully put down the revolt. The victory had exhilarated him. He was now living in the glory of his vindication of royal authority in Virginia, in defiance of his earlier prediction that he would not survive. Indeed his life probably depended as much on his psychological, as on his physical, well-being. An attack on his belief that he had handled the situation justly and courageously might well prove fatal.

What of the personality of the commissioners? Would they understand the shattering experience Berkeley had been through, and his desperate need for justification? All three commissioners had been elevated to positions to which they were in no way accustomed. Thirty-five years earlier Berkeley had received a royal commission as governor of Virginia, and Sir William, of a noble family by birth, was used to command. Now three comparatively undistinguished men—a naval officer, an army officer, and a colonial agent—were commissioned under the Great Seal of England, put in command of a powerful military force, and ordered to put down a rebellion Berkeley was thought unable to suppress, and to collect the grievances the people were thought to have against him. It was only natural that the King's authority should rest uneasily on their shoulders and that they should be doubly sensitive to any apparent slight to their newly-acquired dignity. Francis Moryson, the only Virginia member of the commission and the only commissioner without an additional position of military command, was especially sensitive. Before he left England he wrote Secretary of State Henry Coventry, complaining of the inadequacy of the £1,500 salary that was provided for the commissioners and beseeching Coventry to consider "how strang it will appeare for his Majesties Commissioners, to come from the frigatt to a twelpenny ordinary and mix with those persons they are to judg and inquire of...." [12] Jeffreys, who probably owed his appointment to family connections rather than to military reputation, showed himself equally sensitive to real and imagined slights.[13] Sir John Berry, the most qualified member of the investigating commission, seems to have been a typical, hard-shelled naval captain.[14]

All three were primed to prove their worthiness for the mis-

sion the King had intrusted to them. First they would crush the
rebels in a gallant military campaign. Then, with painstaking
care, they would collect the grievances that would show why
the rebellion occurred. Then they would sail home, make their
recommendations, and receive the King's thanks and commenda-
tions. The last thing in the world they were prepared for was
a situation in which there were no rebels to fight, and no griev-
ances to report.

Berry and Moryson were the first to arrive, dropping anchor
at Kecoughtan, just inside the mouth of the James River, on
January 29, 1677. Berry immediately wrote Governor Berkeley
that he came with ships, ammunition, and soldiers to help the
governor carry on the war against the King's enemies. He also
wrote that he, Colonel Moryson, and the soon-expected Colonel
Jeffreys came as joint commissioners under the Great Seal of
England "for *settling* the greivances and other affaires in Vir-
ginia. . . ." [15] The statement was clearly in violation of the com-
missioners' commission and instructions which gave them only
the right to "enquire into and Report unto us" the grievances
and the power merely to be "assistant" to the governor with their
"advice, whensoever hee shall demand it." [16]

Sir John Berry went on in his letter to say that there were
other matters which he and Moryson wished to communicate to
the governor and "would bee glad it might bee here on board
(if the present state of your health will permitt) or else that
you will please to Nominate unto us some such place of meeting,
as may seeme agreable to the Kings Honour, and your owne
convenience." [17] The tired seventy-year-old governor immedi-
ately and graciously made the long trip to Kecoughtan and came
on board the *Bristol* February 1.[18] The two commissioners read
him their own commission and delivered additional instructions
sent to him from the King together with certain printed procla-
mations of pardon dated October 27, 1676. The proclamations,
designed as propaganda leaflets to aid the governor in breaking
up the rebellion, placed a price on Bacon's head, but promised

pardon to all his followers who would lay down their arms within twenty days of its publication.[19]

The commissioners arrived to find Bacon dead, the rebels crushed, Jamestown burned to the ground, and the country desolate. The appearance of the royal troops caused the governor to be "much amuzed [amazed ?], and the whole people much startled and concern'd, and many ready to desert their Plantations. . . ." The arrival of one thousand troops in a country of scarcely more than forty thousand people was as though four million American troops had suddenly landed in Europe in 1918 after the armistice had been signed. Moreover Berkeley had never asked for troops to help him. To the people of Virginia, who had screamed "No Levies! No Levies!" when their own representatives in the June Assembly attempted to raise one thousand soldiers to fight the Indians, the arrival of a thousand royal troops, who would have to be quartered and supported in idleness at the people's charge, was viewed as a major disaster. Pending the arrival of Colonel Jeffreys and the rest of the soldiers, the two commissioners decided against turning their troops loose "on a naked Shore, to subsist on the poore Loyal party, who have scarce left where with to support themselves at present . . . wherein as there is none has been a greater sufferer than the Governour, soe hath there beene noe one, (under God), a more eminent or active Instrument in suppressing this Rebellion."

Their own plans, they reported to Secretary of State Williamson, were to call for grievances from the counties, "in our Enquiry whereof, Wee can as yet find noe appearance of any; save onely that of the great Salarie paid the Members of the Assembly which wee doubt not but wee shall soone Redresse." [20] After several days of inquiring, the commissioners had been unable to discover any of the serious pre-rebellion grievances they had expected to find. However, the source of the grievances they would find is foreshadowed in the close of their letter, which reported that the governor was "much concern'd about the Distribution of the Forfeited Estates and Possessions of such as have beene concern'd in this Rebellion, which hee would have to bee disposed and given in Restitution to the Loyall partie, that have beene Loosers by it. To which we dare in noe wise give our Advice or opinion as being quite without our Instructions." [21]

In a later discourse with the governor a more serious difference arose when Berry and Moryson found that Berkeley considered it altogether "improper" to publish the King's printed proclamation of pardon of October 27, 1676, now that Bacon was dead. Instead, he talked of issuing another proclamation excepting the ringleaders of the rebellion, including about eight who had not yet been captured. The commissioners, acting on the assumption that the King's pardon was meant to be published, whatever the situation might be in Virginia, strongly urged that it be issued as it stood. [22]

On February 3 the two commissioners sent the governor certain "Interlocutory heads" of such matters as they conceived necessary for His Majesty's service. Their manner was again, as on January 29, hardly that of functionaries who had been sent to "be assistant to" the King's governor. Their attitude was even more surprising since Colonel Herbert Jeffreys, their highest ranking member, had not yet arrived. Instead of outlining plans for collecting the grievances of the people and taking care of the King's troops, they proceeded to tell Berkeley how to run the government. They urged that quarters, food, transportation, and storehouses be immediately provided for the King's troops, that the King's proclamation be immediately published, that the county courts be summoned to give oaths of allegiance and supremacy, that a new assembly be called, that the assembly make due submission to His Majesty, that a good peace be made with the Indians, and that the salary of the burgesses be cut. [23]

In their comment on the Indian peace the commissioners clearly overstepped their authority. They stated that

Whereas his Majestie hath with greatest Earnestnesse *committed to our care* and utmost endeavours the procuring a good and just

peace with the Neighbour Indians...Wee doe therefore con-
ceive, That it doth in a most especiall manner concerne both
you and us, earnestly to endeavour (by all wayes wee can) to
effect such a good and firme peace with the said Indians, as
shall...most conduce to his Majesties honour and interest...
in all which wee doe most heartily assure you, that you shall
find us *ready to assist you*, with a zeale suitable to the enterprize
and the instructions we have received in this particular.[24]

Insofar as Sir John Berry, acting as naval commander, wished
to provide quarters, food, and storehouses for the King's troops,
his recommendations were perfectly legitimate and natural. But
when the two commissioners told Governor Berkeley how to
conduct the political affairs of the colony, they exceeded the
authority of their commission and instructions. It was not that
their recommendations were unreasonable or unjust, but that
it was not in their province to make them. That the commis-
sioners themselves sensed the inappropriateness of their political
requests is shown by the manner in which they avoided mention
of them in the "True and Faithful Account in what Condition
we found Your Majesty's Colony," which they presented to
the King after their return to England. In this report they stated
that the "Interlocutory heads" were "prepared in order to Your
Majestyes immediate service for the landing and Quartering the
Soldiers, and preventing any Demurage to Your Majestie, as
also to desire an answer and account of such other matters as
appertain'd to our Enquiry." [25]

Berkeley had had too much experience with Bacon's double
talk and its consequences calmly to accept the "advice" offered
by the commissioners. The commissioners' prose showed a star-
tling resemblance to that of Bacon in his letters protesting his
obedience and loyalty to the governor and pledging his utmost
efforts to do what he, but not Berkeley, wanted. It was con-
cerning the Indian peace that the commissioners were granted
their greatest authority, but even on this matter they were hardly
being "assistant, to Our Lieut. Governor or Commander in cheife

there, with your Counsel and advice, whensoever hee shall demand it; and particularly in that affaire of renewing a Peace with the Neighboring Indians, in which wee doe particularly order him to demand your assistance." [26]

The commissioners' most pressing problem was to find suitable living quarters. Green Spring, the governor's plantation, was in a shambles. The house, as Lady Berkeley saw it on her arrival with Colonel Jeffreys a few days later, "looked like one of those the boys pull downe at Shrovetide, and was almost as much to repair as if it had beene new to build, and noe signe that ever there had beene a fence about it. . . ." Lady Berkeley, in the following year and a half, spent £300 "to make it habitable, and if I had not bestowed that mony upon it, the Plantation had not beene, worth £100. . . ." To sleep in his own house Berkeley had to borrow a bed "of a gentleman that was plundred, as well as himselfe, tho not soe totallie. . . ." [27]

Despite the ruined condition of the governor's estate, two hundred men—soldiers, prisoners, and officials—were quartered in and around the main house, and forty-one burgesses were soon expected for the assembly that was to meet there February 20. [28] Green Spring had, for the time being, replaced Jamestown as the capital of Virginia. Berkeley, therefore, had no alternative but to look elsewhere for suitable quarters for the commissioners. One of the few undamaged plantations near Green Spring was that of Colonel Thomas Swann at Swann's Point, just across the river in Surry County. Swann had been so involved with the rebels that Berkeley excepted him from his proclamation of pardon of February 10. But as soon as the governor had returned from his meeting with the commissioners on February 1, he wrote Swann asking that he provide accommodations for the commissioners. On February 6 Berkeley received word that Swann would be "Proude of the Honour." [29]

On February 6 Berry and Moryson issued a "Declaration to His Majesty's Loving Subjects." Although they had as yet been unable to discover any important grievances the commissioners assured the people that they had been sent to find grievances and that they expected the people to submit them. In addition to addressing Virginia's very rebellious citizens as His Majesty's "good and Loving Subjects," the declaration reassured the rebels that they could expect the full measure of the King's mercy even though they had never voluntarily relinquished their rebellious designs. Although warning that the King would ever be severe in punishing those who wilfully violated his authority, "soe on the other hand you are to know, that His Most gracious Majestie will be noe lesse Favourable and indulgent to the just Complaints of His Oppressed people. . . ." The people were invited and required, "every of you, without Excepting of any person," to bring in their "Pressures or Grievances," especially those they believed to be the true cause of the rebellion. Swift redress was promised, and punishment for those at fault.[30]

The declaration must have seemed like a godsend to the rebels. They quickly saw that they were assumed to be an "oppressed people" and that they would be excused for their rebellion if they could supply enough grievances to justify the commissioners' assumption.

On February 8 the commissioners wrote Berkeley urging the "timely Publishing" of the King's printed proclamation of pardon of October 27, 1676, so that "the Trembling People [might] be putt out of paine in this particular." As for grievances, the commissioners specifically reported that "to our (as well as your owne) satisfaction noe matteriall Grievance has once bin soe much as whisper'd against you hitherto. . . ." They hoped that none would now arise and warned the governor

not to proceede soe as to give occasion to Merchants and Traders to complaine you obstruct or Retarde their Trading, by causing Hogsheads to bee mark'd with the Broad-Arrowhead, as goods forfeited to the King, which (in our opinion) cannot be justified by any colour of Law, nor can any man be made lyable to seizure as a Delinquent before due Conviction; especially when the King has given restitution of Estates by expresse words in the Proclamation and Pardon.

The commissioners recommended that a stop be put to the seizure and disposal of rebels' estates until the King could rule on the matter.[31]

Later historians have failed to make any distinction between grievances directed at Berkeley *before* the rebellion and those hurled at him *after* it. As the commissioners' letter of February 8 indicates, complaints directed at Berkeley's pre-rebellion record were hard to find. It was in the post-rebellion period that grievances developed. Yet these grievances have, curiously, been applied to Berkeley's conduct before the rebellion to give him his accepted character of "bloodthirsty oppressor" against whom the people were forced to revolt.

Berkeley was physically sick and tired. He had, as a gesture of courtesy, gone all the way to Kecoughtan to meet the commissioners who were sent to assist him. Instead of bringing him help, they brought him problems, problems almost as serious as those he had just overcome. Like a messenger boy he must return to Green Spring and provide out of a desolate country and an empty treasury food and accommodations for a force equal to one-fortieth of the entire population. An even more galling necessity was to have to ask one of Bacon's associates to provide quarters suitable to the dignity of the royal commissioners because of the devastation wrought by the rebels at the homes of the loyalists.

Perhaps the straw that broke the camel's back, however, was the commissioners' insistence that the trading activities of the merchants not be interfered with. Berkeley had from the very moment of his entry into the government in 1642 protested and remonstrated against the avarice of the English merchants who had, with the help of influence at court, monopolized Virginia's trade.[32] In 1662, when he returned to England to protest the

Navigation Acts which had been reintroduced by the restored Charles, he pointed out that "we cannot but resent, that forty thousand people should be impoverish'd to enrich little more then forty Merchants, who being the only buyers of our *Tobacco*, give us what they please for it, and after it is here, sell it how they please; and indeed have forty thousand servants in us at cheaper rates, then any other men have slaves...." [33]

The chief commissioner and the man scheduled to relieve him, Colonel Herbert Jeffreys, was a relative of Alderman John Jeffreys, an important London merchant trader to Virginia and friend of Secretary of State Sir Joseph Williamson. Sir John Berry, the second most important commissioner, was a friend of Giles Bland's "relations," perhaps his father, an important Virginia merchant, or his father-in-law, Thomas Povey, another powerful merchant. Berkeley may well have felt that the merchant interest had at last been able to replace him as governor with one of "their" men as they had been unable to do, despite strenuous efforts by Thomas Povey and others, following the Restoration. [34]

Whatever the reason, Berkeley answered Moryson and Berry's letter of February 8 by asserting angrily that he had not marked one hogshead of tobacco since the commissioners' arrival nor did he intend to until he had the King's permission which he had written Secretary of State Henry Coventry to obtain. Berkeley also notified the commissioners that he had decided to issue the royal proclamation with exceptions "which I have Authority from his Sacred Majesty to make." As to their request that he provide storehouses for the soldiers' food and ammunition, the governor pointed out the difficulties confronting him because of the plundering done by the rebels. "The Rebels left me but one Oxe and six more I have borrowed which is more then they are able to doe to Bring wood and Victuals for two hundred men which I have now in my house and must feed them al and God knowes the Rebels left me not one graine of Corne nor one Cow to feed me...." In a postscript, with what must have been malice aforethought, he wrote: "if you send me word it is lawful for me to presse oxen or Horses for his Majesty's service having none of my owne I wil immediately doe it." [35]

Moryson did not fall into Berkeley's trap. At first he did not reply, on the grounds that Sir John Berry was temporarily absent. But when pressed by Berkeley he answered cautiously, perhaps after rereading the King's commission and instructions, denying that "any thing in ours cann give you the least distast if rightly considered Since itt is noe more than a freindly advice att your own choice to reject or Imbrace as your Reason shall direct you." As for the governor's request for power to commandeer horses and oxen for the King's service "as though you had Power to act nothing because wee are here," Moryson answered: "Sir wee are soe farr from lesseninge your Power and Authoritie, which wee come to vindicate...." [36]

Governor Berkeley's efforts to force the commissioners to be consistent one way or the other about confiscations was thus sidestepped by Moryson. Of course confiscation of rebel property and impressment of private property in general are not the same thing. But Moryson evidently realized their outward similarity enough to desire not to be quoted as saying that cattle and horses might be seized for the use of the King's unneeded troops, but not to supply Berkeley's victorious soldiers or to replace those stolen from the loyalists by the rebels.

The governor wrote Secretary of State Coventry a bitter letter denouncing the commissioners' "indulgence to the Rebels" and their denial to the loyalists of any hopes of recovering even part of their losses. "We very wel know from whome this kindnesse and severyty proceeds and the causes of both," wrote Berkeley, "But we hope his majesty wil not suffer his Loyal subjects to be out of al hope of redresse for it was only to witnesse their Loyalty to his Majesty that they suffered the losse of al they had." [37] Sir William begged Coventry's "protection" for himself and one hundred faithful loyalists who had been plundered of everything they owned. Unless the King were to give the confiscated land and goods of the convicted rebels to the distressed loyalists, they would be undone. "For my part," he wrote, "I have lost at least Eight thousand pounds Sterling in houses goods Plantation servants and Cattle and never looke to be restored to a Quarter of it. But unlesse some part of it be restored I must Begg or starve...." [38]

Berkeley's appeals to Coventry did not produce results. Coventry may have been sympathetic, but he was not on a level with the really "great men" of England. As one of His Majesty's Principal Secretaries of State his function was to supply information and recommendations to the King and his closest advisers, and then to write the necessary letters and proclamations that would carry out the policy determined upon by the King and his great lords. [39] A secretary of state could of course exert great weight in the deliberations of an ill-informed group of nobles, but Coventry suffered recurrent fits of gout and rheumatism which kept him from his duties at crucial times. [40] Furthermore Coventry was not an aggressive councilor, but a faithful upholder of the King's policy even when he felt it to have been determined by bad advice. [41]

On February 10, under pressure from the commissioners, Berkeley finally issued the King's printed proclamation of October 27, 1676. At the same time he issued one of his own, excepting certain notorious rebels from the King's pardon by virtue of "his most sacred Majesty's order and power to mee given to except such persons as I shall think fitt for his Majesty's better service." [42] Berkeley defended the issuance of his own proclamation on the basis of the King's order of October 10, 1676, authorizing him to pardon as he saw fit; [43] the governor was further justified by the terms of the King's additional instructions to him of October 13, 1676. Berkeley was directed, "upon receipt of theise instructions," immediately to summon Bacon "to present himselfe in such manner as you shall judge fitt." When the rebel leader had appeared, he was to be seized and tried in Virginia or sent back to England for trial "as you shall judge most convenient, according to his greater or lesser interest amongst the generality of the people there at this present." "But," continued the King's instructions, "if the said Nathaniell Bacon shall refuse to render himselfe, *then* the proclamation which you shall receive with theise instructions shalbe immediately proclaymed, and all waies of force and designe used to surprise him...." [44] It is obvious from these words that the King's proclamation of pardon was not intended to be issued regardless of the situation in Virginia, but to be used by Berkeley as he saw fit as a means of capturing Bacon *if* other means failed.

The apparent contradiction between the King's printed proclamation of October 27, pardoning all but Bacon, and his authority of October 10, allowing Berkeley to pardon as he saw fit, existed as a real issue only in the commissioners' minds. Throughout the long process of preparing orders to suppress the rebellion, the English authorities conceived of the two documents as complementary. The probable reason they bear different dates is because the Privy Council desired to make a few last-minute changes in the printed proclamation. [45]

Berkeley's proclamation noted that he had already done what the King's printed proclamation offered to do, *i.e.*, to pardon certain rebels who surrendered within a specified period, and he now confirmed them in their pardon. He next granted pardon to all, except certain individuals specifically named, who would come to the county courts within twenty days, take the oath of obedience, and fulfill the other requirements of the King's proclamation. Then he listed the exceptions to his pardon. First he excepted the land and goods of certain named individuals who "dyed in the actuall prosecution of the said Rebellion" or who were condemned and executed for their rebellion and treason. Next he excepted certain rebels like Richard Lawrence who had never been captured and were still at large; these he intended to bring to trial when captured. In addition Berkeley excepted certain rebels like Giles Bland and Anthony Arnold then in prison awaiting trial. Three members of the council, including Colonel Thomas Swann, were excepted as were certain other persons who administered Bacon's oath. Finally Sarah Grindon, "who by her lyeing and scandalous reports was the first great incourager and setter on of the ignorant vulger and hath ever since been an active aider assistor and abettor of the Rebells," was excepted and referred to trial by the commissioners. Berkeley further gave notice that his declaration did not release the rebels from making restitution for horses, cattle, and goods which they had plundered. Sufferers were authorized to bring suits at law to recover such property.[46]

Berry and Moryson denounced Berkeley's proclamation for excluding certain individuals from the King's pardon for "though Bacon bee dead and the faction weakned and falne off, and soe much of his Majesty's Proclamation as concerned the taking of him become uselesse, yet for what remained materiall in itt for the people to have knowne, wee could have heartily wished the timely publishing of itt...." The commissioners insisted that the King's printed proclamation of October 27 nullified the King's authority to Berkeley of October 10 because it was of later date. What conditioned the commissioners' attitude most was not logic but the report "by all hands, as alsoe by the Governors owne report, that of above fifteen Thousand, there are not above five hundred persons untainted in this rebellion." [47] It is impossible to say how much this state of affairs had resulted from a "universall inclination to rebellion" noted by one observer,[48] and how much from Bacon's brilliant strategy of requiring oaths of loyalty from all the people when he had the power to punish any refusal. The effect, at any rate, was to make it difficult to distinguish between the true rebels and the forced supporters. Berkeley, throughout the rebellion, had considered the taking or giving of Bacon's oath as the manifestation of a disloyal attitude.[49] The commissioners took the position, however, that the oath-takers were "seduced" or "forced" into their rebellion, and hence should not be penalized for their actions. But it was not so much the question of force as of numbers that determined the commissioners' attitude on whether the King's pardon should be extended to all. Their attitude was governed most by the fact that "the number of the unconcerned in the late defection were so very few, which in our sense seemed to urge a kind of necessity of opening to them your majesty's royal acts of grace and forgiveness...." [50]

The commissioners' solution to the question of responsibility was to wipe the slate clean and to start afresh from the time of their arrival. Since they considered Berkeley now guilty of violating the King's pardon to his subjects by excepting certain individuals and seizing their estates, they plunged into a defense of the erstwhile rebels against the efforts of the governor to make them disgorge their loot and pay for their rebellion. Although admitting that "noe Jury will be found, to give a faire or just verdict" against the rebels as civil trespassers, the commissioners would not recognize any other way by which the loyalist sufferers might secure justice. Furthermore no one ought to be tried and convicted as a delinquent, they wrote, unless "taken actually such before his Majesty's acts of grace From laying hold whereof there is noe Colour to exclude any that come in to embrace the same...." [51] "Although wee rather Commend what before hee might bee forced to doe in Furore Belli by a martiall power considering how the face of affaires then looked," wrote the commissioners, still His Majesty's instructions required "that the Lawes might returne to their owne proper Channell, and that all future proceedings of his might bee by a Jury...." [52]

It is hardly surprising that the loyalists who had risked their lives and lost their estates upholding and finally vindicating the King's authority should object. Why should they allow the already defeated rebels a questionable pardon which seemed to guarantee them their swollen estates and to debar the loyalist party from any reparation? To be penalized rather than rewarded because they were so few and the rebels so many seemed a double violation of justice. The commissioners were scrupulous and serious-minded men, yet it was their doctrinaire insistence on the letter of the law (misinterpreted in the interests of expediency) which prevented their understanding the broader issues at stake.

The commissioners' attitude was too much for Governor Berkeley to endure. From his bed "expecting fever" he wrote them on February 11 how troubled he was to be admonished for that which was ever practised in all nations. He cited several instances from the English civil wars. One was the case of Colonel "Jarrett" (undoubtedly Charles Gerard, first Baron Gerard of Brandon, later Earl of Macclesfield) who went to Lord Northumberland's house and took away all his horses for the King's service; yet Northumberland, although manifestly against the King, never bore arms and was never convicted. When Berkeley himself was with the King in the pursuit of the Earl of Essex, sometime in the period 1644-1645, the King gave orders to seize the horses, goods, and cattle of many who had declared against him. "And I was by, when Sir Richard Greenevill tooke the house of my Lord Roberts, and out of it at least two thousand poundes sterling in Plate, very rich Hangings and much household stuffe, yet that Lord was soe farr from ever being convicted that at the Kings coming into England he was made Lord Private Seale. . . ." Berkeley was aroused and embittered by the commissioners' growing antipathy towards his course of action. He declared that, though he had seized no goods except at the height of war, "indeed [I] shal doe it hereafter for from divers honest men I heare that those that are Criminally obnoxious dayly and hourely conveigh away their goods and Cattle which can never be distinguished from their goods to whome they are Conveighed." [53]

The legal justification for the commissioners' decision to confirm the rebels in their property (at least until the King's pleasure was known) and to prevent the loyalists from regaining theirs by other than civil court proceedings was derived from the legal writings of Sir Edward Coke. The commissioners noted in their "True and Faithful Account" that they had told Governor Berkeley that it was an "apparent contradiction to the common course of the laws in England to seize or dispose of any man's estate before a lawful tryal and conviction of his crime and shewed him the opinion of the learned lord Coke positively against it, whereof he took little caution or notice, but writ us word he appealed to your majesty and most honourable privy council, and the learned judges of the law...." [54] The commissioners also showed a fondness for a statute of the first year of Richard III, which they described as "against Seisures before Conviction, or attainder." [55]

The commissioners were probably carrying an early edition of Coke's *The First Part of the Institutes of the Law of England: or a Commentary upon Littleton.* The first edition of this work was published in 1628. Eight editions had appeared by 1670. In one section, Coke makes a few incidental comments as to how attainder affects the law of property:

If a felon be convicted by verdict, confession, or recreancie, he doth forfeit his goods and chattels, etc., presently.... And *Stanford* (speaking of a felon convict by verdict) saith, that he shall forfeit his goods which he had at the time of the verdict given, which is the conviction in that case; and by the statute of 1. *R.* 3. *cap.* 3. no sheriffe, bailiffe, etc. shall seise the goods of a felon before hee bee convicted of the felony; whereby it appeareth, that the goods may be seised as forfeit after conviction. [56]

The act of 1 Richard III, cap. 3, knowledge of which the commissioners undoubtedly took from Coke's brief reference, had nothing to do with conviction or attainder for treason. It was entitled "An Act for baylying of persons suspected of Felony," and its purpose was stated in the preamble which read:

Forasmoche as dyvers persones ben daily arested and imprisoned for suspecion of felonie, sumtyme of malice and sumtyme of light suspecion, and so kept in prison without baill or maynepris to their greate vexacion and trouble, it be ordeyned and stablisshed by auctorite of this present parliament...that no Shireff...take or sease the goodes of eny persone arested [for suspicion of felony] afore that the same persone so arested and imprisoned be convycte or atteint of suche felonye accordyng to the Lawe, or ellys the same goodes otherwise lawfully forfeited, uppon peyne to forfeit the dowbull Value of the goodes so takyn, to hym that is so hurt in that behalf....[57]

The commissioners, it will be seen, took some incidental comments of Coke on the law of property and an antiquated law on the unjust use of the police power and threw them into the complex situation of a colonial rebellion and its aftermath in which the authority of a royal governor and a colonial assembly to conduct war, pardon, try, convict, and attaint were all involved. Berkeley, who had been trained in law at the Inns of Court and who had seen the King and his nobles confiscate rebel property without semblance of a trial, took a more permissive view of the rights of government in such situations. Hence his appeal from the antiquated learning of the commissioners to the practice of the men who then ruled England. Unfortunately for him these men did not now see fit to acknowledge that their actions should serve as a precedent for his.[58]

Chapter 8

GOVERNOR BERKELEY *vs.*
LIEUTENANT GOVERNOR JEFFREYS

✧✧✧

ALL OF the activities of the commissioners during the first ten days of February were carried on by Sir John Berry and Colonel Francis Moryson. Colonel Herbert Jeffreys, commander of the King's troops and successor to Berkeley, and therefore the most important member of the commission, finally arrived on February 11 with the troop ships.[1]

The next day Jeffreys presented his credentials to act as lieutenant governor in the governor's absence. Now the real trouble began. Jeffreys' commission of November 11, 1676, stated that Berkeley was to come back with all possible speed and that Jeffreys was to be lieutenant governor with power during Berkeley's absence to exercise the offices of governor and captain general of His Majesty's forces in Virginia.[2] When Jeffreys' commission was read before the governor and council at Green Spring on February 12, Berkeley left it to the council to determine whether he was immediately to resign the government to Colonel Jeffreys or not. The council decided that he should not because, in the words of Jeffreys himself, of a "clause he findes in my Commission that he is to repair speedily into England as soon as he can convenient, which he construes that

[114]

he may take his time for his owne convenience." [3] The commissioners asserted angrily that the council members were maturely to consider whether the word "conveniency" was meant in respect of His Majesty's service or Sir William Berkeley's own private convenience.[4]

The council also made use of another argument, that the commission of oyer and terminer under the Great Seal authorizing Berkeley and the council to try those guilty of insurrection, rebellion, and like offenses bore a later date (November 16, 1676) than the letters of the King and Secretary of State calling him home.[5] The council interpreted the document as continuing Berkeley in, rather than immediately recalling him from, the government.[6] The council thus struck back at the commissioners by using the same arguments the latter had used in the dispute over Berkeley's pardon of February 10, 1677, when they had asserted that the King's proclamation of October 27, 1676, superseded the King's instructions of October 10 and 13, 1676.

The commissioners protested Berkeley's failure to resign the government into the hands of Colonel Jeffreys and sent copies of such parts of their correspondence with Berkeley as would show Secretary Coventry the difficulties they were having. Both Berkeley and the commissioners were sending outraged letters to Coventry at this time enclosing almost identical correspondence with the expectation that their party would be justified. However, as in the case of the earlier problems brought on by Bacon's Rebellion, seventeenth-century communication facilities were too slow to allow the home government to decide the squabble. By the time they knew of the dispute the principals were on their way home. The difference of opinion over the proper time for Berkeley's departure was a serious one, and during the months that followed a continuous wrangle went on between the annoyed commissioners and the embittered governor.

On February 13, 1677, the commissioners complained to the governor of the seizure of people's goods by Berkeley's own servants, and denounced such proceedings as against law, right,

[115]

and His Majesty's royal will.[7] On the same day Berkeley answered that the seizures were beyond his knowledge and that he would punish those responsible. He reminded the commissioners, however, that almost all his neighbors had considerable shares of his goods and that they had been willing to spare some corn and hogs in lieu of what they had stolen.[8]

By the time the assembly met on February 20 relations between the commissioners and the governor had become formal and strained. On that day Colonel Moryson, despite the absence of the other commissioners, wrote Berkeley that various people who were required by the King's proclamation to take the oath of obedience and give security for their future good behavior found themselves unable to get any of the loyal party to stand bound for them. Moryson therefore "desired" Berkeley to take the matter up with the assembly and remedy the situation.[9]

Berkeley answered on February 21 addressing Colonel Moryson, as he usually did the commissioners, as "Right Honorable." "I have received your letter by Capt. Swan," he wrote, "and Shall doe as you Require me." He also noted that he was so perfectly recovered from the sickness that had dogged him from the time of the commissioners' arrival "that I hope to goe for England with the first Ship." [10]

Moryson wrote back sharply saying that the words "I shall doe as you require me" must have been a mistake in Governor Berkeley's reading of his message, not in his writing of it. He defended his right to give advice to the governor (and the governor's right to reject it) without his fellow commissioners being present, although by their instructions none of the commissioners were authorized to offer unsolicited advice to the governor. He also desired that Berkeley should not write him as "Right Honorable," a title that he did not merit, but that he should address him only according to the true title due him.[11] To this Berkeley answered on February 24 that he considered all the King's commissioners of so high a quality that they deserved the title "Right Honorable" and that the others had not taken it ill previously. "For the word Require, truly I know not whether it were Desire, or not." [12]

On February 27 the commissioners sent to the governor, council, and speaker of the house of burgesses a letter to be communicated to the whole assembly. In it they made a strong plea for a just peace with the Indians. They denounced the

inconsiderate sort of men who soe rashly and causelessly cry up a warr, and seem to wish and aime at an utter extirpation of the Indians, (and are yett still the first that Complaine and murmer at the charge and taxes that on any just occasion attends such a warr) wee would wish such to lay their hands on their hearts and seriously to consider with themselves, whether it is not a base ingratitude, a nameless Prodigie of infatuation, and mere madness in such men as would make a breach with, or strive to destroy and extirpate those amicable Indians, who are soe farr from hurting them or us, that we must confess they are our best guards to secure us on the Frontieres from the incursions and suddaine assaults of those other Barbarous Indians of the Continent. . . .

The commissioners urged that the "unreasonable sort" of Virginians should

understand their owne securitie and interest, and to sitt downe satisfyed that they can quietlie enjoye soe large and faire a portion of their possessions as nowe they doe, enough and more then they either will or can ever imploye or cultivate to profitt, and not still Covett and seek to deprive them [the Indians] of more, out of meer Itch of Luxurie rather than any reall lack of it, which shames us and makes us become a Reproach and by-word to those more Morall heathens.

The commissioners further recommended a reduction in the salaries paid burgesses and the withdrawal of their liquor allowance in order to lessen the tax burden on the country. Committee chairmen were urged to write their own reports to save the expense of clerks.[13]

The commissioners sent a second message shortly thereafter to clarify their earlier communication. In the second message they explained that the assembly's function was not to determine whether or not to make an Indian peace or to reduce the salaries of its members, but merely to determine the *manner* in which these aims should be accomplished. The commissioners peremptorily ordered the assembly to put into effect their "recommendations," and had their message signed by Samuel Wiseman, their clerk, "by order of his Majesty's Honorable Commissioners." [14]

The assembly did not take kindly to the commissioners' advice. In fact it never bothered to answer their letter. No effort was made to conclude a formal peace with all the various Indian tribes, although, by orders of the assembly, certain friendly Indian tribes, who had been driven away from their lands, were authorized to return to them and to enjoy their earlier status under the English crown. The Pamunkey, Chiskiac, and Niccomacoe Indians were specifically mentioned in these orders.[15]

The assembly devoted most of its efforts to putting into effect Berkeley's ideas of a just civil settlement. By "An act of indemnitie and free pardon" all persons except notorious actors in the rebellion were pardoned for their rebellion. Fifty-five persons were excepted in some manner from the pardon, either completely or merely to the extent of being debarred from public office. A second act attainted Bacon and certain of the principal leaders of the rebellion of high treason, and declared their estates forfeited to the Crown. However it declared that the estates were only to be inventoried until the King's pleasure might be known. By another act, based on "severall presedents of parliament" in punishing those guilty of treason during the rebellion in England, "and alsoe that such greate and hainous crimes may not passe altogether unpunished," the assembly directed that certain of the previously excepted rebels should beg for their lives on their knees with a rope around their neck either before the governor and council or in county courts.

Another "act for the releife of such loyall persons as have suffered losse by the late rebells" attempted to force the return of looted property. Any person having property belonging to loyalists was to report the fact at the county courthouse so that the owner could claim it. The estates of those already executed for treason were made liable for such property as their owners had previously looted.[16] Unfortunately the loot taken by the rebels did not return as quickly as it left, despite the laws of the assembly.[17]

In accordance with the King's order the assembly declared void all the acts and orders of the June 1676 session. Then it immediately put through most of the "reform" laws of that assembly. The repassage of the reform acts continues to baffle those who see the Bacon-Berkeley struggle as an opposition between "democracy" and "oppression." [18]

During the rebellion, fourteen persons were executed under martial law. The commissioners, after their arrival, joined with Berkeley and the council in civil proceedings which condemned nine persons to death. In all twenty-three persons were hanged for their rebellion.[19] The Virginia historian Campbell thought that the commissioners compromised themselves by agreeing to sit on the trial and condemnation of rebels despite the King's pardon.[20] For the rebels condemned by the commissioners, although captured during the war, would seem to have been just as eligible for the King's pardon as those rebels, also captured during the war, who escaped punishment by pleading the King's pardon after the arrival of the commissioners.[21]

The commissioners, in a letter of March 21, desired Governor Berkeley to make a report of all "seizures, Compositions, amerciaments, Fines and Forfeitures" for their information and for transmittal to the Lord High Treasurer of England. This letter marked an almost final break with the governor. According to Wiseman, the commissioners' clerk, Berkeley did not answer the letter nor did he report the seizures, fines, and forfeitures as requested.[22] Berkeley's refusal may well have been the result of his general disgust with the attitude the commissioners had adopted with more and more insistency. *He* had previously desired that *they* should make a list of what he had seized.[23] Berkeley was proud and he was the King's governor. The commissioners were supposed merely to be assistant to him with their advice. Yet their requests were like directions, and their goal seemed to be to defend the rebels from suffering the same confiscation of estates that the loyalists had previously suffered at their hands. It is little wonder that Berkeley chose to ignore them and to look to the King for his vindication.

Communication did not break down altogether, however. On March 25 Colonel Moryson requested the favor of Lady Berkeley in the case of one Jones, a condemned person, who had sought refuge with the commissioners. Moryson was convinced that his ignorance had led him from his allegiance and that he was "seduced . . . by the Artifices of others." [24] Lady Berkeley assured Moryson the same day that Jones would be pardoned, "Mercy being as inherent in him" (Sir William Berkeley) as in herself. She would forget, she said, how the rebels had once threatened that she would be glad of canvas linen.[25]

The commissioners spent much time in February and March collecting the grievances of the "people": that is, of the people who came to them in February and March of 1677 to complain. One of the most common complaints was directed against the Indians. The writers of many of the grievance petitions, echoing Bacon's former "cause," demanded "an immediate Warr with all Indians in Generall" to be conducted by volunteers. The commissioners noted angrily that "if these very Requesters were to be try'd upon any just occasion they should be the first that would cry out of the Charge, and be unwilling to pay 6: pence towards it." [26]

Another common grievance received by the commissioners concerned too high taxes. When has this not been a grievance! Almost every county complained of the standard two shillings per hogshead tax on exported tobacco, of the fort duties, and of the sixty pounds of tobacco per poll tax levied to support the Virginia agents in England. Some added for good measure taxes necessary to support frequent meetings of the assembly, and local levies for county purposes. The people found little sympathy for their complaints against taxes. The commissioners went to great lengths to explain the necessity of the sixty pounds of tobacco tax, of which Colonel Moryson, one of their number, had been the beneficiary for several years.[27] The commissioners not only defended the tax policy of the Virginia assembly (which alone had the authority to levy taxes) but suggested a new tax, one on liquor, in order to help support the stationing of royal troops in Virginia in the future.[28]

The petition writers also took the occasion of the commissioners' call for grievances to complain of the manner in which taxes were collected. A tax on land was occasionally suggested in place of the customary poll tax. Those historians who cite this proposal as a grievance of the small farmers against the "great men" of the colony will have to explain why it was that Governor Berkeley and the council were the consistent proponents of this reform and why the burgesses were usually opposed to it.[29]

Among the post-rebellion grievances handed in to the commissioners were complaints directed at the vestry system. This system of church government had been made self-perpetuating by an act of March 1662 which provided that on the death of a vestryman the minister and vestry were to appoint a replacement. It is customarily assumed that this act was a deliberate attempt on the part of Governor Berkeley and his oligarchic favorites to restrict the suffrage. Actually the act was passed under the direction of Colonel Francis Moryson himself, who had been left as acting governor when Berkeley went to England to protest against the Navigation Acts. Berkeley had charged Moryson and the clerk of the assembly to peruse the laws and reduce them into as good a form as possible.[30] A complete revision of all the colony's earlier laws was thereupon made under Moryson's direction. It is very probable that the vestry law was merely carelessly drawn without consideration of the long-term effects of having the vestry and minister fill death vacancies. Indeed the fatal clause is tacked on with seeming unconcern to a clause allowing the minister and vestry to choose two churchwardens yearly.[31] The law that it revised, that of Berkeley's assembly of March 1661, contained no such ambiguities but clearly and forthrightly ordered that vestrymen should be "chosen by the major part of the parrish." [32] Therefore, if the 1662 law is to be attributed to a desire to oppress the people, Colonel Moryson will have to take the blame.

A grievance which the commissioners were primed to discover was the "great salarie paid the Members of the Assembly." [33] Sending burgesses to Jamestown had always been costly because of Virginia's many rivers and bays and scattered settlements. In the early days the burgesses had presented bills for their expenses to the counties they represented. Criticisms of their expense accounts were frequent, however, and some persons began to offer themselves as candidates with the promise that they would serve at far less expense to the taxpayers. If "interested persons" were allowed to "purchase votes" in this fashion, declared the assembly of March 1661, the office of burgess might become "both mercenary and contemptible." The assembly therefore enacted that each burgess should receive a fixed compensation of one hundred and fifty pounds of tobacco per day in addition to traveling expenses to and from Jamestown. The act was passed again in Moryson's revisal of the laws in March 1662. Moryson and his fellow commissioners forced the assembly of February 1677 to reduce the amount to one hundred and twenty pounds per day, but enough "extras" were added by the legislators to make the cost of supporting the assembly almost as high as before.[34]

The other "grievances" are startlingly varied. Surry County complained of the exactions of sheriff's and clerk's fees. But, as the commissioners pointed out, the complaint had never been made to the secretary of the council who would have given them relief. Besides, the laws provided against exorbitant fees and so it must have been their own fault, reasoned the commissioners, if they did not apply themselves to such obvious remedies. It is possible that by "exactions" the Surry County gentlemen meant merely that they thought the fixed fees were too high. They also complained of the high cost of legal action.[35] Here again it was under Governor Berkeley's early administration that the fees of the secretary, clerks, sheriffs, and burgesses were first regulated and published for the protection of the people.[36]

James City County demanded in its grievances that Indian slaves taken during the war be disposed of for the public use and profit. The commissioners, however, noted that "The Indian captives being most of them belonging to the Queene of Pamunkey and other friendly nations wee humbly conceive it will be most for his Majestyes honor, that upon the Peace lately concluded, the said Indians may be restored to them. . . ."[37]

Some complained of the lack of able ministers.[38] Others demanded that the capital be moved from Jamestown to Middle Plantation, a move actually made before the turn of the century. However, the commissioners answered that "This is just as if Middlesex should have Petitioned, that London might have beene new-built on High-gate Hill, and removed from the grand river that brings them in their trade."[39] The commissioners were also presented with the "extravagant request" of Lower Norfolk County for liberty to send its tobacco to any of the King's colonies without paying the duty specified by act of Parliament. "This head is wholly mutinous," commented the commissioners, "to desire a thing contrary to his Majesties Royall pleasure and benefitt and also against an Act of Parliament."[40] Also worthy of mention are the grievances of Northampton County that no liquor be sold within a mile of the courthouse on days when the court was in session, and that the Indians of the Eastern Shore "be obliged to kill a certaine Number of wolves yearly."[41]

The difficulty of piercing the veil of secondary interpretation

is illustrated by the grievances signed by seven individuals pur-
porting to represent the views of all the citizens of Isle of Wight
County. The seven petitioners listed twenty-six complaints,
almost all of which concern the "intollerable" tax burden or the
alleged misuse of the tax revenues. Since one of the persons
accused of misappropriation of the public funds was Charles
Moryson, the nephew of Francis Moryson, the commissioners
examined these charges closely and found them utterly un-
justified.[42]

The petition submitted by the seven men was denounced in
another petition of grievance signed by seventy-one persons of
the same county. The "opposing grievances" claimed that the
first complaints received by the commissioners were made with-
out the knowledge of many of the people, and were merely
designed to justify the signers for their rebellion.[43] When the
burgesses from Isle of Wight County in the assembly of Febru-
ary 1677 were asked if the first petition represented the county's
actual grievances, they reported that they did not and that the
signers had used improper methods in collecting and submitting
them. The assembly therefore denounced the first grievances
as "libellous scandalous and Rebellious," and ordered the writers
punished. On April 9 the signers of the petition appeared in the
Isle of Wight courthouse and recanted, promising "never to be
guilty again of being false and scandalous." [44]

Since the accusations of the seven men were challenged by
the commissioners, by the assembly, and by seventy other citizens
of Isle of Wight County, it is difficult to see why editors should
print their petition while omitting the counterpetition against
it, containing ten times as many signatures. The opposing griev-
ances are not, for example, published in McIlwaine's *Journals of
the House of Burgesses*, although they immediately preceded the
other petition from Isle of Wight in the manuscript from which
McIlwaine printed the texts of the county grievances.[45]

In addition to general grievances the people submitted personal
ones. Because the commissioners had expressed the view that

Berkeley's seizures of rebel property without formal trials were illegal, they were inundated with complaints from ex-rebels who saw that, though defeated by Berkeley, they were to be saved, by the King's commissioners, from punishment. The complaints were principally against confiscation of their property by loyalist troops in the final stages of the rebellion. The commissioners made little effort to determine whether their grievances were valid or whether they had anything to do with causing the rebellion. They were particularly annoyed at the actions of Berkeley's lieutenants, William Hartwell and Robert Beverley, in making rough and ready "compositions," or agreements, with the rebels for their pardon in exchange for supplies needed for the King's troops or for the operation of government. When those who had agreed to the compositions heard that the commissioners had stated that they were entitled to their pardons without any penalties whatever, they petitioned the commissioners for relief. Other rebels protested private compositions. Three planters of New Kent County, for example, charged that a loyalist officer had forced them to pay 4,250 pounds of tobacco for killing his hogs during the rebellion. The petitioners did not affirm or deny the accusation but noted merely that they had laid hold of His Majesty's pardon and hence should be protected from prosecution.[46] Because their sympathy was absorbed by the immediate plight of the former rebels, the commissioners paid no attention to the losses suffered by the loyalists in the earlier stages of the rebellion, except to list fifty-one "worthy Persons" who suffered and served the King loyally. In the opinion of the commissioners, only one of these, Major Robert Beverley, made up his losses in the post-rebellion period.[47]

What is astonishing about the grievances presented to the commissioners is that there are almost no charges of graft, corruption, favoritism, or misgovernment against Governor Berkeley or even against most of those closely associated with him. The house of burgesses of the assembly of February 1677 declared that they "doe unanimously agree and Beleive, that there is no Imputation of Corruption or Injustice Can bee agaynst him, many of this house have well knowne his Honnor this five and twenty years and upwards, and doe Affirme and Attest, that they have not knowne nor heard, of any wilfull Injust Judgment given or Action Committed by him in any of his Administrations, And that he hath allwayes had an eare open, to the Complaynt of the meanest or poorest man or weoman, whose access to him hath allwayes been most easy." The burgesses also declared

that in all the greivances of the people, That have been yearly brought to the Assembly, It is observable, that never any of them had the least reflection, uppon him or his goverment, as to the Ill mannagement of it, nor doth any thing Appeare yett of the like nature, against those magistrates that are Appoynted by him, And this his majesties people and Country doe most humbly desire, and would accompt it an high act of favour, that his sacred majesty will graciously please, to Continue him in the Goverment.[48]

This "testimonial" to Berkeley from the house of burgesses was denounced by William Sherwood, who had left Virginia in August 1676 and returned after the rebellion was put down, as a testimony the house "could not avoid giving him . . . that the country might be ridd of him." Sherwood had incurred the governor's ire in February and March by acting as attorney for many of the rebels, and he showed no restraint in denouncing the man he had warmly praised before the rebellion. Most of the burgesses, he charged, were Berkeley's "owne Creatures and Choase by his appointment before the arrivall of the Commissioners."[49] The usual interpretation of the February Assembly, following Sherwood, is that the members were "creatures" of the governor and not representative of the people.[50] However, just as the February Assembly passed again most of the "reform" acts so frequently attributed to Bacon's influence in the previous assembly, so did its justification of Berkeley merely echo that of the June Assembly which no one would assert was made up of Berkeley's "owne creatures."[51]

On March 27, 1677, the commissioners sent a bundle of reports to their agent Mr. Thomas Watkins, for distribution among various of the King's ministers and officials. They enclosed "papers and proofs of some particulars and doe desire that you will inforce the heads of those proofs as occasion offers." [52] The grievances sent back by the commissioners were all minor, disputed, and concerned primarily with post-rebellion confiscations by the loyalists of the property of rebels, or alleged rebels. A typical grievance presented by the commissioners to the English officials was that of Sarah Grindon and her husband complaining that their estate had been seized for what they claimed were reasons unknown. [53] Mrs. Grindon had been one of those who spread false rumors concerning the governor's intentions in the spring of 1676. [54] According to her own petition she assisted Bacon with some powder, but thought it was to be employed against the Indians. She also admitted "(being an Ignorant woman) ... [that] she did speake some foolish and indiscreete words reflecting upon the sloe prosecution of the Indian warr, yett the same were not uttered with Intention of evill against his Majesties governement in this Colony and is most heartily sorrowfull for the same...." [55] The assembly of February 1677 had excepted her from the King's pardon and made her estate liable to such penalties as the next grand assembly, or the General Court upon a legal trial, might levy upon her, on the grounds that she and another "were greate encouragers and assisters in the late horrid rebellion." [56]

No attempt was made to judge the truth or justice of Mrs. Grindon's petition or of others. The claims of those aggrieved were merely forwarded to the highest officials in England unevaluated. It is strange that the commissioners could not find more outrageous and less disputed grievances than those sent back. But as they themselves noted in their letter to Watkins:

The generall Greivances are soe few and triviall That if the Governor and his party would leave off their Depredations and answer to those matters he is by his Majesty instructed and by us desired to doe, wee can see noe further occasion to stay a Fortnight upon the place, but his contrariety and aversion is such, that it begetts new troubles and Obstructions to Our proceedings.[57]

To Secretary Coventry they reported that Berkeley was the main cause of most of the difficulties on the place. Yet they admitted again that "As for the generall Grievances wee are sent hither to Enquire into Report *and Redresse* by what wee can hitherto find, they are like to come within a very narrow compasse...." The only grievances they could find were salaries, fort money, public accounts, and levies, all matters proper for redress by the assembly. Had it not been for Berkeley's obstructions, they reported, "wee verily beleive e're this tyme wee should have fully received and Examined all the Grievances, satisfied the People, Concluded the Peace with the Indians, and finally fulfilled our whole Instructions...."[58] It can be seen that the commissioners had deluded themselves into thinking that their commission and instructions authorized them not only to report but to settle the people's grievances.

The commissioners noted that they had time and again protested Berkeley's "illegall and arbitrarie Proceedings, as to seizures of Estates of Persons not convicted, since the Cessation and laying downe of Armes at West-Point and upon our Arrivall here."

As often as wee urged the illegality of such his Practices in Tyme of Peace hee is still pleased to replie with a story of something done in the late Civil Warrs in England: Asserting that it is the Law of Nations, then that hee Appeales herein to His Majestie, His Councill, and the Learned Judges; and againe that hee has writt home to Your Honors selfe in this behalfe.[59]

Writing to Secretary Sir Joseph Williamson the commissioners were even more harsh. "Wee have still observed here," they wrote, "that those who call themselves the loyall partie are the only chiefe Disturbers and Obstructors of the peace of this

calamitous country...." They explained to Williamson their
theory that just as the governor and the assembly were com-
pelled by force to act against their wills in June 1676, so were
the people in general compelled to act as rebels, including pre-
sumably the five hundred who coerced the governor and as-
sembly. Thus they deserved a royal pardon as much as did
Berkeley and the assembly. The commissioners also charged, on
the basis of two or three disputed incidents, that Governor
Berkeley marked delinquents' tobacco with the broad arrow
(the King's mark) "afterwards altering it to his own private
marke...calling this, securing it to the Kings use." [60]

By April relations between the commissioners and Berkeley
were nearly impossible. On April 5 the commissioners reported
that Berkeley had done nothing to make peace with the Indians
and that he had ignored their request for an account of his sei-
zures. Berkeley in turn had insisted on seeing their instructions
which they refused, finding him "soe criticall and captious at all
advantages to himselfe, that wee are certaine that would rather
more and more retard, than Expedite the Kings Businesse wee
are come aboute...." Berkeley was beginning to strike where
it hurt, and the commissioners now resorted to savage and un-
supported smears. They reported that they would be better able
to accomplish "the Kings Businesse" easily "were hee (the onely
impediment) removed hence For both his Councill, and gener-
ally the whole Assembly and People have bin and are soe over-
awed and byass'd by him, that it is also impossible to expect that
account (from them neither) which our Commission and In-
structions require." Some counties, they charged, had not yet
dared to bring in their grievances "with that Freedome, which
wee have invited them...." Only when Berkeley had left did
they foresee that the "mists, [which] hee by his Artifice casts
before us can bee well cleered, and wee take a plaine and naked
Prospect of things...." [61]

In a postscript to a letter of April 9 to Thomas Watkins,
Colonel Moryson begged Watkins "for Jesus Christ sake to

endeavour for my returne home, for the time draws nigh that you must expect noe more State Letters, for this Country will make us all Fooles and shortly bring us to Cuddy Cuddy!" [62]

On April 13 the commissioners had in effect to announce the failure of their mission, and they did not miss the opportunity to lay the blame where they thought it should lie. The assembly, they reported, had finished its work, and Berkeley had announced that he would leave within a week carrying home his own answers to the commissioners' recommendations and charges. In other words, Berkeley had dissociated himself completely from the commissioners and was determined to report the situation directly to the King and his ministers. The commissioners reciprocated by making their most partisan attack up to that time on the governor, accusing him of keeping "such a Brow upon his Council and Assembly, that what hee approves or dislikes, proposes or perswades is onely done and complied with...." [63] William Sherwood, whose reports in June and August of 1676 had strongly defended Governor Berkeley, joined the commissioners in condemning him. "Itt is most true," wrote Sherwood, "that the great oppressions and abuse of the people by the Governor's arbitrary will hath beene the cause of the late troubles." [64] Neither the commissioners nor Sherwood gave proof of their charges, being content, as Bacon had been, to attack Berkeley in general terms.

Philip Ludwell, on the other hand, wrote the secretaries of state in England denouncing the clamorous "grievances" raised by the former rebels and pointing out that the commissioners had ignored the grievances of the loyalists. Wrote Ludwell:

If to have their whole Estates Seized and Confiscated, and Presently plundered and Carryed away ... If to have the Honor and Reputation of those Loyall persons that Stood to Assert and maintaine His Majesties Intrest here Prostituted to the Base Liberty of Every Scurrilous Tongue, If Tortureing people With Exquisite torments, for what their Law thought faults, If Ravishing Women and Children from their houses and hurrying them about the Countrey, in their Rude Camp and often threatning them with death, because their Husbands and fathers Obeyed his Majesties Lawfull power heer, If these I say and many more like these are Greivances, then I doe Assure your Honor there is a truely and very Sensibly Agreived and Distressed party in Virginia on whose behalfe I most humbly Supplicate your Honors favour to his Most Sacred Majesty and his Royall Highnesse that a Strict Enquirie may be made into the Grievances of all Parties. . . .[65]

The relationship between Governor Berkeley and the commissioners concluded with an incident at once hilarious and tragic. On April 21 Colonel Moryson wrote Berkeley that they intended to pay him a call the next day to take their farewell leave of him, now that he was about to embark for England.[66] The commissioners made the call and were about to leave in the coach provided for them by the governor when they noticed that the postilion was the common hangman of the colony. They walked away in a rage and the next day wrote Berkeley that the King should be the judge of the high indignity they had suffered, purposely they believed, by his order.[67]

Berkeley replied the same day, April 23, expressing sorrow, and insisting he was as "innocent in this as the blessed Angels themselves." Christ and Charles I had also been falsely accused, he commented. He sent his Negro servant and his coachman to be examined by the commissioners. Lady Berkeley similarly protested that neither she nor Sir William knew who their postilion was. She wrote that the governor was dealt with severely to be thought capable of such a vile affront and signed herself "wiffe of the persecuted Sir William Berkelay." [68] The commissioners never forgot the insult, and it served to poison even more their relationship with Berkeley.[69]

On April 27 Colonel Jeffreys, without waiting for Berkeley's departure, proclaimed himself governor. Jeffreys' proclamation stated that the King, "upon the humble representment of the Right Honorable Sir William Berkeley, his great age and bodily weakness, in respect whereof, he held himself unable to perform and execute the Duties of his place and Office and therefore did most humbly and earnestly beseech his Gracious Majesty for leave to retire," had thereupon consented to his retirement. Jeffreys declared that before he left England he took the oath as governor of Virginia, and that anyone who failed to address him as the King's governor and captain general of the colony of Virginia would be considered guilty of contemning His Majesty's royal grant.[70]

Jeffreys' spite called forth a venomous answer from the proud governor. After directing the colony for most of his thirty-five years in Virginia in what he regarded as an able and just manner, after putting down a rebellion when all had seemed lost, Berkeley could regard Jeffreys' proclamation only as a vile public affront. He dashed off a letter to Jeffreys which was not delivered, however, until June 7, after Berkeley's departure. In it Berkeley warned that "Your irresistable desire to rule this Countrey I thinke has precipitated you on that undertakeing which I beleeve can neither be Justified by your Commission, nor mine nor any visible Instructions you have from His most sacred Majestie. . . ." He pointed out that Jeffreys' commission declared that he, Berkeley, should not be answerable for any of Jeffreys' actions in his absence, which Berkeley asserted must mean that he was "intended to weare the stile of Governor of Virginia even in England and that I should returne to my Government when the King thought it fitting."

But in another Paragraffe of your declaration you say that His Majesty out of the knowledge of my inability to Governe did surrogate so able a man as Col. Jeffreys to supply my defects. I wish from my hart Col. Jeffreys were as well knowne to the King and Councel as Sir William Berkeley is, for then the diffrence would be quickly decided. . . .

And no [know] Sir that I may not conceale my owne imperfections and pride of hart from you I will confesse to you that

I beleeve that the inhabitants of this Colony will quickly find a difference betweene your managment and mine. . . .

Berkeley signed himself "Governor of Virginia til his most sacred Majestie shall please to determine otherwise of me," and addressed the letter to Jeffreys as lieutenant governor.[71]

On May 4 Jeffreys vented his grief on Secretary Coventry, reporting that Berkeley "never voutsafed mee the least satisfaction in any thing, Onely for my salary hee has showne himselfe much more concerned than ever I desired or expected, in taking it upon himselfe, as if I had depended (Deputy-like) on him for it. . . ." Berkeley, he reported, had left Jamestown on April 25 but was still in "the lower parts of this Country keeping such an awe upon the People that noe Body dares venture to come at mee. . . ." [72]

It is hard to believe that the people would be in "awe" of a deposed governor (against whom they had previously rebelled) when the lieutenant governor who had deposed him and whose mission was to discover their grievances was in the country with one thousand troops. Jeffreys' pitiful complaint is more a tribute to Berkeley than it is an indictment of him. So accustomed are we to the picture of an oppressive, vindictive Governor Berkeley, that we tend to assume that he was in the wrong in his relations with the commissioners. Yet it was not only Berkeley who could not get along with the commissioners: neither council, burgesses, nor the people generally were able to get along with them, or with Lieutenant Governor Jeffreys alone, in the period after Berkeley's departure. The house of burgesses, under the leadership of its clerk, Robert Beverley, protested the commissioners' seizure of their legislative records, while the council voted consistently against Jeffreys at their meetings. Two members of the council, Philip Ludwell and James Bray, protested Jeffreys' arbitrary rule, Ludwell going so far as to say that Jeffreys was a worse rebel than Bacon because he had broken more laws than Bacon ever did.[73]

In these actions the ex-loyalists, who were the leaders in the fight against Jeffreys' rule, had—as far as can be determined—the support of the people. Historians find it necessary to cease belaboring Philip Ludwell, Robert Beverley, James Bray, and Edward Hill as oppressors of the people, and to speak of them as champions of the people. The contradiction lies solely in the minds of the historians. These men fought the commissioners for the same reason they fought Bacon, which—as Berkeley put it—was to make him "acknowledge [that] the lawes are above him." [74]

Jeffreys, as a new governor and as a colonel, wanted an orderly and contented province with no problems to bother him. He thought the colony would attain this blessed state if everyone forgot about justice and accepted the status quo as of the time the commissioners arrived. Because Berkeley had left the country "full of suites and loud Clamours" Jeffreys closed all the courts until he should receive the King's instructions on how to settle "these new imbroylements of the Country, which the Assembly have opened a gapp for, by leaving a latitude in their Lawes for one person to sue and prosecute another for things acted and done in tyme of the late Rebellion, and instead of making an Act of Oblivion have made a Statute of Remembrance, to last and intayle trouble from one Generation to another. . . ." [75] Similarly, when Philip Ludwell, in accordance with "the Laws and Constant known proceeding of this Colony," appealed from the General Court to the assembly from his conviction of scandalizing the governor, Jeffreys, who wanted the case referred to the King and his Privy Council merely for their determination of the punishment to be inflicted on Ludwell, denounced the council for allowing Ludwell's appeal, whereby the councilors showed themselves to "Vallue the Power and lawes of A few Ignorant Planters mett in An Assembly for this Government to be of greater Authority, then his most Sacred Majesty and his Councill. . . ." [76] Few governors of Virginia have shown themselves more contemptuous of the dignity and authority of the people's representatives.

The one important accomplishment of the commissioners was the conclusion of a general peace with the neighboring tributary Indians whom Bacon had driven from their homes. There is no doubt that Colonel Moryson was the guiding light in this enterprise. Some of the articles were modeled on the Indian act of 1662, passed when he was acting governor.[77]

The ceremony of the signing of the peace took place on May 29, 1677, the King's birthday and day of his restoration to the throne, at an impressive ceremony at Middle Plantation, now Williamsburg. All the Indian kings and queens came and signed the document, "publickly acknowledging to hold their Crownes and Landes of the Great King of England." [78] The treaty re-affirmed Berkeley's principle of recognizing the Indians as subjects of the King of England with a legal title to the lands granted them under the seal of the colony. Bacon's policy of extermination of all Indians as trespassers on the King's domain was thus rejected. The fourth article specifically recognized that the "violent intrusions of divers English into their lands, forceing the Indians by way of Revenge, to kill the Cattle and hoggs of the English," had been one of the important causes of the rebellion. Therefore it decreed that no Englishman should settle nearer than three miles from any Indian town. The fifth article protected the tributary Indians from abuse at the hands of the English. On information from the Indians, the governor was to inflict such punishment "as the lawes of England or this Country permitt, and as if such hurt or injury had bin done to any Englishman, which is but just and Reasonable they owneing themselves to be under the Allegiance of his most Sacred Majestie." [79]

One error was made in the treaty. The twelfth article decreed that each Indian king and queen was to have equal power to govern his or her people, none to have more power than another, "except the Queen of Pomunky: to whom severall scattered Indians doe now againe owne their antient Subjection, and are agreed to come in and plant themselves under [her] power and government...." [80] The commissioners trustingly got their information on the subject from the Queen herself. [81]

By the following January the English had received word that the young men of the several towns under the Queen's subjection were discontented with their status, saying it had been consented to by the old men against their wills. The young men had deserted the towns and established themselves in small parties in the woods "which renders our peace insecure." [82] By June 1678 the situation had deteriorated further. One of the neighboring tribes had refused to pay the Queen's tax and would not do so despite the Virginia government's intervention. The Queen acknowledged that the members of the tribe had paid no tax for thirty years, but insisted on her right to tax them according to the articles of the Indian peace. [83] In the following months other subject nations made identical complaints. Secretary Thomas Ludwell was seriously worried for the peace of the colony, for whichever way the dispute was decided, the other side would have a legitimate grievance. [84]

The Lords of Trade and Plantations approved the treaty in principle but objected to Jeffreys' styling himself "Governor and Captain General" in the treaty. Their Lordships reported to the King "that the Stile and title of Your Lieutenant Governor [in that treaty] is therein mistaken and so fit to be made sutable to that Stile and Character which is given him by your Majesties Commission." [85]

About April 18 ships arrived in England bearing the first news of the commissioners' activities in Virginia. [86] The King and Duke of York were at Newmarket. Secretary Coventry was at his country place at Enfield Chase, Middlesex. The news created a considerable stir. Samuel Pepys, who had received the commissioners' letters of February 2 addressed to the Duke of York and to Sir John Werden, the Duke's secretary, was ordered to hurry to Newmarket from London with all speed. [87] Coventry returned to London to peruse the papers concerning Virginia and to give directions to his secretary Henry Thynne on how the latter should report on the affair to the King at Newmarket.[88]

Further news of Berkeley's "misdeeds" arrived on May 7.[89] The importance of how all this information, and Berkeley's own earlier confident justifications, were represented to the King is obvious. There are several pages of rough notes of recommendations to the King in Coventry's hand which indicate that Coventry took the view of the commissioners against that of Berkeley, especially on the subject of the King's printed proclamation of October 27, 1676. Undoubtedly his attitude as well as that of the King was conditioned most of all by Berkeley's refusal to leave his post at once and return to England. To the King this attitude approached contempt for his commands. To Coventry (who drew the ambiguous orders) it snarled and embarrassed his administration of colonial affairs. Startled by Berkeley's apparent presumption, Coventry and the King may have found it easy to assume that Berkeley had also been unjustified in his other actions.

Coventry's notes are headed "To bee considered of by his Majesty" and suggest the manner in which the questions were put before the King, and how the King reacted. Coventry's first question for the King was "in what manner hee will have his pleasur" for the return of Sir William Berkeley. Coventry similarly asked "In what termes and manner his Majesty will have the proclamation of Sir William Berckley recalled which confisquateth and exemptath men and theyre Estates from pardon that were pardoned by his Majesty." The King was also to be asked how he would "direct the disposall of those goods of those rebells executed or taken prisoner during the warre and still detayned, and that are not within the Compasse of his Majesty's gratious pardon." Again, the King was asked what course was to be taken "to quiett and still evile [avail?] in law concerning Cattle and goods plundered in the Warre and yet detayned by men pardoned by the proclamation."[90]

In the same folder of notes is, apparently, the account of

the King's decisions. These were that a letter be sent particularly recalling Berkeley, that an order be issued calling in Berkeley's proclamation as contradictory to the King's, that Colonel Jeffreys and the council dispose of the confiscated goods of executed or detained rebels "amongst such as they shall Judge meete," and that the Virginia Assembly pass a law "to quiett those disputes" they judge most harmful to the peace of the colony.[91]

On May 13 the actual letters putting the King's decisions into effect went out. Charles informed Berkeley that he was not a little surprised at his failure to return and strictly commanded him to return forthwith.[92] In a letter of the following day to Colonel Jeffreys and the council in Virginia, the King wrote that should Berkeley still refuse to return, he was to be put aboard some vessel and returned without delay.[93] This letter was enclosed in one of May 15 to Jeffreys from Secretary Coventry which explained that Jeffreys was not to show the letter to the council if Berkeley should comply with the King's order, the King not desiring to add more severity than Berkeley's comportment made necessary.[94]

In another letter, of May 15, the King revoked Berkeley's proclamation of February 10 and ordered that his own proclamation of October 27, 1676, should be made known to the people and obeyed.[95]

Secretary Coventry wrote Berkeley the same day congratulating him on putting an end to the rebellion but reporting how upset the King was that he had not returned and that he had not followed the King's proclamation. The King, he wrote, "hath very little hopes that the people of Virginia shall be brought to a right sense of their duty to obey their Governors when the Governors themselves will not obey the King." His long services and great loyalty were all that kept the King from showing more resentment, Coventry reported.[96]

As these letters were being written, Berkeley was at sea, having long since turned over the government to Colonel Jeffreys.

Chapter 9

AFTERMATH OF THE REBELLION
ENGLAND, 1677-1680

❖❖❖

G OVERNOR BERKELEY arrived in England in June 1677 and immediately petitioned the King. He had been totally ruined in his fortunes, he reported, but what was unbearable was that he had been misrepresented to His Majesty. Although weak from his passage he desired to clear his name before he died.[1]

Berkeley never saw the King. He died too soon, on July 9, 1677, and was buried at Twickenham July 13.[2] "He came here alive," wrote Secretary of State Henry Coventry, "but so unlike to live that it had been very inhumane to have troubled him with any interrogations. So he died without any accompt given of his Government."[3]

Berkeley's death is attributed by some to "heartbreak" over the fact that Charles II is supposed to have remarked: "That old fool has hanged more men in that naked country, than I did for the murder of my father." No account of Bacon's rebellion seems to be complete without the story of this remark, the authority for which is the recollection, thirty years after the event, of some gossip that circulated in Virginia at the time.[4]

The Lords of Trade and Plantations met for their first important session on the Virginia situation on August 2, 1677. The laws made by the assembly of February 1677 were discussed, and is was decided that the King's proclamation for general pardon did not hinder proceedings for recovering goods plundered by the rebels, but only pardoned the crime against the King's authority. The Lords accepted the reports of the commissioners at their face value and, remembering the King's reaction of April to the first news from Virginia [5] and forgetting their original intention to allow Berkeley to use the proclamation as he saw fit,[6] they showed irritation and anger that the governor had dared to alter it. They decided to recommend to the King that whatever Berkeley did in derogation of the King's proclamation be annulled.[7]

On August 22 Sir John Berry and Colonel Francis Moryson arrived at Plymouth from Virginia with the King's frigates *Bristol, Rose,* and *Dartmouth.* The commissioners had left Virginia before they received the King's authorization to return, in direct violation of their orders. Fortunately for them the King did not see fit to take their insubordination amiss, as he had Sir William Berkeley's delay in returning.[8]

Shortly after their arrival the commissioners presented several voluminous reports to Secretary Henry Coventry. The most important document was a "True Narrative of the Rise, Progresse, and Cessation of the Late Rebellion in Virginia." In addition the commissioners presented "A Review, Breviary and Conclusion" based on their narrative, "An Exact Repertory of the Generall and Personall Grievances presented to us (His Majesties Commissioners) by the People of Virginia," the "Articles of Peace" between King Charles and the several Indian kings and queens of Virginia, and many other documents.[9] The effect of this mass of material, all written from a point of view antagonistic to Governor Berkeley, was overpowering. No opportunity was lost, even in the phrasing of sentences, to cast blame on Berkeley and the loyal party. In their report of personal grievances the commissioners forgot that they were supposed to be investigating the causes of the rebellion and examined the effects of it, turning in a mass of petitions against Berkeley's confiscations during the latter part of the rebellion.

But Berkeley was not without friends at court. His brother John, Lord Berkeley, one of the Privy Council, made preparations to defend his name. On August 9 he asked for the accusations against his brother in writing that he might answer them, and later he obtained permission to examine the papers relating to Virginia and to take copies of such as most concerned his brother.[10]

Governor Berkeley's cause received a damaging setback on October 9 when Sarah Drummond, wife of one of the leading rebels, presented a bitter petition against Berkeley's alleged confiscation of her property. The Lords were so shocked by the governor's apparent heartlessness that they jumped to a too hasty defense of the rebel party. They denounced the act of the assembly of February 1677 which attainted William Drummond, and recommended that relief be granted his widow. The falsity of Mrs. Drummond's petition was so plain that only the testimony of the commissioners certifying its truth enabled it to succeed.[11]

An amusing sequel to this story and one that throws light on the double standard of morality the commissioners maintained for themselves and for Governor Berkeley concerns Mrs. Drummond's second complaint. When she heard the effect her first petition had on the Lords of Trade, she immediately presented a second "for Goods remaining in the hands of Sir John Berry." This petition was read the following day, October 10. The facts brought out in the examination of her charge showed that Sir John Berry himself had been guilty of plundering her goods for his personal profit as well as for what he claimed was the "King's service." He had concealed his confiscation of her silver plate, dry goods, and bills of exchange while ostentatiously requesting and receiving permission from the King to dispose of £130 worth of her wine and brandy for "the King's service."

Berry was not even reprimanded by the King. Yet Governor Berkeley, whose confiscation of Mrs. Drummond's property was never shown to have profited him personally but to have been, as he claimed, for the King's service, received the unthinking condemnation of Charles and his Lords.[12]

A week after Mrs. Drummond's petitions were presented, Lord Berkeley met Sir John Berry in the Council Chamber of Whitehall and "with an angry voice and a Berklean look" told Berry that he and Moryson had "murdered his brother." He taxed Moryson with ingratitude "and indeed spoke of me as if I had been a servant (and that a mean one too) in the family. . . ." Both commissioners upheld their conduct and their reports. "If we were misinformed," Moryson later wrote, "it was no misinformation of ours, since we took the best means to know the truth of every particular. . . ."[13]

In early November the Lords began to have some second thoughts about their hasty condemnation of Berkeley's actions on the basis of Mrs. Drummond's complaint and the commissioners' harsh reports. Their thought processes were set in motion by a petition for restoration of property, similar to that of Mrs. Drummond, submitted by Richard Carver, son and heir of Captain William Carver, the stout seaman captured by Philip Ludwell off Accomack in August 1676.[14] Governor Berkeley had authorized confiscation of his estate to pay the expenses of the loyalist troops.[15] On November 6, 1677, Richard Carver petitioned the Lords of Trade and Plantations that his father's estate and property were seized and he executed "under colour of the late rebellion." Carver asked that the governor of Virginia be directed to aid him in recovering his estate.[16]

The Lords of Trade debated the petition on November 8. Sir John Berry declared that Carver was a principal actor in the rebellion who had tried to surprise Governor Berkeley at Accomack, but had been taken and soon afterwards executed. Carver's masculine and active role in the rebellion prevented the Lords from pitying his fate as much as they had Mrs.

who Culpeper (and Lord Berkeley) hoped would uphold Sir William's conduct.[24]

Although the facts touched upon by Colonel Culpeper were vitally important to an understanding of the situation, they were presented so poorly that they had little effect. The commissioners defended their narrative by saying that it was "a faithful and impartial account of things as they were related unto them. And that they cannot bee otherwise answerable whether the matter of fact does, in every particular, agree with the same." [25]

Lord Berkeley's attempt to defend his brother's honor went no further than the Lords of Trade and Plantations. On December 6 the Lords of this committee requested the Lord Privy Seal to report to the King in Council that there was lying before them an answer to the objections against Berkeley upon which they desired His Majesty's direction, as also upon what orders to give to the King's commissioners. The message was read in Council on December 7. The King, who had admitted the petitions of numerous rebels to his highest advisory body, directed that no further notice should be taken of Culpeper's paper and dismissed the commissioners from further attendance at court.[26]

The King's order guaranteed a final victory for the commissioners. The previous day, at a meeting of the Lords of Trade and Plantations, they had sharply criticized Berkeley and some of his councilors. The Lords thereupon ordered a list drawn up of those fit to be continued in the council and those who should be excluded.[27] The commissioners turned in a list which not only censured certain members of the council, but added a few poisonous essays about loyalists who were not on the council. Alongside the commissioners' descriptions of the men they disliked are written the words "Putt out" by the hand of higher authority. Those praised by the commissioners were ordered retained. Colonel Thomas Swann, who had been excepted from Governor Berkeley's proclamation of pardon of February 10, a week after the governor had asked him to provide living quarters for the commissioners, was highly praised by them. Despite the evidence of his traitorous activities, Swann was able to convince his high-placed guests that he had done Bacon's bidding involuntarily, and the commissioners reported him worthy of his high office. In discussing Colonel Edward Hill, who was not a member of the council but an official of Charles City County, the commissioners refused to comment on the truth of the charges against him begging lack of time, but remarked that he was the "most hated person of all the County where hee lives, and that not without Cause too." They recommended that he should lay down his position. The hand beside the comment makes the note: "Putt out." [28]

The commissioners also declared that the act of oblivion passed by the assembly was "wholly repugnant to his Majesty's Gracious Proclamation of Pardon." The act of attainder was criticized and the incredible comment made that though some were guilty enough of rebellion, they were not given a fair trial but sentenced by martial law "at a Peaceable Place called Accomack (where a Jury might have pass'd on them)." [29]

Lord Berkeley tried again on December 11, 1677, to defend his brother, criticizing the commissioners for the unusual manner in which they made their inquiries. But the Lords of the committee of Trade and Plantations, asserting that Sir William and several of the council had refused to give the commissioners any account of the state of affairs in Virginia, "seem to remain satisfied with the proceedings of the Commissioners in this regard." The Lords also agreed that the governor, council, and burgesses had extended their authority too far in enacting the various laws that had passed in February 1677 "contrary to justice it selfe." They therefore agreed to report to His Majesty their opinion that all laws contrary to the powers residing in the governor and all laws in derogation of the King's proclamation of October 27, 1676, be annulled and new laws sent in. [30]

On January 18, 1678, the King in Council, acting on the report of the Lords of Trade and Plantations of December 11, 1677, and on several papers presented by the commissioners concerning the laws of the February Assembly, ordered the first three laws of that assembly, those of indemnity, penalties, and attainder, to be rescinded as in derogation of his proclamation of pardon. All persons, whether tried or not, were to be rendered capable of the conditions of the proclamation of October 27, 1676. That is, all were to have the benefits of the King's general pardon and to obtain restitution of all goods confiscated by Governor Berkeley. However, the government of Virginia was authorized to countenance prosecutions against such of the rebellious party as still possessed the goods of honest men. Goods seized by the rebels and "destroyed as soon as taken" or "wasted or made worse" were, however, to be written off as an unfortunate loss for the owners. The Privy Council did note that it was too apparent that many persons had waged horrid rebellion (despite the host of "forced" and "seduced" rebels certified by the latecoming commissioners) and that there were others whose crimes were "very black." So it recommended, and the King approved, that laws should be prepared "as may be fit to be sent over and established in Virginia signifying Your Majesty's just sence of their traitorous designs and enacting such punishments, fines and forfeitures to be inflicted on the several Offenders as to Your Majesty shall seem most equitable and convenient...." [31]

The Privy Council was thus finally recommending what Berkeley and the assembly had long since done, while at the same time forcing the repeal of the very acts by which it had been done.

The result of the King's order was contained in a bill for an "Act of free and generall pardon, indemnitie and oblivion" brought over by Lord Culpeper, the new governor, and passed by the Virginia Assembly in June 1680. [32] The act reiterated the now sacred printed proclamation of October 27, 1676, as the basis for pardoning all the rebels. Yet it went on, as did the act of February 1677, to except from the pardon certain other persons in addition to Nathaniel Bacon, among them Giles Bland, Anthony

Arnold, Richard Turney, Richard Pomfrey, John Isles, Robert Stoakes, John Whitson, William Scarborough, and Richard Lawrence. William Drummond and others executed after trials by courts-martial were not mentioned. Certain persons were disqualified from public office as in the act of February 1677. Loyal sufferers were authorized to recover by legal means any of their goods found in the hands of any other persons, notwithstanding the proclamation of pardon. And since one of the causes of the rebellion was adjudged to be the "false and scandalous reports" raised by "severall ill disposed persons," a year's imprisonment and £500 fine were ordered for anyone convicted of publishing or uttering any word calculated to stir up the people to the dislike or defaming of His Majesty's governor.[33] It is symbolic of the incompetence of the English government in dealing with the matter that the provision against defamation of the governor did not save Berkeley from false accusations, but instead allowed his successors to repress legitimate grievances.[34]

As Hening commented: "It is difficult to reconcile the provisions of this act, with the *professions* of the king, in his proclamation of the 27th of October 1676." He pointed out that Berkeley's proclamation had been revoked because it had excepted persons other than Bacon, contrary to the King's more general pardon. "Yet we find, in this act, several other persons excepted, who were included in Sir William Berkeley's *bloody* act of February, 1676-7...."[35]

One reason the King's "professions" were not carried out in the act of 1680 was the gradual realization that Berkeley had been more nearly right than the King and his advisers had at first imagined. On two central disputes of the post-rebellion period—the right to withhold the King's pardon from rebels other than Bacon and the right of the loyalists to sue the rebels—the government eventually supported Berkeley.[36] But by that time he had long been dead and discredited.

Beginning with their deliberations of February 6, 1679, the Lords of Trade took up the personal grievances reported by the commissioners. None had anything to do with causing the rebellion. The commissioners had not been able to find any legitimate personal grievances for the period prior to the rebellion. So they presented the complaints of admitted and accused rebels whose crops and property had been seized by Berkeley's troops in the final stages of the conflict. Almost all admitted taking or giving Bacon's traitorous oath to be loyal to Bacon and to resist even the King's troops, and most admitted being "seduced" to play other roles in the rebellion. The Lords decided, however, to order restitution of property seized from them after January 16, 1677, which they conceived to have been the date of the surrender of West Point and the end of the rebellion.[37] This was not the date of the surrender of West Point, nor was the rebellion over at this time.[38] The commissioners, anxious to vindicate their condemnation of Berkeley's confiscations and compositions in the final weeks of the rebellion, wrote in their "Narrative" that "about the 16th of January, 1676-7, the whole country had submitted to the Governour. . . ."[39] Since many of Berkeley's seizures occurred in the latter part of January when he had regained the upper hand and was sweeping victoriously inland, the commissioners' statement made them seem to be peace-time seizures.

The commissioners were not in Virginia at the time, of course, nor is there any logical or legal reason why they or the Lords of Trade and Plantations should have any formal right to determine when war in Virginia ended and peace began. Berkeley was captain general of the colony as well as governor, and as the highest military representative of the King in Virginia he certainly had the authority and the knowledge to determine when the rebellion should be declared over. The Lords based their decision not only on the misguided belief that the colony was at peace at the time, but on the mistaken notion that the King's printed proclamation of pardon of October 27, 1676, automatically pardoned all rebels even if they had been captured, tried, and convicted before the proclamation was known or published in Virginia.[40]

On February 10, 1679, the Lords of Trade and Plantations formally decided to order that all injuries committed after January 16, 1677 (when Berkeley had finally obtained the upper hand), should be redressed. Injuries committed before January 16 (when Bacon had the upper hand) were, with certain exceptions, to be pardoned.[41] This startling display of partiality was incorporated into the "Act of free and generall pardon, indemnitie and oblivion" then being made ready for Lord Culpeper to take to Virginia.[42]

The decisions of the Lords of Trade and Plantations and of the Privy Council in the years following the rebellion seemed not only to condemn unjustly the loyalists for their actions during the rebellion, but to exonerate the rebels for theirs. Sir Henry Chicheley, acting governor after the death of Lieutenant Governor Jeffreys, reported that the rebels "bragg themselves to have been in the right" while those who lost their estates faithfully serving the King had become "the scorne and May game of the Rebell partie." [43]

Succeeding governors of Virginia met determined resistance from the people. The leaders of this resistance were not those associated with Bacon's rebels, but those who helped put the rebellion down. Philip Ludwell, Robert Beverley, Edward Hill, and James Bray became the champions of the rights of the people against the arbitrary rule of the King's governors. Historians who see Bacon's Rebellion as a democratic reform movement are placed in a quandary by this apparent reversal of principle. Rather than question their own assumptions about the nature of the rebellion, these writers simply assert that the contradiction is inexplicable. Thus Burk, after denouncing Philip Ludwell and praising Lieutenant Governor Jeffreys throughout his account of the rebellion, notes that in the post-rebellion period Jeffreys attempted to "introduce the influence and prejudices of a remote, ignorant, and unconstitutional power, to control or defeat the end of justice and liberty ... while Ludwell, heretofore, the advocate of high-handed and high-toned principles, and the accessary in a plan of sanguinary proscription, boldly and emphatically asserted the rights of the people, and the independence of the judiciary." [44]

Beverley and Philip Ludwell, the two most active and violent "oppressors of the people," in the eyes of another democratic historian, became in the post-rebellion period "the representative of the dearest rights of the people which they had at one time despised." [45] Thomas Jefferson Wertenbaker concluded that

Strangely enough some of the leading spirits of the old Berkeley party became, by their continued opposition to the executive, champions of representative government in the colony. Had it not been for the active leadership of Robert Beverley and Philip Ludwell the cause of liberty might well have perished under the assaults of Charles II and James II. [46]

Must not the democratic interpreters of Bacon's Rebellion show why those who were supposed to be the worst enemies of democracy overnight became its greatest champions? Must they not show why, in the 1682 resistance to Lord Culpeper over the question of tobacco cutting, "the county of Gloucester, which had been the most loyal during Bacon's rebellion, led the way"? [47] Must they not also show why "definite party divisions in Virginia" did not develop until after Bacon's Rebellion, when governors found themselves "increasingly opposed" by the leading families of Virginia? [48]

Berkeley insisted in his May 29, 1676, remonstrance that he would make Bacon "acknowledge the lawes are above him." [49] We know that the governor was, for thirty-five years, the admitted defender of the rights of the people. We know his pride in the fact that Virginia, under his administration, was a government of laws under which every man could be secure in his property and liberties. May we not also assume that Berkeley and the loyalists were consistent in their beliefs?

It was not in Bacon's Rebellion that resistance to autocratic government was born, but in the post-rebellion fight of the loyalists against the arbitrary injustice of the King's commissioners and governors. The upholders of Virginia's political liberties fought for those rights against Bacon, against Jeffreys, against Culpeper, against Effingham, and against succeeding governors.

Chapter 10

CAUSES OF THE REBELLION

✦✦✦

W HAT was the "cause" of Bacon's Rebellion? What mo-
tivated the 400 foot and 120 horse who marched with
Bacon into Jamestown on June 23, 1676? [1] Romantic
historians like to see the rebellion as "a revolt of the lower classes
of whites against the aristocratic families who governed Vir-
ginia," [2] as "the cause of the poor against the rich, of the humble
folk against the grandees." [3]

Unfortunately such simple solutions of the event are simple
only because of the one-sided moral and intellectual assumptions
of their proponents. Actually, as Professor Craven has written,
"no simple answer can be found for the complex problem of
Bacon's Rebellion . . . but on one point agreement can be had:
the trouble started in a dispute over Indian policy." [4] Craven's
views on the complexity of Bacon's Rebellion mark a return to
the views held of the event at the time. In the intervening period
historians have tended to interpret the rebellion too readily as a
forerunner of 1776.

Robert Beverley, writing when memories of the rebellion were
still fresh in the minds of the people, gave much thought to the
problem of its cause. He wrote:

[153]

The Occasion of this Rebellion is not easie to be discover'd: But 'tis certain there were many Things that concurr'd towards it. For it cannot be imagined, that upon the Instigation of Two or Three Traders only, who aim'd at a Monopoly of the *Indian* Trade,[5] as some pretend to say, the whole Country would have fallen into so much Distraction; in which People did not only hazard their Necks by Rebellion: But endeavor'd to ruine a Governour, whom they all entirely loved, and had unanimously chosen;[6] a Gentleman who had devoted his whole Life and Estate to the Service of the Country; and against whom in Thirty Five Years Experience, there had never been one single Complaint. Neither can it be supposed, that upon so slight Grounds, they would make Choice of a Leader they hardly knew, to oppose a Gentleman, that had been so long, and so deservedly the Darling of the People. So that in all Probability there was something else in the Wind, without which the Body of the Country had never been engaged in that Insurrection.[7]

What this "something else in the Wind" was, Beverley makes a brilliant attempt to answer. He cites the misfortunes suffered by the colony because of the low price of tobacco, the tyranny of the English merchants, the great taxes necessary to throw off the proprietary grants, the restraints on trade caused by the Navigation Acts, and the Indian disturbances. But more important, he relates Virginia's depressed condition to the psychology of the planters and shows how this condition affected their attitude towards the Indians, Governor Berkeley, and the rebel Bacon. It was the Indian disturbances, he finds, which tipped the balance and caused men whose minds were "already full of Discontent" to imagine there was an easy way out by "vent[ing] all their Resentment against the poor *Indians*."[8]

Beverley probably came as close to a successful interpretation of the rebellion as anyone since his time. His analysis is also superior to those made before his time. The men who fought in the rebellion were never able to give a satisfactory explanation of why the troubles arose. Philip Ludwell, for example, wrote

Secretary of State Sir Joseph Williamson that the rebellion "has been of that Intricate unreasonable Texture that I think it a Taske to hard for me to State in all its Circumstances." Ludwell did not attempt to minimize the extent of the revolt. Just as Berkeley had astounded the commissioners with his report that of above 15,000 persons there were not 500 untainted in the rebellion,[9] so Ludwell reported that the defection was "almost general." The gallant loyalist leader could explain the rebellion only in terms of

the Lewd dispositions of some Persons of desperate Fortunes Lately Sprang upp amongst us which meeting with People of like Inclinations Easily seduced their willing mindes From their duty and Allegiance to their King, and Indeed from all feare or Respect of God or man Laying before them the Plunder of the best part of the Countrey and the Vaine hopes of takeing the Countrey wholley out of his Majesty's handes into their owne.[10]

Ludwell probably misjudged the causes of the rebellion because, unlike Beverley, the historian, he assumed that the leaders had thought out their plans and knew what they were after. Thus Ludwell commented on Bacon's pitiful Indian campaigns that "It is most Evident he never Intended anything more in it than a Covert under which to Act all his Villanies." If these rather vaguely defined evil aims had not been the rebels' "Cheife Motives," wrote Ludwell, "they had Certainly Understanding Enough to have ledd them a fairer way to presenting their Greivances than on their Swords points." [11]

Richard Lee, one of the more dignified members of the council, was similarly unable to explain the rebellion. Lee suggested that the reason for the "zealous inclination of the multitude" to Bacon was their "hopes of levelling, otherwise all his specious pretences would not have persuaded them. . . ." [12] Lee thus drew a distinction between the reasons for the "zealous inclination" of the people to Bacon and the causes that led Bacon to start the rebellion in the first place. These are two different things, although historians frequently confuse them.

Others, both at the time and more recently, have concluded that Bacon's purpose was to detach Virginia from the Crown of England. The only evidence to support this view is the comment of the minister who attended Bacon at his death [13] and a dialogue between Bacon and a man named John Goode which took place on September 2, 1676, when the rebel leader questioned the captured Goode about the report that two thousand soldiers were on their way to put down the rebellion. Bacon seems to have been trying to reassure himself that his rebels could defeat them even though outnumbered, but Goode matched every advantage with a disadvantage until Bacon found himself defending the thesis that Virginia could maintain its independence against the Crown itself. [14] The discussion can hardly be taken as proof that Bacon was seriously aiming at the independence of the colony. The most that can be said is that he once speculated on the possibility. To Wesley Frank Craven, also, the dialogue "suggests the desperate graspings of a man who already sensed that his cause was lost, and is of interest primarily for Goode's clear statement of the arguments for Virginia's dependence." Craven also underlines Goode's warning to Bacon that " 'your followers do not think themselves engaged against the King's authority, but merely against the Indians.' " [15]

To Governor Berkeley the cause of the rebellion was to be found in the ungovernable will of Nathaniel Bacon rather than in the grievances of the people. In his letter of February 2, 1677, to Secretary of State Henry Coventry he bitterly remarked that in June 1676

I was Exalted with pride that I had governed this Country fower and twenty yeares in peace and plenty and was most certaine that no pretence of a fault could be alleaged against me. Then did God to humble me and take away the pride of my hart and thoughts rayse this ungrounded (for any real Grevance) and unexpected rebellion against his most sacred Majesty the Country and me....[16]

Berkeley had long prided himself on his justice. In March 1651 he had breathed defiance to the Parliamentary forces that were soon expected to arrive to take over the colony. In a speech to the assembly he urged the burgesses to support him in maintaining the King's government. He asked them

what is it can be hoped for in a change, which we have not allready? Is it liberty? The sun looks not on a people more free then we are from all oppression. Is it wealth? Hundreds of examples shew us that Industry and Thrift in a short time may bring us to as high a degree of it, as the Country and our Conditions are yet capable of: Is it securety to enjoy this wealth when gotten? With out blushing I will speake it, I am confident theare lives not that person can accuse me of attempting the least act against any mans property. Is it peace? The Indians, God be blessed round about us are subdued; we can onely feare the *Londoners*, who would faine bring us to the same poverty, wherein the *Dutch* found and relieved us; would take away the liberty of our consciences, and tongues, and our right of giving and selling our goods to whom we please.[17]

Following Berkeley's impassioned oratory, the assembly unanimously passed a series of resolutions denouncing the attempt of Parliament to coerce the rebellious colony, and reaffirming its loyalty to King Charles.[18]

Berkeley was eventually forced to yield to the Parliamentary forces, but so highly was he thought of that in 1660, before the restoration of Charles II, he was proffered the governorship by the house of burgesses. Berkeley refused the burgesses' first offer explaining that he was willing to hold office from the people of Virginia, but never from any English power except that of the Crown. The burgesses thereupon altered their conditions and once more asked him to accept on his own terms. This he did, and, with the unanimous consent of the council, was chosen governor on March 21, 1660.[19]

Seven years later Thomas Ludwell wrote to Lord Arlington:

nor doe I think there can be a more convincing evidence of his Prudence, and Justice Then that in six years after hee was forced to resign this Country to the Gennerall unhappy fate of our Nation (a Time when the Enemies of his Loyalty and Virtue would have loaden him with reproaches especially had they had Justice on their side) there was not one man that either publiquely or privately charged him with injustice, or any other fault committed in eight years Government....[20]

In 1673 the council wrote to the King that had the people not loved and reverenced Governor Berkeley they would not have defended the country against the Dutch attacks in the previous years.

For in this very Conjuncture had the People had A Distastefull Governor they would have hazarded the losse of this Countrey, and the rather because they doe believe their Condition would not be soe bad Under the Dutch in Point of Traffique as it is under the Merchants who now use them hardly (even to extremity). But this Governo'r Oppresseth them not, but on the Contrary spends all his revenue amongst them in Setting up Manufactures to their advantage....[21]

Even Colonel Moryson, one of the commissioners, wrote in 1676 that fifty years' experience had proved Virginia's government "most easy to the people and advantageous to the Crowne, For in all that time there has not been one lawe complain'd of, burdensome to the one or prejudiciall to the Prerogative of the other...."[22]

Some historians, while admitting Berkeley's justice in his early years, have asserted that after the restoration of Charles II the governor gradually became oppressive, greedy, and corrupt.[23] There is not a shred of responsible evidence to support this supposed change. In his proclamation of May 10, 1676, calling for a new election, Berkeley himself boldly challenged anyone to show a just grievance against him during his years as governor. Wrote Berkeley:

I doe will and require that att the election of the said Burgesses all and every person and persons there present have liberty to present freely to their said Burgesses all such Just Complaints as they or any of them have against mee as Governor for any Act of Injustice by mee done or any reward bribe or present by mee accepted or taken from any person whatsoever and that the same bee by the said Burgesses presented to the Assembly and there duely examined and redressed. And supposeing I whome am head of the Assembly may bee their greatest grevance I will most gladly Joyne with them in a petition to his most Sacred Majesty to appoint a new Governor of Virginia. . . .[24]

He repeated his challenge in his proclamation of May 29, 1676.[25]

Although the many proclamations issued by Bacon and the grievances collected by the commissioners have saturated the consciousness of students of the subject, not one bit of evidence, it should be remembered, was ever found to show that Governor Berkeley was guilty of any act of injustice or bribery. Indeed, he was rarely accused of any specific *act*. Most of the charges against him are the vague political smears with which we are all so familiar today. Historians have accepted them at face value because their own prejudices and assumptions have inclined them to favor a colonial rebel against a representative of imperial Britain. Yet, as Berkeley noted, when he dared the "Baconian" assembly of June 1676 to declare any fault he had ever committed and showed them his petition to the King to send an abler governor, the assembly not only absolved him of all crimes, but begged the King not to remove him from office.[26]

The more prosaic interests of the rebels have rarely been inquired into. It has been assumed that they were selfless patriots fighting a tyrannical government. We are told that Bacon was "a champion of the weak, a rebel against injustice, the forerunner of Washington, Jefferson and Samuel Adams." [27] Others have compared Bacon to Patrick Henry,[28] to Tiberius Gracchus,[29] to Callimachus,[30] and even to Leonidas at Thermopylae.[31]

It is generally assumed, on the other hand, that the governor and his council were the "grandees" of the colony and that they possessed vast holdings of land while the rest of the colonists eked out a precarious existence on their small plantations. Like so many other assertions about Bacon's Rebellion, this one is not based on a study of the evidence. An investigation of the land holdings of the partisans on both sides reveals a surprising equality between them. The leaders on both sides had large holdings. The followers on both sides had more modest holdings. What is most significant is that the leaders of the rebellion against Governor Berkeley almost invariably owned great tracts of land on the frontier, frequently had a record of oppression and aggression against the neighboring Indians, and occasionally had been punished by Berkeley for their crimes against the natives.[32]

Governor Berkeley strove throughout his career to restrain the aggressiveness of the frontier landowners. But his power was limited. For one thing he was not in control of the government from 1652 to 1660 when the most unregulated expansion took place.[33] His ability to control expansion was further restricted when, in 1666, he lost the right to allow or disallow individual grants. The assembly successfully challenged his authority to limit the right to acquire land, and "henceforth it was recognised in practice that the Governor had no more power over land grants than that secured by his individual vote in the Council." [34]

The conventional idea that "Berkeley parceled out some handsome estates in a free and easy manner" [35] is simply untrue. Land, in Berkeley's administration, was granted almost entirely under the headright system which authorized a right to fifty acres for each person brought into the colonies.[36] Headrights could be bought and sold, so that a person of means desiring to acquire large acreage could do so. The governor could not disallow such large grants. But, since land acquisition was tied in a fixed ratio to emigration into the colony, estates were relatively modest by eighteenth-century standards. It was only under later governors, when land came to be saleable without presenting headrights, that enormous tracts were amassed by single owners.

Even when Berkeley did have authority to regulate expansion, he fought a losing battle against frontier disregard of the law. When the Indians were forbidden by English law to sell their lands to the whites, for example, their holdings continued nevertheless to be alienated. "Leases" and extortion were two favorite methods. Thomas Ludwell explained the reason for the law forbidding Indian sale by saying that

whilest the Indians had liberty to sell theire lands the english would ordinaryly either frighten or delude them into a bargaine and for a trifle get away the grownd they should live on, then he comes and settles himselfe there and with his cattle and hoggs destroyes all the corne of the other Indians of the towne. This fills us with complaints and will if not prevented keep our peace for ever uncertaine... *this was a great cause of this last warr, and most of those who had thus intruded and were consequently the principall cause of it were notwithstanding amongst the forwardest in the rebellion and complained most of greivances.*[37]

The commissioners, in their "True and Faithful Account" asserted flatly that the breach of the former peace with the Indians "was the Ground of the Rebellion itselfe." [38] Furthermore, the Indian treaty, which was also written by the Berkeley-hating commissioners, confirms Thomas Ludwell's charge that the cause of the breach was principally on the English side. Article 4 of the treaty states that

Whereas by the mutuall discontents, Complaints, jealousies, and feares of English and Indians occasioned by the violent intrusions of divers English into their lands, forceing the Indians by way of Revenge, to kill the Cattle and hoggs of the English, whereby offence, and injuries being given, and done on boeth sides, the peace of this his Majesties Colony hath bin much disturbed, and

*the late unhappy Rebellion by this means in a great measure be-
gunne and fomented....*[39]

The connection between the colonists' itch for land and the
Indian "troubles" is a close one. Since the Indian troubles set off
the rebellion, it would seem fair to blame the rebellion in great
part on those who caused the Indian troubles. But it seems an
inescapable conclusion that the English, and particularly the re-
bellious frontiersmen themselves, were responsible for the Indian
troubles. It was the frontiersmen's continuing violation of Gov-
ernor Berkeley's efforts to settle the Indian-white relationship
with fairness to both sides that precipitated the rebellion.

Colonel Moryson, one of the commissioners, was well aware
from his period in the Virginia government of the propensity of
the frontiersmen to push the Indians off their land. He wrote in
1676 that there had not been a war with the Indians for the pre-
vious twenty-five years that had not been caused by the English
coveting their land.[40] When, therefore, Moryson and his fel-
low commissioners were presented the "grievance" of Henrico
County that no satisfaction had been obtained against the Indians,
they commented: "These Complainants never consider that the
breach of the Peace and occasion of Bloodshed has still been on
the side of the English, which was publickly Justified and affirmed
in open Court in the face of a very great Assembly, and denied
by none."[41]

The one cause of Bacon's Rebellion that has been consistently
overlooked, then, is the aggressiveness of the frontiersmen. The
careful Hildreth nearly stumbled onto this conception when he
wrote, with unconscious humor, that "the Indian war, the im-
mediate cause of all the late disturbances, seems to have subsided
so soon as expeditions against the Indians were dropped."[42]
What has caused English and American historians to overlook
the frontiersmen's aggressiveness? The reason lies partly in the
white historian's unconscious immersion in his racial bias. Ac-
cording to the mythology of the white view of the world, the

Indian is ever "primitive," "warlike," and "aggressive," while the "civilized" white man is constantly on guard against his attacks.[43] But the aggressiveness of the frontiersmen has been overlooked for another reason, one based on our idea of our political beliefs. Most of the writers and historians who have dealt with Bacon's Rebellion have written from what they regarded as a "liberal" point of view, and it is part of the mythology of this view of history that the American frontiersman symbolizes America's freedom, democracy, and hatred of oppression. Actually the American frontiersman of the seventeenth century paid scant heed to such ideals. As Professor Abernethy has pointed out, frontier democracy

cared little for principles or for the rights of the individual. It wished to carry its point, whatever that point might happen to be at any given moment, by popular action; it cared for numbers more than it did for leadership; it despised the superior man—unless he happened to be useful for the time being—just because he was superior; and it strove to put the bottom rail on top, whereas an enlightened government would attempt, as Jefferson wished, to raise the bottom rail toward the top.[44]

It was the tyranny of the temporarily enraged frontiersmen against which Berkeley was struggling in 1676. He was able to win over the elected representatives of that mob in the assembly of June 1676, a brilliant proof of the force of his superior personality. On the great point at issue—Indian policy—that Baconian assembly was soon giving Berkeleian orders.[45] The record of the June Assembly proves that the real grievance against Governor Berkeley was not that he refused to defend the country from the Indians—a ridiculous charge against the conqueror of Opechancanough—but that he refused to authorize the slaughter and dispossession of the innocent as well as the "guilty."

The assembly of February 1677, like that of June 1676, reflected Berkeley's sentiments on the Indian question when it attempted to explain to the King the causes of the rebellion. The

February Assembly noted that "the distempered humor predomi-
nant in the Common people (the usuall Causes of mutinyes and
Insurrections) grounded uppon false humors, Infused by ill
affected persons," had been excited by the first incursion of In-
dians upon the head of Rappahannock River

wherein about thirty six persons were killed, which Caused
greate murmurrings because so speedy A revenge was not taken
for it, as theire precipitate desires would have exacted, Not Con-
sidering that warrs, are not to bee begunne without Mature de-
liberation Especially with our neighbours that had long lived, in
Amity and good Correspondence with us, and that suddenly it
Could not bee well deserned, whether the mischiefe was by them
perpetrated, or by Forreignors. . . .

The "giddy multitude" wanted action, the assembly continued,
and was not willing to await the meeting of the assembly. Bacon,

finding the multitude in such distempers . . . did with many false,
though specious pretences, declaring to the people, that if they
would follow him, hee would destroy the Indians . . . marched
forth and Killed many of our friend Indians. . . .[46]

The assembly went on to discuss *how* Bacon got recruits for
his design. His method, they noted, was to promise to make the
"meanest" people "equall with or in better Condition than those
that ruled over them. . . ." He tried to fulfill this promise by con-
fiscating the estates of the loyalists and distributing them to the
rebels, by setting prisoners at liberty and declaring freedom to
all servants of loyalists, and by forcing others to follow him,
threatening their ruin if they refused. Bacon's design, the as-
sembly conceived in a wild and improbable guess, was to alienate
Virginia from the King's dominion and "subject it to forreigners
(as it since Appeares by his owne Coffession to the minister that
Assisted at his death . . .)." What motivated Bacon? The as-
sembly could only suggest that "being himselfe of a ruined
fortune, ambitious and desiring Noveltyes" had something to do
with it.[47]

The preamble to the York County grievances gave a similar explanation of the cause of the rebellion. It justified Governor Berkeley declaring, in the commissioners' words, that "noe oppression of his, was the Rise and occasion of the late Distraction: but that the same proceeded from some disaffected persons, spurning against authoritie, and that the pretence of the dilatory Proceedings against the Indians was onely taken up for a Cloake...." The commissioners agreed: "For the first part wee have charity to beleeve it, for before the Warr with the Indians wee can find noe considerable Grievance arising from the Governor, to give the people any just cause of Complaint of his management...." [48]

However difficult it is to judge motives, it is possible to suggest some of the emotions that entered into the rebellion, especially among those who followed Bacon. The Isle of Wight County "opposing grievances" was one of the few documents to express the cause of the rebellion in psychological terms. "Envy, Emulation, Mallice, and Ignorance were the Cheife causes thereof," it stated. [49]

One looks in vain in history books for any recognition that these motives might have had something to do with Bacon's Rebellion. The Bacon-Berkeley fight is traditionally portrayed as another episode in the glorious struggle between the "people" and their "oppressors." As soon as the author's assumptions that Bacon represents the "people" and Berkeley the "oppressors" are established, the narrative rolls smoothly to its intended goal. Actions on the way are judged good or bad not according to what they are but by whom they are done. Bacon's plan to exterminate the weak neighboring Indians is justified by accepting a "guilt" for which there is no proof. Berkeley's attempt to defend the Indian subjects of the King until proof of their guilt might be established is castigated either as administrative incompetency or traitorous greed. Bacon's confiscation of the estates of the loyalists is passed over as one of the necessary steps in the "democratic" revolution. Berkeley's confiscation of the estates of the rebels to support his troops and make up the loyalist losses is denounced as unconscionable, and his hanging of twenty-three of the leading rebels is termed a "reign of terror."

The causes of Bacon's rebellion are complex and profound. They cannot be explained in terms of Berkeley's "greed" and "oppression," Bacon's love of "liberty," the "savagery" of the Indians, or the "patriotism" of the frontiersmen; such explanatory descriptions are meaningless labels pasted on the actors by those who see all history as a morality play. Nor can the rebellion be explained in terms of the concealed identities and mysterious motives of a Gothic romance. Bacon does not change, with the hemispheres, from the spoiled son of a well-to-do English country squire to a dedicated democratic frontier hero. Nor does Governor Berkeley, after being the "Darling of the People" for thirty-five years, suddenly reveal his true identity as their blackest oppressor. Both men remained true to the faults and virtues of their natures.

Nathaniel Bacon would be vastly amused to find himself the sainted hero of the guardians of the liberal traditions of western democratic government. No doubt he would receive the news with an expression of his profane amusement at the idiocy of men. "God damn my blood," he might exclaim; "how easily people are led!"

ESSAY ON THE SOURCES

‹✧✧✧›

I T USED to be thought that Bacon's Rebellion was one of the best documented episodes in American history from the standpoint of published sources. However, the Henry Coventry Papers at Longleat, the estate of the Marquis of Bath in Wiltshire, England, rival in extent and importance not only the published sources for a study of Bacon's Rebellion, but the hitherto-known unpublished sources. The central importance of the Coventry Papers can be judged by the fact that they comprise the official and unofficial papers of the man who was directly in charge of colonial affairs in the period 1674-1680. Henry Coventry was the senior of Charles II's two principal secretaries of state. His province was the "Southern Department" which included the colonies. Coventry never turned his papers over to the newly organized Record Office as the junior secretary, Sir Joseph Williamson, did. Instead, probably through the agency of Henry Frederick Thynne, his personal secretary, the papers were retained in private hands and eventually found their way to Longleat, the estate of the Thynne family. The details of the story of their acquisition, preservation, and discovery is dealt with at greater length elsewhere.[1]

Early in the nineteenth century the documents were examined, arranged, and mounted in volumes by a local clergyman, J. E. Jackson. Two volumes, LXXVII and LXXVIII, of about 450 folios each, contain documents dealing with colonial affairs principally in the period 1675-1680. The bulk of these documents are concerned with the Virginia uprising and its aftermath. Other important letters and documents relating to the rebellion are scattered throughout the 119 volumes of the Coventry Papers. During World War II the British Manuscripts Project of the American Council of Learned Societies, fearful of the destruction of British archives, acquired 2,652 microfilm reels of documentary materials in the British Isles. Fortunately the collections at Longleat were included. Over the years the raw film was processed and positive prints deposited in the Library of Congress. A catalogue was prepared and recently published as *British Manuscripts Project: A Checklist of the Microfilms Prepared in England and Wales for the American Council of Learned Societies, 1941-1945,* ed. Lester K. Born (Washington, 1955).

Most of the documents dealing with Bacon's Rebellion in the Coventry Papers, in addition to material from the Public Record Office, British Museum, and other sources, will be published in a volume I am editing for the Virginia Historical Society. The character of the documents will be sufficiently evident from the references given in the text of this book.

Sir Joseph Williamson's papers form the nucleus of the material relating to Bacon's Rebellion deposited in the Public Record Office, London. Although primary responsibility for the colonies was Coventry's, Williamson played an important role in colonial affairs both because the ill health of Coventry often threw colonial matters into Williamson's hands and because it was customary for subordinate colonial officials to keep both secretaries informed as a matter of courtesy and policy. The documents contained in the Public Record Office are calendared, usually adequately but sometimes inadequately, in the *Calendars of State Papers, Colonial,* and *Calendars of State Papers, Domestic.* The latter series is sometimes neglected by students of colonial affairs, but contains much information of value to the colonial historian. Precise references to the documents in the Public Record Office have been made throughout this work. The Library of Congress possesses a photostatic copy of the important C. O. 5/1371 volume of the commissioners' proceedings in Virginia, and is continually adding to its transcriptions of documents in British archives, although its holdings in the seventeenth century are still inadequate. The Colonial Records Project of the Virginia 350th Anniversary Celebration Corporation, under the chairmanship of Archivist William J. Van Schreeven of the Virginia State Library, Richmond, is at present making a significant effort to microfilm all material relating to colonial Virginia in the Public Record Office and British Museum.

The British Museum contains many of the papers of Thomas Povey, Master of Requests to Charles II, and father-in-law of Giles Bland, one of Bacon's lieutenants. Particularly important among Povey's manuscripts is the famous Egerton 2395 volume, the contents of which demonstrate the important channel of communication Bacon had for disseminating his declarations and letters in England. Other important manuscript volumes include Additional MSS. 25117-25125, which are letter-books of Henry Coventry containing clerks' entries of letters sent to the colonies and elsewhere. The Library of Congress possesses photostatic copies of these volumes. Additional MSS. 4159 and 17018 also contain rebellion material.

The Pepysian Library, Magdalene College, Cambridge, contains one of the three manuscript volumes kept by Samuel Wiseman, clerk of the commissioners sent to Virginia. The volume nearly duplicates another of Wiseman's record books, C. O. 5/1371, in the Public Record Office, but differs in some significant points. Among Pepys' naval manuscripts there are numerous letters relating to the preparations for sending ships and troops to Virginia to put down the rebellion. These letters are adequately calendared in *A Descriptive Catalogue of the Naval*

Manuscripts in the Pepysian Library at Magdalene College, Cambridge, ed. J. R. Tanner, Publications of the Navy Records Society, Vols. 26, 27, 36, 57 (London, 1903-1923).

We are also indebted to the meticulous Pepys for the papers relating to the rebellion that exist in the Bodleian Library, Oxford, in Rawlinson MSS., Series A, Vols. 180 and 185.

In the United States the best collection of original material relating to the period of the rebellion is in the Library of Congress. In the Jefferson Library of the Rare Books Room are several important manuscripts containing transcripts of early Virginia records. Two of the most important are the "Bland Manuscript" containing miscellaneous records dealing with Virginia in the period 1606-1692 and the "Peyton Randolph Manuscript" containing acts of the Virginia Assembly, 1660-1697. These documents are described in E. Millicent Sowerby's *Catalogue of the Library of Thomas Jefferson*, II (Washington, 1953), nos. 1824 and 1828, and their contents have been published in various documentary collections.

The Manuscripts Division of the Library of Congress contains several documents of great significance. The manuscript volume entitled "Instructions commicons letters of Advice and admonitions; and Publique Speeches Proclamations etc: Collected, transcribed and diligently examined by the Originall Records, now extant, belonging to the Assemblie" [1606-1680] may have been made under the supervision of Samuel Wiseman, clerk of the commissioners. It is described by Miss Sowerby, II, no. 1831, who points out that there is no evidence that Jefferson ever possessed it as hitherto believed. Other important manuscript volumes include "Virginia, Acts of the Assembly, 1662-1702," "Virginia, Foreign Business and Inquisitions from 1655 to 1676," and "Virginia, Miscellaneous Papers, 1606-1683 (with Jefferson annotations)." The Library of Congress also possesses the original or rough journals of the Lords of Trade and Plantations for the periods August 3, 1670-December 22, 1674 (Vol. I), March 31, 1677-April 14, 1679 (Vol. II), January 13, 1685-

December 8, 1686 (Vol. III). Before their acquisition by the Library, these journals were in the Sir Thomas Phillips collection. A typewritten calendar of the journals has been prepared by Ruth Anna Fisher of the Library. The rough journals show only minor variations from entry book copies of the journal in the Public Record Office, London. The Jamestown, or Ambler, MSS., consisting of 125 documents (1638-1809) concerned mostly with grants and deeds to land in the Jamestown area, are another valuable collection in the Library of Congress.

The Virginia State Library, Richmond, in addition to possessing original documents or photostatic transcripts of early Virginia land grants and county records, maintains a series of handwritten transcripts of British public records. These transcripts include: (a) the DeJarnette Transcripts (1606-1691), 2 vols., made from original papers in the Public Record Office, London; (b) the Eggleston Transcripts, 1 vol., made by the Rev. Edward Eggleston from Egerton MS. 2395 in the British Museum, London; (c) the McDonald Transcripts (1619-1695), 7 vols., made by Angus W. McDonald from original papers in the Public Record Office, London; (d) the Sainsbury Abstracts (1606-1740), 20 vols., made by William Noel Sainsbury from original papers in the Public Record Office, London; and (e) the Winder Transcripts (1607-1678), 2 vols., made by F. A. Winder from original papers in the Public Record Office, London. The Virginia State Library possesses the deed to Bacon's plantation, bought from Thomas Ballard in 1674, which contains the only known signature of the rebel.

The New York Public Library contains the original manuscript of William Sherwood's important account of Bacon's Rebellion entitled "Virginias Deploured Condition; Or an Impartiall Narrative of the Murders committed by the Indians there, and of the Sufferings of his Majesty's Loyall Subjects under the Rebellious Outrages of Mr. Nathaniell Bacon Junior to the tenth day of August Anno Domini 1676." The document was evidently "borrowed" from the British public records by George

Chalmers, the eighteenth-century annalist, in the course of his work on the history of the colonies. On his death Chalmers' papers were dispersed among the booksellers of London. The document was bought by an American, Mr. Thomas Aspinwall, and published along with other Aspinwall Papers in the Massachusetts Historical Society's *Collections*, 4th ser., IX (Boston, 1871), 162-176. It was published, however, without a very important endorsement, which is in the original. This endorsement, on the last sheet, reads: "Virginia. State of it. August 1676. formed by Mr. Sherwood." Sherwood never signed the document, but it is in his hand and in two places he signed his name to testify to the accuracy of the copies he had made of certain documents included in the narrative. The importance of the authorship of this document lies in the fact that *after* the rebellion Sherwood, who then incurred the enmity of Sir William Berkeley by serving as legal counsel for many former rebels, blamed the rebellion on Berkeley's "arbitrary will." [2] Yet in this account of August 1676 he places all the blame on Bacon. After writing "Virginias Deploured Condition," Sherwood fled the country for England. He returned in February 1677 with the fleet that carried the soldiers and the commissioners. His later accusations can undoubtedly be explained by the bitter feud that developed between him and Berkeley over his ignominious flight from the country, and what to Berkeley were his unethical and unjustifiable attempts to save undeserving rebels. I hope to take up the strange career of this "Newgate Burd, Jayle Burd Roague," as Berkeley, in alluding to his former criminal record, called him,[3] in a later article.

The Henry E. Huntington Library, San Marino, California, contains several important items hitherto unused in any study of Bacon's Rebellion. These items are Governor Berkeley's commission to Captain Thomas Larrimore of August 30, 1676 (HM 21810), a letter of James Scott, Duke of Monmouth, to [Sir Joseph Williamson], October 26, 1676, ordering an extract to be made of all directives concerning the armed expedition to

Virginia (HM 21811), an order from Governor Berkeley to Captain Larrimore, November 9, 1676 (HM 21812), a letter from Andrew Marvell to Sir Henry Thompson, November 14, 1676, giving an account of Bacon's Rebellion as received from a ship just arrived from Virginia (HM 21813), and a copy of Bacon's "Declaration of the People" in the Blathwayt Papers (BL 85).

The Alderman Library of the University of Virginia, Charlottesville, contains a few items bearing on Bacon's Rebellion, most notable of which is a contemporary copy of Berkeley's declaration of May 10, 1676, dissolving the assembly, made by Gideon Macon, sub-sheriff of York County, with his comments on the declaration. The Library also possesses a letter sent by the commissioners for Virginia to Lord Treasurer Danby on March 27, 1677. It is a "covering letter" announcing the sending of transcripts of some of the commissioners' correspondence with Governor Berkeley and "Copies of Petitions etc. relating to his Majestyes Revenue." The enclosures do not exist in the Alderman Library, but the covering letter, in Samuel Wiseman's hand, has the authentic signatures of the three commissioners upon it.

The Virginia Historical Society, Richmond, possesses Edmund Randolph's manuscript "History of Virginia" which contains some interesting comments on the rebellion of 1676 by a participant in the revolution of 1776. The portion of the "History" for the years 1774-1782 was published in the *Virginia Magazine of History and Biography* during the years 1925-1937. The earlier portion has never been published.

The printed sources for a history of Bacon's Rebellion are dealt with in the text. The most important collections of printed material are to be found in Charles McLean Andrews, ed., *Narratives of the Insurrections, 1675-1690* (New York, 1915), pp. 1-141. Andrews reprints T. M. [Thomas Mathew], "The Beginning, Progress, and Conclusion of Bacons Rebellion in Virginia in the Years 1675 and 1676" [1705], "A True Narrative of the Rise, Progresse, and Cessation of the Late Rebellion in Virginia,

Most Humbly and Impartially Reported by his Majestyes Commissioners Appointed to Enquire into the Affaires of the Said Colony" [1677], and "The History of Bacon's and Ingram's Rebellion," or Burwell Manuscript [1676].

Lawrence C. Wroth, in his introduction to "The Maryland Muse by Ebenezer Cooke" in the American Antiquarian Society's *Proceedings,* new ser., XLIV (Worcester, 1935), gives excellent evidence to prove that the Burwell Manuscript was written by John Cotton, the husband of Mrs. An. Cotton, whose letter, published in Peter Force's *Tracts and Other Papers Relating Principally to the Origin, Settlement, and Progress of the Colonies in North America* (Washington, 1836-1846), I, no. 9, it so closely resembles.[4] In this opinion Wroth follows Moses Coit Tyler, *A History of American Literature* (New York, 1878), I, 79-80 n. Jay B. Hubbell agrees with Wroth and Tyler as to Cotton's authorship of the account. See Hubbell's "John and Ann Cotton, of 'Queen's Creek,' Virginia," *American Literature,* X (1938), 179-201. Howard Mumford Jones has discussed the document and concludes that the poems attributed to a partisan and to an opponent of Bacon which are included in the Burwell account "should in all probability be viewed as rhetorical exercises" from the same pen, presumably that of the author of the whole manuscript (*The Literature of Virginia in the Seventeenth Century* [Memoirs of the American Academy of Arts and Sciences, Vol. XIX, pt. 2], Boston, 1946, p. 45 n.). Jay B. Hubbell, in *The South in American Literature, 1607-1900* (Durham, N. C., 1954), p. 25, also takes this view.

Other important documents dealing with the rebellion have been printed in William Waller Hening, ed., *The Statutes at Large ... A Collection of All the Laws of Virginia from the First Session of the Legislature in ... 1619,* 13 vols. (Richmond, [etc.] 1819-1823); John Daly Burk, *The History of Virginia from its first Settlement to the Commencement of the Revolution,* 3 vols. (Petersburg, 1804-1805); the *Virginia Magazine of History and Biography* (1893 to date); the *William and Mary Quarterly*

(1892 to date); H. R. McIlwaine, ed., *Journals of the House of Burgesses of Virginia, 1659/60-1693* (Richmond, 1914); H. R. McIlwaine, ed., *Minutes of the Council and General Court of Colonial Virginia, 1622-1632, 1670-1676, with notes and excerpts from original Council and General Court Records, into 1683, now lost* (Richmond, 1924); and in other periodicals and books. A particularly interesting account of the rebellion was published in the *Virginia Gazette* of Alexander Purdie and John Dixon on February 23, 1769. Specific references to many aspects of Bacon's Rebellion are to be found in Earl G. Swem, *Virginia Historical Index*, 2 vols. (Roanoke, 1934-1936).

The rebellion, because of its dramatic character, has appealed to many historians. The most recent full-length historical study is Thomas Jefferson Wertenbaker, *Torchbearer of the Revolution: The Story of Bacon's Rebellion and Its Leader* (Princeton, 1940), which includes a useful "Essay on Authorities," pp. 215-225. Wesley Frank Craven's *The Southern Colonies in the Seventeenth Century, 1607-1689* (Baton Rouge, 1949), contains a brilliant brief account of the rebellion.

Bacon's rebellion has provided a never-ending source of inspirational history for writers of fiction. More than twenty works of fiction use the rebellion as a theme, and it is mentioned in many others. For a partial listing of these works, see Jay B. Hubbell, *Virginia Life in Fiction* (Dallas, 1922).

NOTES

‡‡

Chapter 1

1. The changing literary conception of the rebellion will also be ignored in this essay; the change is adequately summarized in Bertha Monica Stearns, "The Literary Treatment of Bacon's Rebellion in Virginia," *Virginia Magazine of History and Biography* (hereafter cited as *Virginia Magazine*), 52 (1944), 163-179.

2. See also "Essay on the Sources," pp. 171-172.

3. *Ibid.*, p. 174.

4. "The Widow Ranter" is most conveniently available in Montague Summers, ed., *The Works of Aphra Behn* (London, 1915), IV, 215-310.

5. See later, chap. ii.

6. See, for example, chap. iv.

7. See later, chap. x.

8. I would apply the same praise to Beverley's interpretation of Bacon's Rebellion that Wesley Frank Craven gives to his interpretation of the dissolution of the Virginia Company: that "strangely enough" it was "the most accurate explanation...to appear for two centuries" (*Dissolution of the Virginia Company: The Failure of a Colonial Experiment* [New York, 1932], p. 4).

9. John Oldmixon, *The British Empire in America, Containing the History of the Discovery, Settlement, Progress and present State of all the*

British Colonies on the Continent and Islands of America (London, 1708), I, 257-258; passage omitted in 1741 edition, I, 389.

10. Lawrence C. Wroth, ed., "The Maryland Muse by Ebenezer Cooke": A Facsimile, American Antiquarian Society, *Proceedings,* new ser., 44 (1934), 313.

11. *Ibid.,* p. 307.

12. Pp. 154, 157.

13. Vol. I, 201.

14. *The Works of Edmund Burke* (Boston, 1839), IX, 361. Burke, who became a champion of colonial rights during the American Revolution, did not change the treatment of Bacon's Rebellion in later editions of the *Account.*

15. *An Universal History, from the Earliest Account of Time to the Present; Compiled from Original Authors*..., 1st edn., 23 vols. folio (London, 1736-1765); 2d edn., 65 vols. (London, 1747-1766); 3d edn., 60 vols. (London, 1779-1784). The Virginia section is in the *Modern Part of the Universal History* and is identical in both first (Vol. XV) and second (Vol. XLI) editions. Both appeared in 1764. John Campbell, LL.D. (1708-1775) was probably the author of the Virginia section. See Robert Watt, *Bibliotheca Britannica; or A General Index to British and Foreign Literature* (Edinburgh, 1824), s.v. "Campbell, John."

16. Vol. XLI, 537. There are slight changes in the third edition, XXXV (1783), 259.

17. Vol. XLI, 538. The phrase "though they disliked the principles of it" is omitted in the 1783 edition and the phrase "its authors" is changed to "the insurgents."

18. Pp. 67-68.

19. See the documents printed in appendices to the second volume of John Daly Burk's *History of Virginia from its first Settlement to the Commencement of the Revolution* (Petersburg, Va., 1804-1805); in William W. Hening, *The Statutes at Large...A Collection of All the Laws of Virginia* (Richmond, [etc.], 1819-1823), II, 528-533; and in W. Noel Sainsbury, ed., *Calendar of State Papers, Colonial Series, America and West Indies, 1675-1676* (London, 1893), nos. 892, 893, 935.

20. *Political Annals,* p. 335.

21. *Ibid.* See also *Introduction to the History of the Revolt* (published in London, 1782, but suppressed; later published in Boston, 1845), I, 161.

22. *Introduction to the History of the Revolt,* I, 162.

23. See "Essay on the Sources." For a brief discussion of Chalmers see Wesley Frank Craven, *The Legend of the Founding Fathers* (New York, 1956), pp. 51-55.

24. E. Millicent Sowerby, comp., *Catalogue of the Library of Thomas Jefferson*, I (Washington, 1952), no. 534.

25. *Ibid.*, no. 464. In a "Postscript" to the Preface to Burk's first volume he noted that "since writing the above, several interesting papers have been added to my collection, by the friendship and public spirit of several citizens, of which all the use possible shall be made in the notes and general appendix." The *History* was dedicated to Jefferson.

26. Dixon Wecter, *The Hero in America* (New York, 1941), p. 27.

27. Prefatory letter accompanying text in Peter Force, ed., *Tracts and Other Papers Relating Principally to the Origin, Settlement, and Progress of the Colonies in North America* (Washington, 1836-1846), I, no. 8, 4.

28. 1804 edn., p. 197; 1824 edn., p. 159.

29. 1824 edn., p. 160; revised stylistically but not in content from 1804 edn., pp. 198-199.

30. 1824 edn., p. 162, with stylistic changes from 1804 edn., pp. 201-202. Jefferson denounced Marshall's *Life of Washington* for distorting truth, at least unconsciously, in the interest of "party feelings" (Sowerby, *Catalogue*, I, no. 496).

31. A fourth volume of Burk's *History* was issued by Skelton Jones and Louis Girardin following Burk's death in a duel in 1808. For an account of Burk's activities in the United States see James Morton Smith, *Freedom's Fetters: The Alien and Sedition Laws and American Civil Liberties* (Ithaca, N.Y., 1956), pp. 204-220. See also Charles Campbell, *Some Materials to Serve for a Brief Memoir of John Daly Burk* (Albany, N.Y., 1868).

32. *History of Virginia*, II, 155-158.

33. *Ibid.*, p. 168.

34. *Ibid.*, p. 212. Burk's strong republican bias is discussed by Craven, *Legend of the Founding Fathers*, pp. 69-71. Craven hazards the guess that it was in Burk's *History* that Bacon became "for the first time a forerunner of the Revolution." In the Preface to Vol. I, Burk expressed the intention of showing "the slow and gradual transition of the mind from barbarism, to taste, from tyranny to freedom...."

35. Moncure Daniel Conway, *Omitted Chapters of History Disclosed in the Life and Papers of Edmund Randolph* (New York, 1888), pp. 360, 369.

36. Edmund Randolph, MS "History of Virginia" [ca. 1809-1810], pp. 94, 96-97, in the Virginia Historical Society, Richmond.

37. *Ibid.* See also Conway, *Omitted Chapters of History*, pp. 360, 369, and Irving Brant, "Edmund Randolph, Not Guilty!" *William and Mary Quarterly*, 3d ser., 7 (1950), 179-198.

38. See later, chap. iv, footnote 52.

39. Curtis Carroll Davis, *Chronicler of the Cavaliers: A Life of the Virginia Novelist Dr. William A. Caruthers* (Richmond, 1953), p. 187; Jay B. Hubbell, *The South in American Literature, 1607-1900* (Durham, N.C., 1954), p. 501.

40. George Bancroft, *History of the United States*, II (Boston, 1856), 219-221. In the author's last revision, I (New York, 1883), 460-461, he modifies slightly the praise extended to Bacon.

41. Robert S. Bright, *The Address of Robert S. Bright at the Unveiling of the Memorial Window to Nathaniel Bacon in the Powder Horn at Williamsburg, Virginia, November Fourteenth, Nineteen Hundred and One* (Richmond, 1941), p. 12. Southern historians of the nineteenth and twentieth centuries universally deplore this ungenerous act against Southern womanhood.

42. "The Conquering cause pleased the gods, but the conquered one pleased Cato"—Lucan, *Pharsalia*, Lib. I, line 128. The plaque was erected by the Society of the Colonial Dames of America in the State of Virginia. An even more flattering tablet was erected in the court room of the Gloucester County Court House in 1904. It hails Bacon as "the Washington of his day, popular and patriotic, whose magnanimity strongly contrasts with Berkeley's malignity. A soldier, a statesman, a Saint" (John H. Gwathmey, *Twelve Virginia Counties: Where the Western Migration Began* [Richmond, 1937], p. 34; Gloucester County Court Common Law Order Book No. 2, p. 370).

43. Pp. v, 14, 32.

44. See his "A Red Sinking Sun: Bacon's Rebellion," in Earl Schenck Miers, ed., *The American Story* (New York, 1956), pp. 55-60; and his *Bacon's Rebellion, 1676* [Jamestown 350th Anniversary Historical Booklet, Number 8] (Williamsburg, 1957).

Chapter 2

1. Frances Culpeper, Lady Berkeley, the governor's wife, was a cousin of Nathaniel Bacon. Fairfax Harrison, "The Proprietors of the Northern Neck," *Virginia Magazine*, 33 (1925), 145-150, 343-352; Charles Hervey Townshend, "The Bacons of Virginia and their English Ancestry," *New England Historical and Genealogical Register*, 37 (1883), 191.

2. The quoted phrase is from Robert Beverley, *The History and Present State of Virginia* [1705], ed. Louis B. Wright (Chapel Hill, 1947), p. 74 (Bk. I, chap. iv, sec. 92).

3. John Ray to Peter Courthope of Danny, from Friston Hall, n.d. [1662?], in Robert W. T. Gunther, *Further Correspondence of John Ray* (London, 1928), no. 19.

4. Thomas Jefferson Wertenbaker, *Torchbearer of the Revolution: The Story of Bacon's Rebellion and Its Leader* (Princeton, 1940), p. 49; Chancery Proceedings, *Jarvis* v. *Jason* (1681-1684), in *Virginia Magazine*, 14 (1907), 411-419, and 15 (1907-1908), 65-70, 306-312. Bacon's role in the defrauding of the youth seems to have been more than that of "catspaw" as his biographer charitably asserts.

5. The early letters that passed between the governor and Bacon will be published in a collection of documents I am editing for the Virginia Historical Society.

6. The original deed is in "Colonial Papers, 1652-1689," Folder "1674" in the Virginia State Library, Richmond. The deed is reproduced in *Virginia Magazine*, 37 (1929), opposite p. 354, but not transcribed. It is similarly reproduced in John Fiske, *Old Virginia and her Neighbours*, illus. ed. (Boston, 1900), between pp. 74 and 75 of Vol. II. Other information is contained in Henrico County court records, *Virginia Magazine*, 37 (1929), 354-357; Lyon Gardiner Tyler, *The Cradle of the Republic: Jamestown and James River* (Richmond, 1900), p. 138; and Wertenbaker, *Torchbearer of the Revolution*, pp. 52-53.

7. See, for example, the Bacon letter printed in *William and Mary Quarterly*, 1st ser., 9 (1900), 6-10. One of the perquisites of the governor's office was income derived from the granting of authority to trade with the Indians. There was nothing illegal about this source of the governor's income. See later in this chapter, p. 29 and note 58.

8. Bacon to Berkeley, n.d., in Henry Coventry Papers at Longleat, estate of the Marquis of Bath (hereafter cited as Longleat), LXXVII, fol. 100.

9. Commissioners' "Narrative" [1677], in Charles McLean Andrews, ed., *Narratives of the Insurrections, 1675-1690* (New York, 1915), p. 110.

10. Throughout this work I have, with reluctance, used the word "frontiersman" to describe the inhabitants in the outer area of English settlement. The word has so many *meanings* that it has no *meaning*. For some twentieth-century readers it conjures up the picture of uncouth, illiterate, "white savages" of the eighteenth-century Appalachian frontier. For others it brings to mind pious, industrious dirt-farmers of the nineteenth-century Great Plains frontier. The seventeenth-century tidewater Virginia frontiersman was neither of these. He was not only in contact with the Indians but with Europe. In great measure he retained European conceptions of the distinction between "mean" persons and persons of "quality." Bacon was a gentleman and accepted as such by the men he fought with and by the men he fought against. That he made the "Grand Tour" of the European continent as a young English gentleman was not held against him by his poor Henrico neighbors whose only overseas travel had been from a London dock to Jamestown. Indeed it is doubtful whether the "vulgar" would have followed him in rebellion against Governor Berkeley unless he had been a gentleman. It may be misleading to some, therefore, to talk about the rebellion as a "frontier" revolt. Yet it was a frontier revolt, so I have used the terms "frontier" and "frontiersman." My hope is that the reader will restrain his impulse to associate his images of eighteenth- and nineteenth-century frontiersmen with the seventeenth-century planters of the "out-settlements" depicted in this work. There are many points of similarity, but also many of dissimilarity.

11. H. R. McIlwaine, ed., *Minutes of the Council and General Court of Colonial Virginia, 1622-1623, 1670-1676* (Richmond, 1924), *passim.*

12. Wesley Frank Craven, *The Southern Colonies in the Seventeenth Century, 1607-1689* (Baton Rouge, 1949), p. 270; Governor Berkeley's reply to the 1670 "Enquiries" of the Lords of Trade and Plantations, in William W. Hening, *The Statutes at Large ... A Collection of All the Laws of Virginia* (Richmond, [etc.], 1819-1823), II, 515.

13. Hening *Statutes*, II, 274-275.

14. Thomas Ludwell to "Right Honorable," Sept. 17, 1666, *Virginia Magazine*, 5 (1897), 58.

15. Reply to "Enquiries" of Lords of Trade, Hening, *Statutes*, II, 513.

16. See, for example, the orders of the General Court in April 1674 concerning encroachments on the lands of the Nottoway, Pamunkey, and

Chickahominy Indians. McIlwaine, *Minutes of the Council*, pp. 365, 370-371.

17. This paragraph is based on the commissioners' "Narrative" [1677], in Andrews, *Narratives*, pp. 117-118, and on T. M. [Thomas Mathew], "The Beginning, Progress and Conclusion of Bacons Rebellion in Virginia in the Years 1675 and 1676" [1705] (hereafter cited as Mathew's "Narrative," in Andrews, *Narratives*), 15-16. T. M. has been identified as Thomas Mathew, a Northumberland planter, in *Virginia Magazine*, 1 (1893), 201-202, and in Andrews, *Narratives*, p. 13, and from internal evidence it seems obvious that he was the very man accused by the Indians of fraudulent dealing. He was later a burgess at the assembly of June 1676, and aided Bacon sufficiently to be excepted from Governor Berkeley's pardon to the rebels of February 10, 1677 (DeJarnette Transcripts, II, no. 104, in Virginia State Library, Richmond).

18. Mathew's "Narrative," in Andrews, *Narratives*, p. 17.

19. *William and Mary Quarterly*, 1st ser., 4 (1895), 86. My italics.

20. Washington and Allerton to governor and council of Maryland, Sept. 6, 1675, in William Hand Browne, ed., *Archives of Maryland*, Vol. XV: *Proceedings of the Council of Maryland, 1671-1681* (Baltimore, 1896), 48.

21. Governor and council of Maryland to Washington and Allerton, Sept. 14, 1675, in *Archives of Maryland, op. cit.*, XV, 48-49.

22. Longleat, LXXVII, fol. 3.

23. Testimony of John Shankes, Truman's interpreter and messenger to the Indians, May 19, 1676, to upper house of the Maryland Assembly, in *Archives of Maryland*, Vol. II: *Proceedings and Acts of the General Assembly of Maryland, April 1666 - June 1676* (Baltimore, 1884), 481.

24. Anonymous "Complaint from Heaven, with a Huy and crye and a petition out of Virginia and Maryland..." in *Archives of Maryland*, Vol. V: *Proceedings of the Council of Maryland, 1667-1687/8* (Baltimore, 1887), 134. For a discussion of this document see footnote 33.

25. Testimony of John Shankes, *Archives of Maryland*, II, 481.

26. Testimony of John Gerrard, June 14, 167[6], sworn before Nicholas Spencer and Richard Lee by order of Governor Berkeley, *William and Mary Quarterly*, 1st ser., 2 (1893), 40.

27. Testimony of John Shankes, *Archives of Maryland*, II, 482.

28. *Archives of Maryland*, II, 475 ff.

29. Depositions in *William and Mary Quarterly*, 1st ser., 2 (1893), 38-43.

30. *Archives of Maryland*, II, 500-501, 504.

31. Berkeley to assembly of June 1676, reported in Mathew's "Narrative," in Andrews, *Narratives*, p. 23.

32. Depositions in *William and Mary Quarterly*, 1st ser., 2 (1893), 39-43.

33. Journal of the Lords of Trade and Plantations, Dec. 6, 1677, in Public Record Office, London, Colonial Office, Series 391, Vol. 2, p. 176. Hereafter such references will be written C. O. 391/2, p. 176, etc. A diatribe explaining the Indian troubles in terms of a Catholic plot to overthrow the Protestants of Virginia and Maryland is the subject of a "Complaint from Heaven, with a Huy and crye and a petition out of Virginia and Maryland: To our great Gratious Kinge and Souveraigne Charles the II, King of Engeland, etc. with his Parliament." This is a twelve-page document, abominably written, dated only 1676, in C. O. 1/36, no. 78. It is printed, with many errors of transcription, in the *Archives of Maryland*, V, 134-152. The "Complaint" is so full of absurd and false accusations as to be of little use as a source of reliable information on the Susquehannock fight. It is sometimes cited by anti-Berkeley historians, however, because the author asserts that the troops murdered the chiefs because they knew them to be "som of the Murtherers," and because it provides the juicy scandal that Berkeley was "Altered by marrying a young wyff, from his wonted publicq good, to a covetous tode-age" (printed in *Archives of Maryland* as "fools-age" instead of "tode-age").

34. "The History of Bacon's and Ingram's Rebellion," or Burwell MS., in Andrews, *Narratives*, pp. 48-49.

35. Commissioners' "Narrative," Andrews, p. 107.

36. In a letter to Secretary of State Sir Joseph Williamson, April 1, 1676, Berkeley wrote that following the raid the Susquehannocks "fled towards the mountains from whence we have heard no more then this from them that they live only on Acornes that they have robd other lesser nations of the Indians of and so made them their Ennimies and we have now such a strength on the frontiers of al our Plantations that we cannot feare them if they were ten times more in number then they are" (C. O. 1/36, no. 36, fol. 66; the letter has been printed, with several serious errors of transcription, in the *Virginia Magazine*, 20 [1912], 243-246).

37. Colonel Francis Moryson to Attorney-General Sir William Jones, October 1676, C. O. 5/1371, pp. 9-10.

38. Thomas Jefferson Wertenbaker makes this suggestion in his *Torchbearer of the Revolution*, p. 85. In his *Virginia under the Stuarts* (Princeton, 1914), p. 151, Professor Wertenbaker suggests that fear of mutiny among the troops may have caused Berkeley to abandon the expedition.

39. Burwell MS., in Andrews, *Narratives*, p. 49.

40. *Ibid.*

41. The post-rebellion grievances of Sittingbourne Parish, Rappahannock County, state that Sir Henry Chicheley, Philip Ludwell, and Matthew Kemp issued such a warrant Feb. 14, 1676, and make the complaint quoted (Winder Transcripts, II, 221-222, Virginia State Library, Richmond).

42. Abstract of letter from Berkeley to "Mr. Secretary" [Thomas Ludwell], Feb. 16, [1676], Longleat, LXXVII, fol. 56.

43. Berkeley to Williamson, April 1, 1676, C. O. 1/36, no. 36. See also Wilcomb E. Washburn, "Governor Berkeley and King Philip's War," *New England Quarterly*, 30 (September 1957), 363-377.

44. See, for example, Berkeley's proclamation and justification of May 29, 1676, printed in Edward D. Neill, *Virginia Carolorum: The Colony under the Rule of Charles the First and Second, A.D. 1625 - A.D. 1685* (Albany, 1886), p. 357.

45. Abstract of letter from Berkeley to "Mr. Secretary," Feb. 16, [1676], Longleat, LXXVII, fol. 56.

46. Hening, *Statutes*, II, 326.

47. *Ibid*, p. 327.

48. *Ibid.*, pp. 331-332.

49. *Ibid.*, pp. 336-337.

50. *Ibid.*, pp. 336-337. Historians antagonistic to Governor Berkeley usually say that he himself was to appoint the men commissioned to conduct this trade. See, for example, John Spencer Bassett's introduction to *The Writings of "Colonel William Byrd of Westover in Virginia Esqr."* (New York, 1901). p. xx. Actually, of course, the individual county courts were given this authority.

51. Hening, *Statutes*, II, 337.

52. William Sherwood, "Virginias Deploured Condition; Or an Im-

partiall Narrative of the Murders committed by the Indians there, and of the Sufferings of his Majesty's Loyall Subjects under the Rebellious outrages of Mr. Nathaniell Bacon Junior to the tenth day of August Anno Domini 1676" (hereafter cited as Sherwood, "Virginias Deploured Condition"), in Massachusetts Historical Society, *Collections*, 4th ser., Vol. IX (Boston, 1871), 165-166; Bacon letter in *William and Mary Quarterly*, 1st ser., 9 (1900), 6-8. For a discussion of the authorship of "Virginias Deploured Condition," see "Essay on the Sources."

53. Charles City County post-rebellion grievances, signed by seven men, in *Virginia Magazine*, 3 (1895), 137.

54. "Report of examinations and depositions" in support of Charles City County grievances, Winder Transcripts, II, 409, in Virginia State Library, Richmond.

55. Hening, *Statutes*, I, 236-237; Thomas Ludwell to Lord [Arlington?], Sept. 17, 1666, *Virginia Magazine*, 21 (1913), 40.

56. Beverley, *History of Virginia*, p. 74 (Bk. I, chap. iv, sec. 92).

57. See footnote 1. See also genealogical notes in *Virginia Magazine*, 15 (1907), 181; and 35 (1927), 230. The Byrd-Culpeper link was through Mary Horsmanden, wife of William Byrd.

58. Bacon to Berkeley, Sept. 18, 1675, Longleat, LXXVII, fol. 6; William and Frances Berkeley to Bacon, Sept. 21, 1675, Longleat, LXXVII, fol. 8. Berkeley sent back to England the letters concerning his fur trade agreement with Bacon; he would not have done so had it involved something underhanded. The fee for the privilege to trade was set by negotiation. Berkeley's authority to license traders was specified in the King's instructions to him of 1642, *Virginia Magazine*, 2 (1895), 284, and in the act "Concerning Indians" of the assembly of March 1662, Hening, *Statutes*, II, 140. The "Act lycensing trading with Indians" of the assembly of October 1677, passed while Herbert Jeffreys, one of the commissioners sent to inquire into grievances against Berkeley, was governor, provided that "the dues belonging to the governour be reserved as formerly" (Hening, *Statutes*, II, 411). One should not be upset at the informality and uncertainty of the licensing arrangements. Both salaries and fees were extremely elastic in the seventeenth century, a phenomenon which creates suspicion among twentieth-century observers, but which was a matter of course in the seventeenth century.

59. Sherwood, "Virginias Deploured Condition," Mass. Hist. Soc., *Collections*, 4th ser., IX, 167-168.

60. Address of March 24, 1676, Longleat, LXXVII, fol. 66.

61. See later, p. 34.

62. Address of March 24, 1676, Longleat, LXXVII, fol. 66.

63. Berkeley to Thomas Ludwell, Apr. 1, 1676, *Virginia Magazine*, 20 (1912), 248-249. Berkeley mentions in this letter that he "appeased two mutinies this last yeare" caused by rumors that the fifty pounds of tobacco tax to support the Virginia agents in England was intended for the enriching of private individuals. In the days before the withholding tax and the machine gun, "mutinies" were frequent in all countries. They were usually on a small scale and without the social or military significance attached to the word "mutiny" today. See, for example, the fourteen-man mutiny in Surry County in December 1673, *William and Mary Quarterly*, 1st ser., 3 (1894), 122-125, and John B. Boddie, chapter on "America's First Tax Strike," in his *Colonial Surry* (Richmond, 1948), pp. 101-107.

64. George Louis Beer, *The Old Colonial System, 1660-1754*, Part I: *The Establishment of the System, 1660-1688* (New York, 1912), II, 142-147, asserts that the Navigation Acts were in no way responsible for Bacon's Rebellion; Thomas Jefferson Wertenbaker, *The Planters of Colonial Virginia* (Princeton, 1922), pp. 92-94, disagrees. For another opinion, see Charles McLean Andrews, *The Colonial Period of American History*, Vol. IV: *England's Commercial and Colonial Policy* (New Haven, 1938), 138-139. For instances of Berkeley's attempts to relieve the economic distress of the colony, see his *Discourse and View of Virginia* (London, 1663), reprinted Norwalk, Conn., 1914; and Wertenbaker, *Virginia under the Stuarts*, pp. 122-123.

65. Philip Ludwell to Thomas Ludwell, June 13, 1676, Longleat, LXXVII, fol. 121.

66. Mathew's "Narrative," in Andrews, *Narratives*, p. 38.

67. Berkeley to "Mr. Secretary" [Thomas Ludwell], July 1, 1676, Longleat, LXXVII, fol. 145.

68. Governor Francis Nicholson of Virginia, writing to the Lords of Trade and Plantations on July 1, 1699, suggested that Bacon would not have dared to lead a rebellion had not Governor Berkeley grown ill and infirm. He also pointed out that had Berkeley been capable of taking the field against the Indians he would have saved himself from the vicious rumors and accusations that circulated among the people (Cecil Headlam, ed., *Calendar of State Papers, Colonial Series, America and West Indies, 1699* [London, 1908], no. 579 [hereafter cited as *Cal. State Papers, Colonial*]).

69. Hening, *Statutes*, II, 331, but the words "Continually" and "motion" are used as in the Longleat copy of the act (LXXVII, fol. 58) in place of Hening's "constantly" and "action."

70. Longleat, LXVII, fol. 445. For a more complete description of the "Appeal," see later, pp. 36-37. Sherwood, "Virginias Deploured Condition," Mass. Hist. Soc., *Collections*, 4th ser., IX, 166, also asserts that "the forts' being settled, the forces were dayly out in p'suit of the Indians...."

71. Wesley Frank Craven, "Indian Policy in Early Virginia," *William and Mary Quarterly*, 3d ser., 1 (1944), 75; Craven, *Southern Colonies in the Seventeenth Century*, p. 392; Hening, *Statutes*, II, 433-440; letters of Nicholas Spencer to Henry Coventry, Sept. 17, 1680, and Aug. 20, 1680, and to Sir Leoline Jenkins, May 13, 1681, in *Virginia Magazine*, 25 (1917), 144, 147, 271.

72. William Sherwood, "Virginias Deploured Condition," Mass. Hist. Soc., *Collections*, 4th ser., IX, 166.

73. Berkeley to Thomas Ludwell, Apr. 1, 1676, *Virginia Magazine*, 20 (1912), 247-249.

74. Commissioners' "Narrative," in Andrews, *Narratives*, p. 108.

75. Berkeley to Coventry, July 1, 1676, Longleat, LXXVII, fol. 144.

76. Thomas Mathew's "Narrative," in Andrews, *Narratives*, p. 20.

77. "Report of examinations and depositions" in support of Charles City County grievances, Winder Transcripts, II, 407-410, in Virginia State Library, Richmond.

78. *Ibid.*, pp. 407-408; commissioners' "Narrative," in Andrews, *Narratives*, p. 109; "Petition of your poor distressed subjects in the upper parts of James River in Virginia to Governor Sir William Berkeley," C. O. 1/36, no. 66, summary in W. Noel Sainsbury, ed., *Cal. State Papers, Colonial, 1675-1676* (London, 1893), no. 921. Sainsbury incorrectly dates the petition "?May" but the depositions in support of the Charles City County grievances state that it was presented in April.

79. "Report of examinations and depositions" in support of Charles City County grievances, Winder Transcripts, II, 408. Berkeley's attitude towards the petitioners has not enhanced his reputation with later historians, but his policy differs little from that of his later critic Colonel Francis Moryson, one of the King's commission of investigation into the causes of Bacon's Rebellion. Moryson, acting governor of Virginia in 1661 when Berkeley was in England, was responsible for a council order laying a fine of five thousand pounds of tobacco and one year's imprison-

ment on "whosoever shall falsely raise any rumor or reports that may tend to the disturbance of the Countrey." This order was made at a meeting of the General Court, June 12, 1661, recorded in the Charles City County Court Order Book and printed in Beverly Fleet, ed., *Virginia Colonial Abstracts*, Vol. XI: *Charles City County Court Orders, 1658-1661* (Richmond, 1941 [mimeographed]), p. 97. In a letter or proclamation that accompanied the order Moryson noted that "the annuall feares of the Indians which distract the Inhabitants of this Country proceed more from their own Jealousies than any reall dangers, most people looking upon the Indians as a people that are provoked and by consequence likely to be inclined to revenge...But then, would they reflect not onely upon the inconsiderable number of our neighbouring Indians, but upon the dependency they have upon us, and the enmity they by that meanes contract to themselves from the most potent nations, But upon the levity of the reporters and vanity of the reports which though for so many yeares they have been raised yett there never yet appeared a person to verifie or hardly to patronize them, they would soon find upon how light foundations they grounded their jealousies; But yet these Panick feares stop not with the particular trouble of the authors but for the most part breake out into murmurings and repinings against their Governours and the Government for not following their rash humours and immediately involveing the Countrey in a destructive warr, which should they be assented to, would soon discover the temper of those spirits...." ("By the Governor and Captain Generall of Virginia," Francis Moryson, recorded in the Charles City County Court Order Book, July 15, 1661, printed in *Virginia Magazine*, 43 [1935], 347-349).

80. Charles City County post-rebellion grievances, *Virginia Magazine*, 3 (1895), 137.

81. "Report of examinations and depositions" in support of Charles City County grievances, Winder Transcripts, II, 408.

82. Commissioners' "Narrative," in Andrews, *Narratives*, p. 109; Journal of the Lords of Trade and Plantations, Dec. 6, 1677, C. O. 391/2, pp. 176-177.

83. Commissioners' "Narrative," in Andrews, *Narratives*, pp. 110-111.

84. Berkeley's letters are not extant, but their content can be deduced from Bacon's answers to them, copies of which, sent by Philip Ludwell, acting secretary of the colony, to Secretary of State Coventry in June 1676, are now at Longleat, LXXVII, foll. 99-101. Three of the letters of Bacon to Berkeley are undated but, from internal evidence and from

corroborative evidence in "Virginias Deploured Condition" and other documents, seem to belong to this period which is probably early April to April 27, 1676, date of the first dated Bacon letter of 1676 in the Coventry Papers. It is possible that these letters belong to the period May 29 to June 5, 1676, but after first favouring this view I have rejected it.

85. Bacon letters cited in previous note, Longleat, LXXVII, foll. 99-101; Sherwood, "Virginias Deploured Condition," Mass. Hist. Soc., *Collections*, 4th ser. IX, 166.

86. Longleat, LXXVII, foll. 100-101. My italics.

87. C. O. 5/1371, pp. 247-254. A copy of the "Appeal" is in Longleat, LXXVII, fol. 445, and in Egerton MS. 2395, fol. 544, in the British Museum, London. A resume is in *Cal. State Papers, Colonial, 1675-1676*, no. 909, dated by Sainsbury "April? 1676." For similar views on the Indians' right to their land, discussed by Bacon in his letters and in his "Manifesto," see pp. 46, 58, 71-72.

88. C. O. 5/1371, pp. 247-254.

89. Berkeley to Coventry, Feb. 2, 1677, Longleat, LXXVII, foll. 350-351; statement of Lady Berkeley, undated, Longleat, LXXVII, fol. 41. Berkeley's February 2 letter to Coventry has been edited, with an introduction, by Wilcomb E. Washburn under the title of "Sir William Berkeley's 'A History of Our Miseries,'" *William and Mary Quarterly*, 3d ser., 14 (July 1957), 403-413.

90. Spotswood to Council of Trade and Plantations, July 25, 1711; to William Blathwayt, May 8, 1712; to Council of Trade and Plantations, June 4, 1715; and to Lords of the Treasury, July 15, 1715; in R. A. Brock, ed., *The Official Letters of Alexander Spotswood, Lieutenant-Governor of the Colony of Virginia, 1710-1722* [Virginia Historical Society, *Collections*, new series, I, II] (Richmond, 1882, 1885), I, 94-95, 157-158; II, 116, 118. See also Beverley W. Bond, Jr., *The Quit-Rent System in the American Colonies* (New Haven, 1919), pp. 234, 240, 405. The Privy Council, on March 14, 1679, recommended what Spotswood later urged, that the quit-rents of Virginia be kept as a reserve there for use in times of rebellion, invasion, and similar emergencies. See W. L. Grant and James Munro, eds., *Acts of the Privy Council of England, Colonial Series*, Vol. I, *A.D. 1613-1680* (Hereford, England, 1908), no. 1250.

91. Sherwood, "Virginias Deploured Condition," Mass. Hist. Soc., *Collections*, 4th ser., IX, 166. In one of his undated letters Bacon describes

the flight of an Indian tribe, probably the Pamunkeys, and the occupation of their town by his "volunteers" (Longleat, LXXVII, fol. 101).

92. Philip Ludwell to Coventry, June 28, 1676, Longleat, LXXVII, fol. 134. An almost identical statement appears in Ludwell's letter of the same date to Secretary Williamson, *Virginia Magazine,* 1 (1893), 180.

93. Bacon's "Manifesto," *Virginia Magazine,* 1 (1893), 56-57.

94. "Petition of your poor distressed subjects in the upper parts of James River in Virginia to Governor Sir William Berkeley," C. O. 1/36, no. 66; "The humble Appeal of the Volunteers to all well minded and charitable people," C. O. 5/1371, pp. 247-254; "The Virginians' plea for opposing the Indians without the Governor's order," C. O. 1/37, no. 14. Summaries of all these documents appear in *Cal. State Papers, Colonial, 1675-1676,* nos. 909, 921, 962.

Chapter 3

1. Governor Berkeley to "Mr. Secretary" [Thomas Ludwell] to be communicated to the King's Secretaries of State, July 1, 1676, in the Henry Coventry Papers at Longleat, estate of the Marquis of Bath (hereafter cited as Longleat), LXXVII, fol. 144; Colonel Edward Hill's defense against the Charles City County grievances, in *Virginia Magazine,* 3 (1896), 345.

2. Bacon to Berkeley, Apr. 27, 1676, Longleat, LXXVII, fol. 73; Berkeley to [Thomas Ludwell], July 1, 1676, Longleat, LXXVII, fol. 144.

3. William Sherwood, "Virginias Deploured Condition," in Massachusetts Historical Society, *Collections,* 4th ser., Vol. IX (Boston, 1871), 167. Governor Berkeley prepared his will the day before he began this march. It is printed in William W. Hening, *The Statutes at Large . . . A Collection of All the Laws of Virginia* (Richmond, [etc.], 1819-1823), II, 558-559.

4. Bacon to Berkeley, May 2, 1676, Longleat, LXXVII, fol. 76.

5. Egerton MS. 2395, fol. 539, in British Museum, London.

6. Colonial Office, Series 1, Vol. 36, no. 64, fol. 137, in Public Record Office, London (hereafter cited as C. O. 1/36, etc.). There is a copy of the proclamation in Egerton MS. 2395, fol. 540, in the British Museum, and another in the Alderman Library, University of Virginia, made in June 1676 by Gideon Macon, sub-sheriff of York County.

7. Unsigned, unaddressed letter of May 23, 1676, by someone reporting

information that Berkeley had received "About a weeke a goe," Longleat, LXXVII, fol. 86.

8. Berkeley had earlier in May instructed Goodrich to raise a force to destroy the Susquehannocks, but not any other Indians. See Colonel William Travers to Giles Cale, May 13, 1676, C. O. 1/36, no. 65, summary in W. Noel Sainsbury, ed., *Calendar of State Papers, Colonial Series, America and West Indies, 1675-1676* (London, 1893), no. 920 (hereafter cited as *Cal. State Papers, Colonial*).

9. Longleat, LXXVII, fol. 85.

10. That all the reports Berkeley received at this time were utterly false is suggested by the commissioners' absolute assertion of the innocence of the Queen of Pamunkey (commissioners' "Narrative," in Charles McLean Andrews, ed., *Narratives of the Insurrections, 1675-1690* [New York, 1915], p. 123); by Berkeley's later execution of one Wilford, an interpreter who had reported Indian atrocities to the governor at this time, as one "that frighted the Queen of Pamunkey from the lands she had granted to her by the Assembly, a month after peace was concluded with her" (Berkeley's list of those executed during the rebellion, in Peter Force, ed., *Tracts and Other Papers Relating Principally to the Origin, Settlement, and Progress of the Colonies in North America* [Washington, 1836-1846], I, no. 10); by Berkeley's later report that no Englishman was killed during April and May (Berkeley to "Mr. Secretary" [Thomas Ludwell], July 1, 1676, Longleat, LXXVII, fol. 144); by his later excepting Colonel Goodrich, the man who reported—falsely it seems—the death of "those poore innocents" about May 15, from his proclamation of pardon of Feb. 10, 1677 (DeJarnette Transcripts, II, no. 4, in Virginia State Library, Richmond, and in C. O. 5/1371, pp. 276-286); and by the acts and orders of the Assembly of June 1676 which carefully distinguished between guilty and innocent Indians (see later, p. 55).

11. Commissioners' "Narrative," in Andrews, *Narratives*, p. 112.

12. Article on Occaneechee Island in *William and Mary Quarterly*, 1st ser., 11 (1902), 121-122.

13. Council of Virginia to Lords of Trade and Plantations, May 31, 1676, Longleat, LXXVII, foll. 95-96.

14. Philip Ludwell to Secretary of State Sir Joseph Williamson, June 28, 1676, *Virginia Magazine*, 1 (1893), 180-181; Sherwood, "Virginias Deploured Condition," Mass. Hist. Soc., *Collections*, 4th ser., IX, 167. T. M. [Thomas Mathew], "The Beginning, Progress and Conclusion of Bacons Rebellion in Virginia in the Years 1675 and 1676," in Andrews,

Narratives, p. 21, states that the Occaneechees promised the English food but kept putting them off. T. M.'s "Narrative," written thirty years after the event, has numerous errors and must be treated with particular caution. One of Bacon's soldiers (see footnote 19) reported a later refusal on the part of the Indians to supply food but his words do not necessarily imply an initial refusal. The Occaneechees probably refused to *continue* to supply food to their unwanted guests after the initial cordial reception reported by Ludwell and Sherwood.

15. Philip Ludwell to Coventry, June 28, 1676, Longleat, LXXVII, fol. 135, and to Williamson, same date, *Virginia Magazine*, 1 (1893), 180-181.

16. *Ibid.*; Sherwood, "Virginias Deploured Condition," Mass. Hist. Soc., *Collections*, 4th ser., IX, 167.

17. Sherwood, "Virginias Deploured Condition," Mass. Hist. Soc., *Collections*, 4th ser., IX, 167-168.

18. Philip Ludwell to Williamson, June 28, 1676, *Virginia Magazine*, 1 (1893), 181-182.

19. "A description of the fight between the English and the Indians in May 1676, Nathaniel Bacon being their General and the number of his men 211," C. O. 1/36, no. 77. The narrative of the fight is printed in *William and Mary Quarterly*, 1st ser., 9 (1900), 1-4, from a transcription of the Egerton MS. 2395, fol. 542, copy in the British Museum, London. The Egerton copy is full of errors, all of which, and a few more, are reproduced in the printed version. A copyist's error is also responsible for the fact that the chief of the Occaneechees is sometimes called "Rossechy" instead of "Persicles." In the original manuscript the king's name is written "Posseclay" which is, of course, close to Ludwell's "Persicles." The person who made the copy of this account in Egerton MS. 2395, however, put a tail on the "P" and confused several other letters of the name, thereby converting it to "Rossechy." "Rossechy" then found its way into the printed version.

20. "Mr. Bacon's account of their troubles in Virginia by the Indians. June the 18th [28], 1676," *William and Mary Quarterly*, 1st ser., 9 (1900), 7. For comment on date, see footnote 20 of chapter iv.

21. Wood to Berkeley, May 24, 1676, Longleat, LXXVII, fol. 88.

22. Berkeley to Coventry, Feb. 2, 1677, in *William and Mary Quarterly*, 3d ser., 14 (July 1957), 407.

23. William E. Dodd, *The Old South: Struggles for Democracy* (New York, 1937), p. 242.

24. Thomas Perkins Abernethy, ed., *More News from Virginia: A Further Account of Bacon's Rebellion*, reproduced in facsimile (Charlottesville, Va., 1943), Introduction.

25. So unheroic and incomprehensible did this action appear to the author of *Strange News from Virginia; Being a full and true Account of the Life and Death of Nathaniel Bacon, Esq.* (London, 1677), p. 5, reprinted in Harry Finestone, ed., *Bacon's Rebellion: The Contemporary News Sheets* (Charlottesville, Va., 1956), p. 12, that he has Bacon assaulting the Susquehannocks in their fort before dealing with the Occaneechees, although not even Bacon's men pretended they had fought the Susquehannocks. The idea that Bacon fought the Susquehannocks has found its way into more recent publications, e.g., Richard B. Morris, ed., *Encyclopedia of American History* (New York, 1953), p. 28.

26. Bacon seized an Indian called Jack Nessam and his family from the custody of Major General Abraham Wood following his return from the Occaneechee campaign. See postscript to Bacon's letter of May 25, 1676, to Berkeley, in Longleat, LXXVII, fol. 89, and Wood to Berkeley, May 24, 1676, Longleat, LXXVII, fol. 88.

27. Bacon to Berkeley, May 25, 1676, Longleat, LXXVII, fol. 89. A copy of this letter, minus its postscript and with numerous minor differences is in Egerton MS. 2395, fol. 541, in the British Museum, London.

28. Document signed by Berkeley, Sir Henry Chicheley, John Clough, and James Crewes (Bacon's messenger), May 26, 1676, Longleat, LXXVII, fol. 90.

29. Council to Bacon, two letters of May 27, 1676, Longleat, LXXVII, foll. 91-92. Berkeley was fully aware of the need for caution, consideration, and strength in dealing with rebellious outbreaks. In a letter of December 7, 1664, to Richard Nicolls, governor of New York, the Virginia governor commented on a mutiny that had broken out there in Nicolls' absence. "I dare not meddle though but in a censure with any thing out of my owne spheare but me thought it was something intempestive (in your absence) to erect instruments of punishment for soldiers without pay for such things should be donne in the moment ther was need of them and not give them time that were to suffer to consider whether they were able to resist the punishment intended them or not. But since this is past without any manifest rupture of the obedience of the soldiers to your person and commands I thinke two things wil be necessary the one to give a free and General pardon for what is past the other severely to punish the next slight fault of this nature to shew that punishing is

yet in your power and if you find that the Dutch have had a hand in this disorder it wil be best to begin with them and as many of them has [*sic*] have deserved it to have their farmes taken from them and given to the soldiers which wil content them in steade of pay. But my Deare General tis miserable condition of honor to command without mony to pay. For my part I had rather plough but this few consider but those that feels it." The letter is in the Huntington Library, San Marino, California, BL 69. "Intempestive" means "unseasonable."

30. Bacon to Berkeley, May 28, 1676, Longleat, LXXVII, fol. 93.

31. The original of the May 29 declaration in Berkeley's hand is at Longleat, LXXVII, foll. 157-158. Two copies are also in Longleat, LXXVII, fol. 43 ff. and fol. 181 ff. The document is printed in Edward D. Neill, *Virginia Carolorum: The Colony under the Rule of Charles the First and Second, A.D. 1625 - A.D. 1685* (Albany, 1886), pp. 351-357, and in the Massachusetts Historical Society, *Collections*, 4th ser., Vol. IX (Boston, 1871), 178-181. Neither printed copy is authentic, however, for numerous copyists' errors crept into transcriptions of the document as soon as it left Berkeley's hand, e.g., "sickly" for "rashly." A correct transcription will be published in the collection of documents I am editing for the Virginia Historical Society.

32. Longleat, LXXVII, fol. 94; copy, fol. 179.

33. Sherwood to Secretary Williamson, June 1, 1676, *Virginia Magazine*, 1 (1893), 169.

34. Sir Henry Chicheley to Colonel Nathaniel Bacon, Sr., June 2, 1676, Longleat, LXXVII, fol. 102.

35. Commissioners' "Narrative," in Andrews, *Narratives*, pp. 113-114.

36. Philip Ludwell to Lady Berkeley, June 12, 1676, Longleat, LXXVII, fol. 117.

37. Longleat, LXXVII, fol. 103. The last portion of this letter is printed in the *Virginia Magazine*, 26 (1908), 200.

Chapter 4

1. "An Answer to the Objections against Sir William Berkeley, in justification of his proceedings," signed by Alexander Culpeper, and read before the Lords of Trade and Plantations, Dec. 4, 1677. The original is in Colonial Office, Series 1, Vol. 41, no. 19, in Public Record Office, London (hereafter cited as C. O. 1/41, etc.). There is a copy in C. O.

5/1355, pp. 230-239. The document is printed in John Daly Burk, *The History of Virginia* (Petersburg, 1804-1805), II, 259-264, and in the *Virginia Magazine*, 6 (1898), 139-144. The Burk and *Virginia Magazine* copies show important variations from the Public Record Office documents. The *Virginia Magazine* copy, for example, has the word "infused" instead of the word "infected" in the passage quoted.

2. Governor Berkeley to Secretary of State Henry Coventry, July 1, 1676, in the Henry Coventry Papers at Longleat, estate of the Marquis of Bath (hereafter cited as Longleat), LXXVII, fol. 144; Col. Francis Moryson to Coventry, Sept. 6, 1676, Longleat, LXXVII, fol. 204.

3. William W. Hening, *The Statutes at Large ... A Collection of All the Laws of Virginia* (Richmond, [etc.], 1819-1823), II, 280. Hereafter cited as Hening, *Statutes*.

4. Commissioners' "Narrative," in Charles McLean Andrews, ed., *Narratives of the Insurrections, 1675-1690* (New York, 1915), p. 113.

5. Jordan to Moryson, dated only "June, 1676," Longleat, LXXVII, fol. 138.

6. Berkeley to Coventry, Feb. 2, 1677, in *William and Mary Quarterly*, 3d ser., 14 (July 1957), 408.

7. Allerton to Thomas Ludwell, Aug. 4, 1676, Longleat, LXXVII, fol. 160.

8. Hill's defense against the Charles City County grievances, *Virginia Magazine*, 3 (1896), 249. Hill is probably referring not to the reform acts but to the forced acts of the assembly, such as that disabling him personally from holding office. See later, p. 62.

9. Berkeley to "Mr. Secretary" [Thomas Ludwell], July 1, 1676, Longleat, LXXVII, fol. 144.

10. Philip Ludwell to Secretary of State Sir Joseph Williamson, June 28, 1676, *Virginia Magazine*, 1 (1893), 182-183.

11. Berkeley to Gardner, June 7, 1676, C. O. 5/1308, fol. 67. After the rebellion Gardner applied for a suitable reward for his services, which, not coming in adequate measure, the captain continued to petition for more, claiming particularly a £200 reward Berkeley was alleged to have offered for Bacon's capture at this time. Though Gardner presented a copy of the governor's order to seize Bacon he did not submit any proclamation in which Berkeley offered a reward for the deed. Numerous documents on the matter dating from 1676 to 1693 are contained in C. O. 5/1308, foll. 61-73, 83-84, 203, 210-211.

12. William Sherwood to Williamson, June 28, 1676, *Virginia Magazine*, 1 (1893), 170-171.

13. Berkeley to Coventry, Feb. 2, 1677, in *William and Mary Quarterly*, 3d ser., 14 (July, 1957), 408; Philip Ludwell to Lady Berkeley, June 12, 1676, Longleat, LXXVII, fol. 117.

14. Philip Ludwell to Lady Berkeley, June 12, 1676, Longleat, LXXVII, fol. 117. A copy of Bacon's confession is in Longleat, LXXVII, fol. 116; a printed copy is in Hening, *Statutes*, II, 543-544.

15. T. M. [Thomas Mathew], "The Beginning, Progress and Conclusion of Bacons Rebellion in Virginia in the Years 1675 and 1676," in Andrews, *Narratives*, p. 23. Hereafter cited as Mathew's "Narrative," in Andrews, *Narratives*.

16. Longleat, LXXVII, fol. 116; H. R. McIlwaine, ed., *Minutes of the Council and General Court of Colonial Virginia, 1622-1623, 1670-1676* (Richmond, 1924), p. 516.

17. Philip Ludwell to Lady Berkeley, June 12, 1676, Longleat, LXXVII, fol. 117; Philip Ludwell to Williamson, June 28, 1676, *Virginia Magazine*, 1 (1893), 182-183. The commissioners, in their "Review, Breviary and Conclusion," state that Bacon was restored to his council seat on June 11 (C. O. 5/1371, p. 413). Thomas Mathew, writing thirty years after the event, places Bacon's restoration to his council seat on the same day that he begged and received his pardon, which would be June 9 (Mathew's "Narrative," in Andrews, *Narratives*, p. 23).

18. Journal of the Lords of Trade and Plantations, Dec. 6, 1677, C. O. 391/2, p. 177.

19. Berkeley to Thomas Ludwell, July 1, 1676, Longleat, LXXVII, foll. 144-145.

20. "Mr. Bacon's account of their troubles in Virginia by the Indians. June the 18th, 1676," from the copy in Egerton MS. 2395, fol. 551, in the British Museum, London, printed in the *William and Mary Quarterly*, 1st ser., 9 (1900), 6-10. Actually the date is probably an error of the original copyist for June 28 because the letter mentions the forced commission and forced justificatory letter of the governor to the King which were obtained between June 23 and June 25, 1676. See later, pp. 65-66.

21. Ludwell to Lady Berkeley, June 12, 1676, Longleat, LXXVII, fol. 117. Lady Berkeley had left Virginia for England two weeks earlier.

22. Ludwell to Coventry, June 28, 1676, Longleat, LXXVII, fol. 136; also expressed in a letter of same date to Secretary Williamson, *Virginia*

Magazine, 1 (1893), 183. William Sherwood, in a letter to Secretary Williamson, June 28, 1676, wrote that Bacon was promised "upon his good behaviour he should have a commission..." (*Virginia Magazine*, 1 [1893], 171). The author of the Burwell Manuscript wrote that on Saturday, June 10, Bacon was promised a "Commission signed the Monday following...as Generall for the Indian war..." but was refused by Berkeley ("The History of Bacon's and Ingram's Rebellion," or Burwell MS., in Andrews, *Narratives*, pp. 54-55). The commissioners' "Narrative" remarked that "the Governor is said to have promised" Bacon "a commission...to goe out against the Indians..." (Andrews, *Narratives*, pp. 115-116).

23. H. R. McIlwaine, ed., *Journals of the House of Burgesses of Virginia, 1659/60-1693* (Richmond, 1914), p. 65.

24. "Mr. Bacon's account of their troubles in Virginia by the Indians. June the 18th [28], 1676," *William and Mary Quarterly*, 1st ser., 9 (1900), 8.

25. Ludwell to Lady Berkeley, June 12, 1676, Longleat, LXXVII, fol. 117.

26. Philip Ludwell to Thomas Ludwell, June 12, 1676, with postscript written June 13, Longleat, LXXVII, fol. 121. Bland's troubles in Virginia and his connections in England are both complicated and involved. Details of the former are set forth in the *Virginia Magazine*, 20 (1912), 350-352, 21 (1913), 133-134, McIlwaine, *Journals of the House of Burgesses, 1659/60-1693*, p. 63, and McIlwaine, *Minutes of the Council, 1622-1623, 1670-1676*, pp. 423, 435. I have gone more fully into this matter and into Bland's influence at the court of Charles II through his father-in-law, Thomas Povey, in my doctoral dissertation, Harvard University, 1955, entitled "Bacon's Rebellion, 1676-1677." The extent of Bland's authority in relation to Governor Berkeley's was never clearly defined and the two were frequently at odds. See, for example, the Virginia agents' remarks to the Lord Treasurer, July 28, 1676, in William A. Shaw, ed., *Calendar of Treasury Books, 1676-1679*, Vol. V, Part I (London, 1911), p. 67.

27. Commissioners' "Narrative," in Andrews, *Narratives*, p. 116. The commissioners report the rumor that Bacon fled because of a plot against his life, "but being rais'd after Bacon was gone we suppose it false." According to the author of the Burwell MS., Bacon pretended that his wife was sick and got permission from the governor to visit her (Andrews, *Narratives*, p. 55). According to William Sherwood, Bacon left James-

town four days after his submission (Sherwood to Williamson, June 28, 1676, *Virginia Magazine*, 1 [1893], 171).

28. Ludwell to Williamson, June 28, 1676, *Virginia Magazine*, 1 (1893), 183.

29. Mathew's "Narrative," in Andrews, *Narratives*, p. 27.

30. *Ibid.*, p. 23. See earlier, p. 23.

31. See earlier, p. 53.

32. Hening, *Statutes*, II, 341-343.

33. See earlier, p. 41.

34. Berkeley to Coventry, Feb. 2, 1677, in *William and Mary Quarterly*, 3d ser., 14 (July 1957), 408.

35. McIlwaine, *Journals of the House of Burgesses, 1659/60-1693*, p. 66.

36. Allerton to Thomas Ludwell, Aug. 4, 1676, Longleat, LXXVII, fol. 160; assembly to agents, Longleat, LXXVII, foll. 140-141, with note by Philip Ludwell.

37. Philip Ludwell to Williamson, June 28, 1676, *Virginia Magazine*, 1 (1893), 183; William Sherwood to Williamson, June 28, 1676, *ibid.*, 171. Ludwell estimated Bacon's forces at 500; Sherwood at 400 foot and 120 horse.

38. Commissioners' "Narrative," in Andrews, *Narratives*, pp. 116-117; Mathew's "Narrative," *ibid.*, p. 29. Mathew wrote that he had a servant near enough to hear these words.

39. William Sherwood to Williamson, June 28, 1676, *Virginia Magazine*, 1 (1893), 171-172.

40. Philip Ludwell to Williamson, June 28, 1676, *Virginia Magazine*, 1 (1893), 184.

41. Mathew's "Narrative," in Andrews, *Narratives*, p. 29.

42. William Sherwood to Williamson, June 28, 1676, *Virginia Magazine*, 1 (1893), 172; see also Ludwell to Williamson, June 28, 1676, *ibid.*, p. 184, and commissioners' "Narrative," in Andrews, *Narratives*, p. 116. While Bacon was demanding a commission, his men were shouting "No levies" to protest against the taxes necessary to raise troops for the Indian war.

43. Mathew's "Narrative," in Andrews, *Narratives*, pp. 29-30. The comment on Bacon's "new coyned oaths" appears in Ludwell's letter to Williamson, June 28, 1676, *Virginia Magazine*, 1 (1893), 184.

44. See earlier, p. 55.

45. "Mr. Bacon's account of their troubles in Virginia by the Indians. June the 18th [28], 1676," in *William and Mary Quarterly*, 1st ser., 9 (1900), 8-9.

46. Hening, *Statutes*, II, 349.

47. Longleat, LXXVII, foll. 106-109; Hening, *Statutes*, II, 348-349; Sherwood to Williamson, June 28, 1676, *Virginia Magazine*, 1 (1893), 172.

48. Philip Ludwell to Williamson, June 28, 1676, *Virginia Magazine*, 1 (1893), 184.

49. Mathew's "Narrative," in Andrews, *Narratives*, p. 30.

50. Sherwood to Williamson, June 28, 1676, *Virginia Magazine*, 1 (1893), 173.

51. William Sherwood, "Virginias Deploured Condition," in Massachusetts Historical Society, *Collections*, 4th ser., Vol. IX (Boston, 1871), 171.

52. Hening, *Statutes*, II, 341-365. Hening printed the June laws from the Peyton Randolph MS. now in the Jefferson Collection, Rare Book Room, Library of Congress. Someone has inserted the heading "Bacon's Laws" at the tops of the pages of the June section of the manuscript. In the opinion of Miss E. Millicent Sowerby, in a letter to the writer of Jan. 5, 1956, the hand is not Hening's.

53. For the acts of the two assemblies, see Hening, *Statutes*, II, 341-406.

54. See later, pp. 121-122.

55. Governor Berkeley is frequently seen as an enemy of a broad franchise, yet it was under his administration, in October 1646, that Virginia's most liberal suffrage law was passed. Not only were freemen (including "covenanted servants") allowed to vote as they had previously, but freemen who failed to vote were to be fined one hundred pounds of tobacco (Hening, *Statutes*, I, 333-334). The first restriction of Virginia's suffrage came not during Berkeley's governorship, but during the period when Virginia was under Parliamentary control. It was in 1655 that the vote was, for the first time, restricted to housekeepers. The reaction was immediate, and the next year all freemen were again admitted to the suffrage, although by an act of March 1658 they were allowed to vote only provided they did not do so "in tumultous manner" (Hening, *Statutes*, I, 403, 412, 475; Philip Alexander Bruce, *Institutional History of Virginia in the Seventeenth Century* [New York, 1910], II, 409-411). Freemen continued to vote until 1670 when the assembly restricted the privilege once more to freeholders and housekeepers because of the tu-

multuous behavior of many propertyless men at elections, and to bring Virginia's laws into conformity with the laws of England (Hening, *Statutes*, II, 280). That the problem of disorder at the polls was a real one is suggested by the fact that three counties had protested the influx of criminals into the colony at this time as a danger to the security of the colony, and six months before the 1670 act was passed the Virginia council forbade the entry of criminals (Thomas Ludwell to Lord Arlington [?], Apr. 29, 1670, *Virginia Magazine*, 19 [1911], 355 and ed. note). In the light of these circumstances, as Bruce has remarked, "the General Assembly's action in restricting the suffrage appears to have been neither unwise nor unjust" (Bruce, *Institutional History*, II, 412-413). Since Berkeley allowed all freemen to vote in the election *to* the assembly of June 1676 (see earlier, pp. 49-50), there seems little reason to assume that he was a violent opponent of liberal voting laws.

56. Philip Ludwell to Williamson, June 28, 1676, *Virginia Magazine*, 1 (1893), 184-185; Ludwell's letter to Coventry of the same date, Longleat, LXXVII, fol. 137, describes the event in similar terms; for the date of the episode, see William Sherwood to Williamson, June 28, 1676, *Virginia Magazine*, 1 (1893), 172.

57. Sherwood to Williamson, June 28, 1676, *Virginia Magazine*, 1 (1893), 172.

58. Sherwood, "Virginias Deploured Condition," Mass. Hist. Soc., *Collections*, 4th ser., IX, 171. For an account of the authorship of this work, see "Essay on the Sources," pp. 171-172. Sherwood became one of Governor Berkeley's great enemies following the rebellion.

59. William Sherwood to Williamson, June 28, 1676, *Virginia Magazine*, 1 (1893), 174. Sherwood places the scene of the eight murders "att the heade of Chickahomony and in New Kent (from whence most of this rabble came)." Philip Ludwell, in the letter quoted next in the text, asserted that the eight were killed "at two severall places on York River, one within 23 miles of us, neer 40 miles within our Fronteir plantacons."

60. Philip Ludwell to Williamson, June 28, 1676, *Virginia Magazine*, 1 (1893), 185.

61. Hening, *Statutes*, II, 365.

62. Ludwell to Williamson, June 28, 1676, *Virginia Magazine*, 1 (1893), 185.

63. C. O. 5/1371, pp. 241-246; copy in Longleat, LXXVII, foll. 442-443. "Bacon's Letter," as this is called, is undated. It is placed in the June 1676 section of W. Noel Sainsbury, ed., *Calendar of State Papers, Colonial*

Series, America and West Indies, 1675-1676 (London, 1893), no. 941 (hereafter cited as *Cal. State Papers, Colonial*). Its peculiar style and tenses as well as its vaguely general character make it difficult to date, but it seems to have been written after the dissolution of the June Assembly because of its reference to the elections to, and failure of, the assembly, and because the agents which it speaks of sending to England seem to have been arranged for after the assembly had ended its work. See Giles Bland's letter discussed in next paragraph of text.

64. Giles Bland to Thomas Povey, July 8, 1676, C. O. 1/37, no. 27; copy in Egerton MS. 2395, fol. 555, in the British Museum, London; abstract in *Cal. State Papers, Colonial, 1675-1676*, no. 980.

65. "Mr. Bacon's account of their troubles in Virginia by the Indians. June the 18th [28], 1676," *William and Mary Quarterly*, 1st ser., 9 (1900), 9.

66. Longleat, LXXVII, foll. 224-225. The endorsement on the document indicates that it was received by Thomas Bacon, the father of the rebel, on Sept. 21, 1676. Words in brackets are missing in the Longleat copy and are supplied from the Public Record Office copy. See *Cal. State Papers, Colonial, 1675-1676*, no. 962.

67. John Fiske, *Old Virginia and her Neighbours* (Boston, 1897), II, 70.

68. Mathew's "Narrative," in Andrews, *Narratives*, p. 24.

69. *The Lawes of Virginia Now in Force* (London, 1662), Dedication. Thomas Ludwell, writing to "Right Honorable" [Lord Arlington?], Sept. 17, 1666, stated that Berkeley was the "sole author of the most substantial parts of . . . [the government] either for Lawes, or other Inferiour institutions. . . ." (*Virginia Magazine*, 21 [1913], 37).

70. Thomas Jefferson Wertenbaker, *Virginia under the Stuarts* (Princeton, 1914), p. 207.

71. The fact that King Charles ordered all the laws of the June Assembly declared null and void because of the force Bacon had used against it has encouraged the assumption that Bacon forced through the laws. The assumption is understandable but invalid.

72. Hening, *Statutes*, II, 391 n.

73. Armistead C. Gordon, "The Laws of Bacon's Assembly. An address delivered before the Beta of Virginia Chapter of the Phi Beta Kappa Society at the University of Virginia, June 17, 1914," University of Virginia, *Alumni Bulletin*, 3d ser., 8 (1914), 575-576. Gordon's belief that the

NOTES TO PAGE 69

reform laws were re-enacted gradually in later assemblies is an interesting example of how assumptions can condition facts. The laws which were later re-enacted were not done so "by degrees, and from year to year," but in a block in the assembly of February 1677.

Chapter 5

1. Berkeley to "Mr. Secretary" [Thomas Ludwell], July 1, 1676, in the Henry Coventry Papers at Longleat, estate of the Marquis of Bath (hereafter cited as Longleat), LXXVII, fol. 145. On Bland and Ingram see later, pp. 85-89, 92-93.

2. Colonel Thomas Ballard, one of the council, issued warrants on July 6, July 10, and August 25, 1676, for pressing men and provisions for Bacon's service (*Virginia Magazine*, 21 [1913], 235). According to the commissioners, Ballard assured the people that the commission was freely granted by Governor Berkeley (Commissioners' "Review, Breviary and Conclusion," in Colonial Office, Series 5, Vol. 1371, pp. 413-414, in Public Record Office, London [hereafter cited as C. O. 5/1371, etc.]).

3. George Jordan to Thomas Ludwell, July 19, 1676, Longleat, LXXVII, fol. 156.

4. "The History of Bacon's and Ingram's Rebellion," or Burwell MS., in Charles McLean Andrews, ed., *Narratives of the Insurrections* (New York, 1915), p. 56.

5. Commissioners' "Review, Breviary and Conclusion," C. O. 5/1371, p. 414.

6. William Sherwood, "Virginias Deploured Condition," in Massachusetts Historical Society, *Collections*, 4th ser., Vol. IX (Boston, 1871), 173. Sherwood's account of this period receives support in many particulars from a narrative published in Alexander Purdie and John Dixon's *Virginia Gazette*, Feb. 23, 1769, by a writer whose name we do not know because the beginning and end of his account appeared in issues of the *Virginia Gazette* not extant, but a writer, nevertheless, who seems to have been thoroughly acquainted with the facts of the rebellion and with the actions of the commissioners following the rebellion. Part of the narrative is quoted in Charles Campbell, ed., *The Bland Papers: Being a Selection from the Manuscripts of Colonel Theodorick Bland, Jr. of Prince George County, Virginia* (Petersburg, 1840-1843), Appendix A, I, 146-147 n.

7. Burwell MS., in Andrews, *Narratives*, pp. 56-57; commissioners' "Narrative," in Andrews, pp. 120-121.

8. Allerton to Thomas Ludwell, Aug. 4, 1676, Longleat, LXXVII, fol. 160.

9. Burwell MS., in Andrews, *Narratives*, p. 56.

10. Sherwood, "Virginias Deploured Condition," Mass. Hist. Soc., *Collections*, IX, 174.

11. Berkeley to Coventry, Feb. 2, 1677, in *William and Mary Quarterly*, 3d ser., 14 (July 1957), 409.

12. Frank Monaghan, *Heritage of Freedom: The History and Significance of the Basic Documents of American Liberty* (Princeton, 1947), p. 17. Bacon's "Declaration of the People" was displayed on the "Freedom Train" as one of the important documents in America's heritage of freedom.

13. Lyon G. Tyler, "Bacon's Rebellion," in *Tyler's Quarterly Historical and Genealogical Magazine*, 23 (1941), 23.

14. The *Calendar of State Papers, Colonial Series, America and West Indies, 1675-1676*, ed. W. Noel Sainsbury (London, 1893), no. 1010 (hereafter cited as *Cal. State Papers, Colonial*), lists the document under the date of August 3. Actually, however, the Public Record Office copy bears no date. Two facts show that the "Declaration" preceded the conference. First, the copy sent by William Sherwood to Secretary of State Sir Joseph Williamson along with his account of the period, "Virginias Deploured Condition," is endorsed by Sherwood in his own hand "Copie of Mr. Bacon's Declaration of the People, July 30th 1676" (George Chalmers Collection, Papers Relating to Virginia, I, fol. 76, in New York Public Library; see also "Essay on the Sources"). Second, the "Declaration" advises certain "pernicious councellors" such as Thomas Ballard to surrender themselves within four days. Ballard actually did surrender himself in time to sign certain other declarations of Bacon on August 3 and 4 (Longleat, LXXVII, foll. 165-166; C. O. 1/37, no. 42).

15. Bacon's "Declaration of the People" exists in numerous copies, many of them corrupt, owing to the ease with which copyists got lost in Bacon's interminable subordinate clauses. There are four copies of the "Declaration" in the Coventry Papers, Longleat, LXXVII, foll. 184, 199, 200-201, 202-203; two in the Bodleian Library, Oxford, Rawlinson MSS., Class A, Vol. 180, foll. 306-307, and Vol. 185, fol. 257; four in the British Museum, London, Egerton MS. 2395, foll. 547-550, Additional MS. 17018, fol. 110, and Additional MS. 4159, no. 393, fol. 177; one in the Public Record Office, London, C. O. 1/37, no. 41; one in the Huntington Library, San Marino, California, among the Blathwayt Papers, BL 85;

one among the Blathwayt Papers in Colonial Williamsburg, Williamsburg, Virginia; and one in the New York Public Library, George Chalmers Collection, Papers Relating to Virginia, I, fol. 76. The "Declaration" has been printed in Edward D. Neill, *Virginia Carolorum: The Colony under the Rule of Charles the First and Second, A.D. 1625-A.D. 1685* (Albany, 1886), pp. 361-365; Mass. Hist. Soc., *Collections*, 4th ser., IX, 184-187; *Virginia Magazine*, 4 (1896), 55-63; and Merrill Jensen, ed., *English Historical Documents: American Colonial Documents to 1776* (New York, 1955), no. 94A.

16. Bacon's "Declaration of the People." Bacon's use of the term "traitors to the people" against the loyalists reminds one of Stalin's use of the term "enemies of the people" against opponents he desired to liquidate. As Khrushchev pointed out in his famous denunciation of Stalin in the spring of 1956, the psychological impact of the accusation is so overwhelming that it obviates the need to prove the specific charges made against the accused.

17. *Virginia Magazine*, 1 (1893), 55-58. W. Noel Sainsbury, who paraphrases the document in *Cal. State Papers, Colonial, 1675-1676*, no. 1031, dates the manifesto "September 15? 1676" but the author of the Burwell MS., in Andrews, *Narratives*, pp. 58-59, is probably right in placing it right after Bacon's arrival at Middle Plantation. Bacon's assertion that the Indians cannot be prosecuted or "Complained against" is, of course, false. See, for example, earlier, pp. 19-20. Bacon always spoke as though he were championing the rights of the King and the King's "loyal subjects" against the treasonable activities of the governor. Similarly the Parliamentary forces in England in 1642 professed the aim of upholding the Protestant religion, the King's person, dignity and authority, the laws of the land, the peace of the kingdom, and the privileges of Parliament. Charles I, to mock his antagonists, professed the same ends in the same words. See Thomas May, *A Breviary of the History of the Parliament of England* [1650], in Francis Maseres, *Select Tracts relating to the Civil Wars in England* (London, 1815), Part I, pp. 49-50.

18. Sherwood, "Virginias Deploured Condition," Mass. Hist. Soc., *Collections*, 4th ser., IX, 174. Governor Berkeley, in his commission to Captain Thomas Larrimore, Aug. 30, 1676, in the Huntington Library, San Marino, California, HM 21810, gives the date of the seizure of Larrimore's ship as "on or about the 1st day of August."

19. Commissioners' "Narrative," in Andrews, *Narratives*, pp. 121-122.

20. Burwell MS., in Andrews, *Narratives*, pp. 60-63.

21. *Ibid.,* pp. 63-64.

22. C. O. 1/37, no. 42, fol. 130, printed in Robert Beverley, *The History and Present State of Virginia* [1705], ed. Louis B. Wright (Chapel Hill, 1947), pp. 82-84 (Bk. I, chap. iv, secs. 106-107).

23. C. O. 1/37, no. 42, fol. 131; also Longleat, LXXVII, fol. 165.

24. C. O. 1/37, no. 43, fol. 133; also Longleat, LXXVII, fol. 166.

25. Commissioners' "Narrative," in Andrews, *Narratives,* p. 122; also Longleat, LXXVII, fol. 437.

26. C. O. 1/37, no. 43; also Longleat, LXXVII, fol. 164. Apparently nothing ever came of this summons.

27. Account published in Purdie and Dixon's *Virginia Gazette,* Feb. 23, 1769.

28. Commissioners' "Narrative," in Andrews, *Narratives,* p. 123. Attempts were made by the frontiersmen at the time and by some later historians to implicate the Pamunkeys in the attacks on the colony but no evidence exists to sustain the belief, and there is much evidence positively against it. The commissioners, for example, in their "Narrative" cited above, state categorically that "it was well knowne to the whole country that the Queene of Pamunkey and her People had nere at any time betray'd or injuryed the English. But among the Vulgar it matters not whether they be Friends or Foes Soe they be Indians." I have dealt with the subject of the Pamunkeys' alleged guilt in my "Bacon's Rebellion, 1676-1677" (Harvard Univ. doct. diss., 1955), chaps. viii and x.

29. Commissioners' "Narrative," in Andrews, *Narratives,* pp. 126-127.

30. *Ibid.,* p. 125.

31. Commissioners' "Narrative," C. O. 5/1371, p. 393. This is a marginal comment of the commissioners which is not printed either in the Andrews, *Narratives,* or *Virginia Magazine,* 4 (1896), 119-154, copy of the document. It is, however, listed as one of the "Heads" of papers presented by the commissioners to the English government (*Cal. State Papers, Colonial, 1677-1680* [London, 1896], no. 433).

Chapter 6

1. Berkeley to Secretary of State Henry Coventry, Feb. 2, 1677, in the Henry Coventry Papers at Longleat, estate of the Marquis of Bath (hereafter cited as Longleat), LXXVII, fol. 353. The letter is printed in the *William and Mary Quarterly,* 3d ser., 14 (July 1957), 403-413.

2. Account of Bacon's Rebellion in Alexander Purdie and John Dixon's *Virginia Gazette*, Feb. 23, 1769. For a description of this document, see footnote 6 in previous chapter.

3. Berkeley to Coventry, Feb. 2, 1677, in *William and Mary Quarterly*, 3d ser., 14 (July 1957), 410.

4. *Ibid.*

5. *Virginia Gazette* (Purdie and Dixon), Feb. 23, 1769.

6. Berkeley to Coventry, Feb. 2, 1677, in *William and Mary Quarterly*, 3d ser., 14 (July 1957), 410.

7. *Virginia Gazette* (Purdie and Dixon), Feb. 23, 1769.

8. Berkeley to Coventry, Feb. 2, 1677, in *William and Mary Quarterly*, 3d ser., 14 (July 1957), 410. Carver's reputation for aggressiveness seems to have been deserved. In 1672 he stabbed to death a man sitting next to him at dinner, apparently without realizing what he was doing (*William and Mary Quarterly*, 1st ser., 3 [1895], 163).

9. Berkeley to Coventry, Feb. 2, 1677, in *William and Mary Quarterly*, 3d ser., 14 (July 1957), 410. T. M. [Thomas Mathew], "The Beginning Progress and Conclusion of Bacons Rebellion in Virginia in the Years 1675 and 1676," in Charles McLean Andrews, ed., *Narratives of the Insurrections, 1675-1690* (New York, 1915), pp. 36-37, is the authority for the belief that Carver was deceived by Berkeley's word, lured into a conference, and his ship captured. The commissioners, in their "Narrative," in Andrews, p. 128, tell the story without imputing bad faith to the governor. If Berkeley's letter is to be believed, there is no basis for the charge of bad faith. "The History of Bacon's and Ingram's Rebellion," or Burwell MS., in Andrews, p. 65, mentions the report given by some of Bacon's men that the expedition was betrayed by Captain Carver! No contemporary account accuses Berkeley of deceit, although such a rumor might logically have developed, and no doubt it did develop in time for Mathew, writing thirty years after the event, to include it in his narrative.

10. Berkeley's commission to Captain Thomas Larrimore, Aug. 30, 1676, in the Huntington Library, San Marino, California, HM 21810.

11. Berkeley to Coventry, Feb. 2, 1677, in *William and Mary Quarterly*, 3d ser., 14 (July 1957), 410-411. Other estimates state that Berkeley's armada consisted of four ships and thirteen sloops plus six hundred men (*Virginia Gazette* [Purdie and Dixon], Feb. 23, 1769; commissioners' "Narrative," in Andrews, *Narratives*, p. 129).

12. Commissioners' "Narrative," in Andrews, *Narratives*, p. 135.

13. Burwell MS., in *ibid.*, pp. 65-66.

14. Unfortunately we have no copy of this proclamation and so are unable to state the exact conditions under which Berkeley authorized condemnation of rebel prizes. The proclamation is mentioned, however, in Berkeley's commission to Captain Larrimore of August 30, 1676, empowering and commanding him to attack the rebels and promising him and his men that "whatsoever prizes you shall take, and shall be Condemned, you shall have, and receive your due shares and proportions thereof," according to the proclamation of August 8 (Huntington Library, San Marino, California, HM 21810). It is probable that the land troops were also authorized to share captured rebel property.

15. Commissioners' "Review, Breviary and Conclusion," in Colonial Office, Series 5, Vol. 1371, p. 417, in the Public Record Office, London (hereafter cited as C. O. 5/1371, etc.).

16. Berkeley to Coventry, Feb. 2, 1677, in *William and Mary Quarterly*, 3d ser., 14 (July 1957), 411. According to the Burwell MS., in Andrews, *Narratives*, p. 66, Bacon had 700 or 800 men in Jamestown. According to Mrs. An. Cotton, "An Account of our late Troubles in Virginia," in Peter Force, ed., *Tracts and Other Papers Relating Principally to the Origin, Settlement, and Progress of the Colonies in North America* (Washington, 1836-1846), I, no. 9, 7, Bacon had 900 men in Jamestown.

17. Mrs. An. Cotton, "An Account of our late Troubles in Virginia," in Force, *Tracts*, I, no. 9, 7.

18. Berkeley to Coventry, Feb. 2, 1677, in *William and Mary Quarterly*, 3d ser., 14 (July 1957), 411. The author of the Burwell MS., in Andrews, *Narratives*, p. 65, reported that "(as it is saide)" Berkeley was supposed to have 1,000 men aboard five ships and ten sloops. Mrs. An. Cotton in her "Account" in Force, *Tracts*, I, no. 9, 7, also reported Berkeley's forces to number 1,000. The commissioners, in their "Narrative," in Andrews, *Narratives*, p. 130, similarly reported 1,000 men as the "Intelligence coming to Bacon" at the time concerning the size of Berkeley's forces.

19. Berkeley to Coventry, Feb. 2, 1677, in *William and Mary Quarterly*, 3d ser., 14 (July 1957), 411. Berkeley's proclamation was similar to that being prepared in London at the time. The King's proclamation, however, arrived after the rebellion was over, and served merely to complicate Berkeley's post-rebellion activities. See later, pp. 107-111.

20. Burwell MS., in Andrews, *Narratives*, pp. 66-67.

21. *Ibid.*, p. 67.

22. Berkeley to Gardner, Sept. 9, 1676, C. O. 5/1308, fol. 65.

23. In the George Chalmers Collection, Papers Relating to Virginia, I, fol. 49, in the New York Public Library, are Chalmers' notes concerning a letter from Virginia of Sept. 19, 1676, which reported that "Bacon's followers having deserted him he had proclaimed liberty to the Servants and Slaves which chiefly formed his army when he burnt James Towne." There were at least eighty Negroes fighting with Bacon at the end of the war (see later, p. 88). The assembly of February 1677 reported that Bacon recruited followers by promising freedom to servants of loyalists (see later, p. 164). The poet, Andrew Marvell, on the basis of a ship captain's report, wrote that two days after Berkeley had captured Jamestown, "Bacon came before it having first proclam'd liberty to all Servants and Negros" (Marvell to Sir Henry Thompson, Nov. 14, 1676, Huntington Library, San Marino, California, HM 21813).

24. Berkeley gives this figure in his Feb. 2, 1677, letter to Secretary Coventry, *William and Mary Quarterly*, 3d ser., 14 (July 1957), 411. The commissioners, in their "Narrative," in Andrews, *Narratives*, pp. 129-130, wrote that at the time Berkeley took Jamestown, Bacon had but "136 tyr'd men" in his camp, but that he increased his numbers to 300 before arriving at Jamestown. The author of the Burwell MS., in Andrews, p. 68, puts Bacon's forces at this time at 150, as does Mrs. An. Cotton in her "Account" in Force, *Tracts*, I, no. 9, 8. The fact that the Burwell MS. and Mrs. Cotton agree should not be taken as added proof that their figures for the opposed forces are correct, for the Burwell MS. was undoubtedly written by John Cotton, the husband of An. Cotton. See "Essay on the Sources," p. 174. The *Virginia Gazette* (Purdie and Dixon) gives Bacon 800 men at this time.

25. Berkeley to Coventry, Feb. 2, 1677, in *William and Mary Quarterly*, 3d ser., 14 (July 1957), 411.

26. *Virginia Gazette* (Purdie and Dixon), Feb. 23, 1769.

27. Commissioners' "Narrative," in Andrews, *Narratives*, p. 131.

28. *Virginia Gazette* (Purdie and Dixon), Feb. 23, 1769.

29. *Ibid.*

30. Mrs. An. Cotton, "Account," in Force, *Tracts*, I, no. 9, 8. Note that the wives of Colonel Bray and Colonel Ballard were seized at this time. Their husbands had shortly before signed some of Bacon's orders at the Middle Plantation conference. Bacon's action indicates that they had almost immediately returned to their loyalty.

31. Bacon's letter of Sept. 17, 1676, intercepted by the loyalists, in commissioners' "Narrative," in Andrews, *Narratives*, pp. 133-134; copy in Longleat, LXXVII, fol. 216.

32. Commissioners' "Narrative," in Andrews, *Narratives*, p. 130.

33. *Virginia Gazette* (Purdie and Dixon), Feb. 23, 1769.

34. Burwell MS., in Andrews, *Narratives*, p. 70. A description of the fight is also given by Bacon in the intercepted letter mentioned in footnote 31 above. The date of the fight is given in the commissioners' "Review, Breviary and Conclusion," C. O. 5/1371, p. 417.

35. *Virginia Gazette* (Purdie and Dixon), Feb. 23, 1769.

36. *Ibid.*

37. Berkeley to Coventry, Feb. 2, 1677, in *William and Mary Quarterly*, 3d ser., 14 (July 1957), 411-412.

38. Berkeley to Coventry, Feb. 2, 1677, *ibid.*, p. 412. The account in the *Virginia Gazette* (Purdie and Dixon), Feb. 23, 1769, states that most of Berkeley's troops one night crowded on board the small vessels lying at the town, deserting the governor, who "thus left alone, determined to sell his life at as dear a rate as possible, but his friends persuaded him to accompany them, which after some time he consented to."

39. Commissioners' "Review, Breviary and Conclusion," C. O. 5/1371, p. 417. See also letter of Philip Lanyon to Secretary of State Sir Joseph Williamson, Jan. 21, 1677, giving an account of the burning of Jamestown as reported by the captain of a merchantman which arrived in James River the day after the conflagration, in F. H. Blackburne Daniell, ed., *Calendar of State Papers, Domestic Series, March 1st, 1676, to February 28th, 1677* (London, 1909), p. 517.

40. *Virginia Gazette* (Purdie and Dixon), Feb. 23, 1769.

41. Burwell MS., in Andrews, *Narratives*, pp. 72-73.

42. See footnote 52.

43. Bacon's oath is inserted in the commissioners' "Narrative," in Andrews, *Narratives*, pp. 136-137.

44. Commissioners' "Narrative," in *ibid.*, p. 136.

45. Burwell MS., in *ibid.*, p. 74.

46. Bacon's "Appeal to the People of Accomac," C. O. 5/1371, pp. 254-263; copy in Longleat, LXXVII, fol. 444. The "Appeal" is dated by W. Noel Sainsbury in the *Calendar of State Papers, Colonial Series, America and West Indies, 1675-1676* (London, 1893) (hereafter *Cal.*

State Papers, Colonial), no. 969, as "? July, 1676," but internal evidence and the Burwell MS. suggest it was written in September 1676.

47. Hill's defense against Charles City County grievances, C. O. 1/40, no. 73, in *Virginia Magazine*, 3 (1896), 250-251.

48. Commissioners' "Narrative," in Andrews, *Narratives,* p. 138.

49. For the date of Bacon's death, see commissioners' "Review, Breviary and Conclusion," C. O. 5/1371, p. 418. The Burwell MS., as printed in Force, *Tracts,* I, no. 11, 28, and in the Massachusetts Historical Society, *Collections,* 2d ser., Vol. I (Boston, 1814), 57, gives October 1 as the date of his death in a marginal heading. For the manner of his death, see commissioners' "Narrative," in Andrews, *Narratives,* p. 139. The account in the *Virginia Gazette* (Purdie and Dixon), Feb. 23, 1769, remarks that in addition to the two diseases cited Bacon fell sick of dysentery while lying exposed in the trenches outside Jamestown.

50. Berkeley to Coventry, Feb. 2, 1677, in *William and Mary Quarterly,* 3d ser., 14 (July 1957), 412.

51. Burwell MS., in Andrews, *Narratives,* pp. 77-78.

52. Journal of the ship *Young Prince,* Robert Morris commanding, from Sept. 19, 1676, to Jan. 29, 1677, C. O. 1/37, no. 52; summary in *Cal. State Papers, Colonial, 1675-1676,* no. 1035.

53. Berkeley's warrant to Captain Larrimore, Nov. 9, 1676, Huntington Library, San Marino, California, HM 21812.

54. Burwell MS., in Andrews, *Narratives,* p. 80.

55. Testimony of Berkeley in favor of Beverley, Nov. 13, 1676, in William W. Hening, *The Statutes at Large ... A Collection of All the Laws of Virginia* (Richmond, [etc.], 1819-1823), III, 567. The date is confirmed by an entry in the Journal of the *Young Prince,* Robert Morris commanding, C. O. 1/37, no. 52, fol. 184.

56. Burwell MS., in Andrews, *Narratives,* p. 80.

57. George Bancroft seems to have originated Hansford's title. In his *History of the United States,* II (Boston, 1856), 230, Bancroft wrote that "Hansford perished, the first native of America on the gallows, a martyr to the right of the people to govern themselves." He omitted the sentence, however, in his last revised edition, I (New York, 1883), 467. Mrs. Annie Tucker Tyler wrote an account of "Thomas Hansford, the First Native Martyr to American Liberty," Virginia Historical Society, *Collections,* new ser., Vol. XI (Richmond, 1892), 191-202. Thomas Jefferson Wertenbaker, *Torchbearer of the Revolution: The*

Story of Bacon's Rebellion and Its Leader (Princeton, 1940), p. 188, also refers to Hansford as a "martyr to the cause of American freedom." This man, so "keenly sensitive to honor" as Bancroft described him, was fined in the General Court on March 21, 1676, for smuggling tobacco out of Virginia on his own vessel (H. R. McIlwaine, *Minutes of the Council and General Court of Colonial Virginia, 1622-1623, 1670-1676* [Richmond, 1924], p. 449).

58. Commissioners' "Exact Repertory of the General and Personal Grievances Presented to us," C. O. 5/1371, p. 346.

59. Burwell MS., in Andrews, *Narratives*, pp. 84-85. The commissioners, following the rebellion, ordered a stay on the seized goods of Howard and presented his grievances to the King (commissioners' "Exact Repertory of the General and Personal Grievances Presented to us," C. O. 5/1371, p. 346). Howard seems to have been well enough off, despite the plundering, to go to London and petition the King directly for restitution of the £500 he claimed to have lost (petition of William Howard to the King, Nov. 23, 1677, *Cal. State Papers, Colonial, 1677-1680*, no. 489). Beverley sent in "4 scandalous petitions," as Colonel Francis Moryson, one of the commissioners, put it, in answer to the complaints of Howard's clerks and secretaries, but they do not survive in the English archives despite Moryson's assertion that the commissioners handed them in (Moryson to Thomas Ludwell, Nov. 2, 1677, in MS. no. 6, "Virginia. Miscellaneous Records, 1606-1692" ["The Bland Manuscript"], Jefferson Collection, Library of Congress, p. 335, printed in John Daly Burk, *The History of Virginia* [Petersburg, 1804-1805], II, 268, with the date Nov. 28, 1677). Another complaint by Beverley against the commissioners also failed to survive (commissioners' "Exact Repertory of the General and Personal Grievances Presented to us," C. O. 5/1371, p. 351). The Lords of Trade and Plantations asked Sir John Berry whether he had possession of papers concerning Beverley and Colonel Edward Hill, but in a letter to William Blathwayt, Secretary to the Lords, January 17, 1682, Berry reported that all the Virginia papers were in the custody of Colonel Moryson who had, he thought, delivered them to the Privy Council before his death (*Virginia Magazine*, 26 [1918], 136).

60. Captain Thomas Grantham's "Accompt of my Transactions," Longleat, LXXVII, fol. 301. There is a reference to the broken truce agreement in an excerpt from a letter probably from Captain Grantham to Gregory Walklett, one of the leading rebels, in *Cal. State Papers, Colonial, 1677-1680*, no. 20.

61. Grantham's "Accompt of my Transactions," Longleat, LXXVII, fol. 301.

62. *Ibid.* The author of the Burwell MS. recounts this tale of deception of the servants and slaves in almost identical terms, claiming to have heard the story from Grantham himself (Andrews, *Narratives*, pp. 94-95).

63. Burwell MS., in Andrews, *Narratives*, pp. 92-93. The account in the *Virginia Gazette* (Purdie and Dixon), Feb. 23, 1769, also states that "Walkelate [another rebel leader] knew his case to be desperate, and cheerfully accepted the governor's offer."

64. Hening, *Statutes*, II, 545-546; Burwell MS., in Andrews, *Narratives*, p. 97.

65. Berkeley's list of those executed during the rebellion, in Force, *Tracts*, I, no. 10, 3-4; Hening, *Statutes*, II, 545-546.

66. Berkeley's list of those executed during the rebellion, in Force, *Tracts*, I, no. 10, 4.

67. Journal of the ship *Young Prince*, Robert Morris commanding, entry for Jan. 14, 1677, C. O. 1/37, no. 52, fol. 185. Bacon's plantation had been stripped and abandoned by its rebel garrison under Thomas Whaley shortly after the surrender of West Point.

68. Burwell MS., in Andrews, *Narratives*, pp. 96-98.

69. Berkeley to Beverley, Jan. 18, 1677, in Hening, *Statutes*, III, 569.

70. Burwell MS., in Andrews, *Narratives*, p. 98; Hening, *Statutes*, II, 546. For an account of the execution and its aftermath, see Wilcomb E. Washburn, "The Humble Petition of Sarah Drummond," *William and Mary Quarterly*, 3d ser., 13 (July 1956), 354-375.

71. Berkeley to Beverley, Jan. 21, 1677, in Hening, *Statutes*, III, 569; Berkeley's list of those executed during the rebellion, in Force, *Tracts*, I, no. 10, 4.

72. Commissioners' "Review, Breviary and Conclusion," C. O. 5/1371, p. 419.

73. Berkeley to Colonel Francis Moryson and Sir John Berry, Feb. 9, 1677, Longleat, LXXVII, fol. 386; copy in C. O. 5/1371, pp. 62-64. See later, p. 102.

74. Hening, *Statutes*, II, 547-548.

Chapter 7

1. For a detailed account of the reception of the news of Bacon's Rebellion in England, see Washburn, "Bacon's Rebellion, 1676-1677" (Harvard University doct. diss., 1955), chap. vii. The quotation from Giles Bland is from his letter to Secretary of State Sir Joseph Williamson, April 28, 1676, *Virginia Magazine*, 20 (1912), 352-357.

2. Berkeley to Secretary of State Henry Coventry, July 1, 1676, in the Henry Coventry Papers at Longleat, estate of the Marquis of Bath (hereafter cited as Longleat), LXXVII, fol. 145.

3. Undated petition of Sir William Berkeley to the King, in Colonial Office, Series 1, Vol. 40, no. 110, in Public Record Office, London (hereafter cited as C. O. 1/40, etc.). There is a full summary of the petition in W. Noel Sainsbury and J. W. Fortescue, eds., *Calendar of State Papers, Colonial Series, America and West Indies, 1677-1680* (London, 1896), no. 304 (hereafter cited as *Cal. State Papers, Colonial*). See also Giles Bland to Williamson, April 28, 1676, *Virginia Magazine*, 20 (1912), 353.

4. William A. Shaw, ed., *Calendar of Treasury Books, 1676-1679*, Vol. V, Part II (London, 1911), Appendix I, especially prefatory note, p. 1316.

5. Courtin to Louis XIV, Nov. 9 and 30, 1676, in Correspondance Politique, Angleterre, 120, foll. 174, 244, in Foreign Office Archives, Paris; Louis XIV to Courtin, Dec. 8, 1676, in *ibid.*, 120 B, fol. 243 (microfilmed by Colonial Records Project of Virginia 350th Anniversary Celebration Corporation). The financial "squeeze" caused by Bacon's Rebellion may well have been the decisive factor in forcing the King to recall Parliament in the spring of 1677. William Harbord, in a letter to the Earl of Essex, Dec. 17, 1676, wrote that "ill news from *Virginia and New England* doth not only *alarm us* but extreamly *abate* the *customs* so that notwithstanding *all the shifts Treasurer can make this Parliament or another must sitt....*" (Clement Edwards Pike, ed., *Selections from the Correspondence of Arthur Capel, Earl of Essex, 1675-1677* [Camden Society, 3d ser., Vol. XXIV], [London, 1913], p. 87.)

6. The King's commission to Herbert Jeffreys, Sir John Berry, and Francis Moryson, Oct. 3, 1676, C. O. 5/1371, pp. 83-85.

7. The King's instructions to Jeffreys, Berry, and Moryson, Nov. 11, 1676, C. O. 5/1355, pp. 117-120; also in C. O. 389/6, pp. 161-165; summary in *Cal. State Papers, Colonial, 1675-1676*, no. 1130. The phrase "Lieutenant Governor" in the King's instructions may be wondered at. As Leonard W. Labaree, *Royal Government in America: A Study of the British*

Colonial System before 1783 (New Haven, 1930), p. 19, points out, this phrase was sometimes used in the King's commissions to his governors. However, its use in the commissioners' instructions was meant to cover any eventuality, whether it was the death of Berkeley or his continuance in office. For a detailed discussion of the meaning of the phrase, see Washburn, "Bacon's Rebellion, 1676-1677" (Harvard University doct. diss., 1955), chap. x, pp. 378-381.

8. The number of troops to be sent was constantly revised upward during the summer and fall of 1676 until it reached 1,130. See the Admiralty Journal, Oct. 29, 1676, in J. R. Tanner, ed., *A Descriptive Catalogue of the Naval Manuscripts in the Pepysian Library at Magdalene College, Cambridge*, IV [Publications of the Navy Records Society, LVII] (London, 1923), 366.

9. Berry and Moryson to Coventry, Nov. 19, 1676, Longleat, V, fol. 91; Hugh Salesbury to Secretary of State Sir Joseph Williamson, Nov. 21, 1676, in F. H. Blackburne Daniell, ed., *Calendar of State Papers, Domestic Series, March 1st, 1676, to February 28th, 1677* (London, 1909), p. 426 (hereafter cited as *Cal. State Papers, Domestic*); various letters in Tanner, *Descriptive Catalogue*, III [Publications of the Navy Records Society, XXXVI] (London, 1909), nos. 3450, 3455, 3553. Charles McLean Andrews, ed., *Narratives of the Insurrections, 1675-1690* (New York, 1915), p. 102, states that the *Bristol* left Nov. 24. It is believed, however, on the basis of the references given in this note, that the true date was Nov. 19.

10. Various letters of Samuel Pepys in Tanner, *Descriptive Catalogue*, III, nos. 3491, 3492, 3493, 3500, 3501, 3503, 3506, 3513, 3526, 3528, 3530, 3553, and letters of Pepys in Helen Truesdell Heath, ed., *The Letters of Samuel Pepys and His Family Circle* (Oxford, 1955), nos. 47, 48, 49, 50.

11. See earlier, p. 48. For Berkeley's deafness, see Berry and Moryson to Berkeley, Feb. 8, 1677, Longleat, LXXVII, fol. 379.

12. Moryson to Coventry, Sept. 28, 1676, Longleat, LXXVII, fol. 54. For commissioners' salary see Coventry to Lord High Treasurer, Sept. 29, 1676, in *Cal. State Papers, Colonial, 1675-1676*, no. 1043.

13. See Jeffreys' letters cited in the next chapter. Jeffreys' correspondence will be published in a documentary collection on Bacon's Rebellion which I am editing for the Virginia Historical Society. For Jeffreys' political connections see Andrews, *Narratives*, pp. 101-102.

14. Sir John Berry had conducted an investigation of the Newfound-

land colony in the fall of 1675 (*Cal. State Papers, Colonial 1675-1676*, nos. 628, 665, 666, 731, 744, 769, 870, 1015).

15. Berry to Berkeley, Jan. 29, 1677, C. O. 5/1371, pp. 17-19. My italics.

16. Commissioners' commission, Oct. 3, 1676, C. O. 5/1355, pp. 83-85, copy in McDonald Transcripts, V, 58-61, in Virginia State Library, Richmond; commissioners' instructions, Nov. 11, 1676, C. O. 5/1355, pp. 117-120, copies in C. O. 389/6, pp. 161-165, and C. O. 5/1371, pp. 365-367.

17. Berry to Berkeley, Jan. 29, 1677, C. O. 5/1371, p. 19.

18. Commissioners' "Particular Account how wee...have observed and Comply'd with our Instructions," C. O. 5/1371, p. 365.

19. Commissioners' "True and Faithful Account in what Condition we found Your Majesty's Colony," C. O. 5/1371, p. 423, printed in John Daly Burk, *The History of Virginia* (Petersburg, 1804-1805), II, 254. For further comment on the pardon of Oct. 27, 1676, see later, pp. 107-110, and Wilcomb E. Washburn, "The Humble Petition of Sarah Drummond," *William and Mary Quarterly*, 3d ser., 13 (July 1956), 372-374.

20. Moryson and Berry to Williamson, Feb. 2, 1677, C. O. 5/1371, pp. 29-30; copy at Longleat, LXXVII, foll. 364-365. The grievance of the great salaries was not found by the commissioners in Virginia, but brought by them from England. It had originally been reported by Giles Bland in a letter to Secretary Williamson, April 28, 1676, printed in the *Virginia Magazine*, 20 (1912), 352-357, and had had an influence on the policy adopted by the English government to deal with the rebellion. See chap. vii of my 1955 Harvard doctoral dissertation entitled "Bacon's Rebellion, 1676-1677."

21. Moryson and Berry to Williamson, Feb. 2, 1677, C. O. 5/1371, pp. 29-30; copy at Longleat, LXXVII, foll. 364-365.

22. Moryson and Berry to Thomas Watkins, Feb. 2, 1677, Longleat, LXXVII, fol. 349. Similar condemnation of Berkeley's stand on the proclamation is expressed in Berry and Moryson to Sir John Werden, secretary to the Duke of York, Feb. 2, 1677, C. O. 5/1371, pp. 34-35.

23. C. O. 5/1371, pp. 23-24; copy in Longleat, LXXVII, foll. 370-371. There is some confusion as to the exact date and manner in which these "heads" were presented. They were probably sent to Berkeley on February 3 as the written outline of what the commissioners discussed with him on board the *Bristol* February 1 and 2.

24. C. O. 5/1371, pp. 23-24; copy in Longleat, LXXVII, foll. 370-371. My italics. There are some minor variations in the two copies. For

example, in the Longleat copy the words "and just" are omitted in the phrase "a good and just peace." This quotation shifts between the copies to obtain the clearest possible sense and most logical syntax.

25. C. O. 5/1371, p. 423.

26. Commissioners' instructions, C. O. 5/1355, pp. 117-120.

27. Lady Berkeley to her cousin, the wife of Sir Abstrupus Danby, June 27, 1678, in Cunliffe-Lister Muniments, Bundle 69, Section 11, in the Bradford Art Gallery and Museum, Bradford, England; microfilm copies in the Virginia Historical Society, Richmond.

28. Moryson and Berry to Coventry, Feb. 2, 1677, Longleat, LXXVII, foll. 364-365; copy in C. O. 5/1371, pp. 27-33. Berkeley to Moryson and Berry, Feb. 9, 1677, Longleat, LXXVII, fol. 386; copy in C. O. 5/1371, pp. 62-64. Most of the men must have lived in outbuildings or camped in the yard, for the main house was of only moderate proportions. See Louis R. Caywood, *Excavations at Green Spring Plantation* (Yorktown: Colonial National Historical Park, 1955), his "Green Spring Plantation," *Virginia Magazine*, 65 (Jan. 1957), 67-83, and Lyon G. Tyler, *The Cradle of the Republic: Jamestown and James River* (Richmond, 1900), p. 108. Each county sent two burgesses to the assembly and Jamestown normally sent one.

29. Berkeley to Moryson and Berry, Feb. 6, 1677. This letter is in one of the three large books of their proceedings kept by Samuel Wiseman, the clerk of the commissioners. Wiseman, petitioning the Lords of Trade and Plantations in January 1678 for more money, mentions the fact of keeping three such books (*Cal. State Papers, Colonial, 1677-1680*, no. 562). This particular volume is located in the Pepysian Library, Magdalene College, Cambridge, and is unpaged. It is in general a duplicate of much of the material in C. O. 5/1371 in the Public Record Office, London. Both are entry books in which the documents were copied. But this one letter of February 6 seems to exist only in the Pepysian copy. It is probable that the third book originally kept by Wiseman is in the Manuscripts Division of the Library of Congress. See "Essay on the Sources," p. 170. Colonel Thomas Swann was the first signer of the orders issued by Bacon at his Middle Plantation conference in August 1676 (see earlier, p. 74). Thomas High accused Swann of sitting on the council of war for burning Jamestown and of other traitorous actions (depositions from Surry County records, Nov. 15, 1677, in *William and Mary Quarterly*, 1st ser., 9 [1902], 80-81). Swann's son, Captain Samuel

Swann, married the daughter of William Drummond, one of the leaders of the rebellion, in 1673 (*Virginia Magazine*, 28 [1920], 30-31).

30. Longleat, LXXVII, fol. 376; copy in C. O. 5/1371, pp. 39-44.

31. Longleat, LXXVII, fol. 378; copy in C. O. 5/1371, pp. 55-60.

32. William Waller Hening, *The Statutes at Large ... A Collection of All the Laws of Virginia* (Richmond [etc.], 1819-1823), I, 230-235. Berkeley's denunciation, in the assembly of March 1651, of the Parliamentary act of Oct. 3, 1650, prohibiting Virginians from trading with foreign nations except as the Parliamentary government should allow, contains one of the most bitter attacks on the London merchants ever delivered. Following his speech, the assembly voted unanimously to reject the act as illegal and to continue in allegiance to Charles II. See later, p. 157, and H. R. McIlwaine, ed., *Journals of the House of Burgesses of Virginia, 1619-1658/59* (Richmond, 1914), pp. 75-78.

33. Sir William Berkeley, *A Discourse and View of Virginia* (London, 1663), reprinted Norwalk, Conn., 1914, pp. 6-7.

34. Andrews, *Narratives*, pp. 101-102, discusses Jeffreys. Berry's acquaintance with Bland's relations is mentioned in Berry's letter of Feb. 2, 1677, to Sir John Werden, secretary to the Duke of York (C. O. 5/1371, pp. 34-35), as reported in a contemporary newsletter, *More News from Virginia, Being A True and Full Relation of all Occurrences in that Countrey, since the Death of Nath. Bacon* (London, 1677), reprinted Charlottesville, Va., 1943 (ed. Thomas Perkins Abernethy), and 1957 (ed. Harry Finestone). The merchants' success in placing their own candidates in colonial governorships is discussed by Charles McLean Andrews, *British Committees, Commissions, and Councils of Trade and Plantations, 1622-1675* (Baltimore, 1908), pp. 55, 61-65.

35. Berkeley to Moryson and Berry, Feb. 9, 1677, Longleat, LXXVII, fol. 386; copy in C. O. 5/1371, pp. 62-64.

36. Moryson to Berkeley, Feb. 11, 1677, Longleat, LXXVII, fol. 395; copy in C. O. 5/1371, pp. 65-67.

37. Berkeley to Coventry, Feb. 9, 1677, Longleat, LXXVII, fol. 382. Berkeley may be attributing the commissioners' policy to the Bland family and to its close associate, Thomas Povey, but this is by no means certain. See chap. vii of my 1955 Harvard doctoral dissertation entitled "Bacon's Rebellion, 1676-1677."

38. Berkeley to Coventry, a second letter dated Feb. 9, 1677, Longleat, LXXVII, fol. 384.

39. Florence M. Greir Evans (Mrs. C. S. S. Higham), *The Principal Secretary of State: A Survey of the Office from 1558 to 1680* (Manchester, England, 1923), pp. 139-140; Sir William Anson, *The Law and Custom of the Constitution*, Vol. II: *The Crown* (3d ed.; Oxford, 1907), Part I, 78.

40. Coventry's correspondence at this period is filled with references to his illnesses. See later, footnote 7 of chap. ix.

41. Bishop Gilbert Burnet, *History of His Own Time* (Oxford, 1823), I, 531-532.

42. DeJarnette Transcripts, II, no. 104, in Virginia State Library, Richmond; also in C. O. 5/1371, pp. 276-286.

43. Hening, *Statutes*, II, 423-424.

44. *Ibid.*, pp. 424-426, dated incorrectly by Hening Nov. 13, 1676. My italics.

45. W. L. Grant and James Munro, eds., *Acts of the Privy Council of England, Colonial Series*, Vol. I, *A.D. 1613-1680* (Hereford, England, 1908), nos. 1094, 1095, 1097; Washburn, "Bacon's Rebellion" (Harvard University doct. diss., 1955), chap. vii.

46. Berkeley's proclamation of Feb. 10, 1677, DeJarnette Transcripts, II, no. 104, in Virginia State Library, Richmond. The commissioners did not try Mrs. Grindon but instead presented to the King her complaint against confiscation of her goods by the Virginia government (commissioners' "Exact Repertory of the General and Personal Grievances Presented to us," C. O. 5/1371, p. 339). Berkeley's proclamation, despite the attacks made against it by the commissioners, contains all the proper exceptions that the Lords of Trade and the King and his Privy Council were forced to make when they finally realized some of the injustices their blanket printed pardon had inadvertently caused. See later, pp. 147-148.

47. Berry and Moryson to Thomas Watkins, Feb. 10, 1677, Longleat, LXXVII, fol. 389.

48. Isaac Allerton to Thomas Ludwell, Aug. 4, 1676, Longleat, LXXVII, fol. 160.

49. After the rebellion Berkeley relieved some justices for giving Bacon's oath and pardoned others. See, for example, the petition of the York County justices, March 23, 1677, and Berkeley's reply, in York County MS. volume, "Deeds, Orders, Wills, etc., No. 6, 1677 to 1684," p. 5.

50. Commissioners' "True and Faithful Account in what Condition wee found Your Majesty's Colony," in Burk, *History of Virginia*, II, 254. The commissioners expressed similar sentiments in a March 27, 1677, letter to Thomas Watkins (C. O. 1/39, no. 52) and in their comments on the grievances of Lancaster and Nansemond counties (C. O. 5/1371, pp. 314, 329). The commissioners showed their inconsistency and partiality by aiding William Sherwood to sue the rebels after he had switched his support from Berkeley to the commissioners. See Washburn, "Bacon's Rebellion" (Harvard University doct. diss., 1955), chap. x. The dispute over penalizing takers of Bacon's oath recalls the dispute over whether American prisoners in Korea who collaborated with the Chinese Communists after being "brainwashed" should be punished.

51. Moryson and Berry to Thomas Watkins, Feb. 10, 1677, Longleat, LXXVII, fol. 389. Note the ambiguity of the commissioners' phraseology. Does "before his Majesty's acts of grace" mean before the pardons were printed in England on October 27, 1676, before they were handed to Governor Berkeley on February 1, 1677, or before they were published (along with Berkeley's qualifying proclamation) on February 10, 1677? Or does it mean that the commissioners themselves were not sure which date was proper and wished to conceal their uncertainty?

52. *Ibid.*, with slight alterations taken from the copy of the letter in Longleat, LXXVII, fol. 391.

53. Longleat, LXXVII, fol. 426; copy in C. O. 5/1371, pp. 68-70. Berkeley was sent to England by the assembly of June 1644 to implore the King's assistance to the colony following the great Indian massacre of April of that year (McIlwaine, *Journals of the House of Burgesses of Virginia, 1619-1658/59*, p. 71). He gave more assistance to the King, who was having his own troubles, than he received, however. On June 7, 1645, he arrived back in the colony (H. R. McIlwaine, ed., *Minutes of the Council and General Court of Colonial Virginia, 1622-1632, 1670-1676, with notes and excerpts from original Council and General Court Records, into 1683, now lost* [Richmond, 1924], p. 503). An example of the confiscation policy of Sir Richard Grenville, "Generall of his Majesties Forces in the Weste of Cornwall," is revealed in a warrant dated August 5, 1644, from Truro, to Captain Edward Roscarrocke, to seize six horses belonging to the Earl of Bath on the grounds that he has "Fortie or Fiftie able horses and men whoe live about thes partes and Neyther himselfe nor anie of them have Appeared att the Posse in their persons nether himselfe given us anie advises or incouragementes by Letters or otherwise but as I am credibly informed hath obtayned his protection from the Earle

of Essex...." This document is in a bundle of "Warrants, petitions, Parliamentary reports" among the papers of the Barons of Sackville, Knole Park, microfilmed by the British Manuscripts Project of the American Council of Learned Societies, and deposited in the Microfilm Reading Room of the Library of Congress under the heading Camb 673/2. For a discussion of Grenville's seizure of Lord Robartes' (or Roberts) house, and conflict with Sir John Berkeley, William's brother, over the confiscation of other estates, see Edward, Earl of Clarendon, *The History of the Rebellion and Civil Wars in England Begun in the Year 1641*, ed. W. Dunn Macray (Oxford, 1888), IV, 29-33, 64-68 (Bk. IX, secs. 24-27, 61-64).

54. Burk, *History of Virginia*, II, 255-256.

55. Commissioners to Berkeley, March 6, 1677, copy "For my Lord Treasurers Inspection," Longleat, LXXVIII, fol. 1. Alexander Walker, complaining against Berkeley's seizure of twenty-three hogsheads of tobacco which the governor insisted was his due, based his appeal to the commissioners on this statute (copies of Walker's letters to Berkeley and to the commissioners "For my Lord Treasurer's inspection," Longleat, LXXVIII, foll. 3-4).

56. All editions, Lib. 3, Cap. 13, sec. 745, 391a.

57. *The Statutes of the Realm,* Printed by Command of His Majesty King George the Third, II (1816), 478-479. The commissioners may also have had a copy of Coke's *Third Part of the Institutes of the Laws of England* (London, 1644). *Cf.* Cap. 1, p. 12, of this work with the commissioners' comment on the assembly's bill of attainder condemning William Hunt after his death, in their "Exact Repertory of the General and Personal Grievances Presented to Us," C. O. 5/1371, p. 343; the act of assembly is in Hening, *Statutes,* II, 375-377.

58. Despite the commissioners' condemnation of Berkeley's actions in putting down the rebellion and seizing rebel property, he was undoubtedly justified in law and, indeed, might have used more extreme methods than he did. See, for example, George Webb, *The Office and Authority of a Justice of Peace...Collected from the Common and Statute Laws of England, and Acts of Assembly, now in Force; And adapted to the Constitution and Practice of Virginia* (Williamsburg, 1736), s.v. "Treasons" and "Attainder and Conviction."

Chapter 8

1. Jeffreys to Secretary of State Henry Coventry, Feb. 14, 1677, in the Henry Coventry Papers at Longleat, estate of the Marquis of Bath (hereafter cited as Longleat), LXXVII, fol. 403; memorandum of Samuel Wiseman, the commissioners' clerk, that on Feb. 11 Jeffreys "came up" to Swann's Point, in Colonial Office, Series 5, Vol. 1371, p. 70, in Public Record Office, London (hereafter cited as C. O. 5/1371, etc.). Lady Berkeley, who had left Virginia early in June 1676, returned from England with Colonel Jeffreys (Berkeley to Coventry, Feb. 9, 1677, Longleat, LXXVII, fol. 384; Berkeley to Moryson, Feb. 11, 1677, C. O. 5/1371, pp. 69-70).

2. King's warrant to the attorney general, Nov. 7, 1676, to prepare Jeffrey's commission, C. O. 389/6, p. 122; Jeffreys' commission, Nov. 11, 1676, *Virginia Magazine*, 14 (1907), 356-359.

3. Jeffreys to Coventry, Feb. 14, 1677, Longleat, LXXVII, fol. 403.

4. Memorandum, C. O. 5/1371, p. 83; full abstract in W. Noel Sainsbury and J. W. Fortescue, eds., *Calendar of State Papers, Colonial Series, America and West Indies, 1677-1680* (London, 1896), no. 60 (hereafter cited as *Cal. State Papers, Colonial*). The "conveniency" phrase mentioned by Jeffreys does not appear in his commission as printed in the *Virginia Magazine*, 14 (1907), 356-359.

5. Commission to Berkeley and council, Nov. 16, 1676, *Virginia Magazine*, 17 (1909), 349-351.

6. Commissioners to Coventry, Feb. 14, 1677, Longleat, LXXVII, fol. 401; copy in C. O. 5/1371, pp. 90-94.

7. C. O. 5/1371, pp. 78-80; copy in Longleat, LXXVII, fol. 400.

8. C. O. 5/1371, pp. 81-82; copy in Longleat, LXXVII, fol. 397.

9. Longleat, LXXVII, fol. 424.

10. Longleat, LXXVII, fol. 424. Captain Samuel Swann was the son of Colonel Thomas Swann, and the husband of Sarah, daughter of the rebel leader William Drummond (*Virginia Magazine*, 28 [1920], 30-31).

11. Moryson to Berkeley, Feb. 23, 1677, Longleat, LXXVII, fol. 425.

12. Longleat, LXXVII, fol. 425.

13. *Virginia Magazine*, 14 (1907), 271-277; the letter is also printed in H. R. McIlwaine, ed., *Journals of the House of Burgesses of Virginia, 1619-1658/59* (Richmond, 1915), pp. 90-93.

14. McIlwaine, *Journals of the House of Burgesses, 1619-1658/59*, p. 94.

15. *Ibid.*, pp. 70, 89.

16. William W. Hening, *The Statutes at Large ... A Collection of All the Laws of Virginia* (Richmond, [etc.], 1819-1823), II, 366-386.

17. See, for example, the declaration of William Randolph of Turkey Island, Nov. 19, 1677, in Clayton Torrence, ed., *The Edward Pleasants Valentine Papers, Abstracts of Records in the local and general Archives of Virginia* (Richmond, [1927]), III, 1377-78.

18. See earlier, pp. 60-62, 66-67.

19. Commissioners' "True and Faithful Account in what Condition we found Your Majesty's Colony," C. O. 5/1371, p. 424; Governor Berkeley's list of those executed during the rebellion, in Peter Force, ed., *Tracts and Other Papers Relating Principally to the Origin, Settlement, and Progress of the Colonies in North America* (Washington, 1836-1846), I, no. 10; the record of courts-martial and civil trials in Hening, *Statutes*, II, 545-558; Mrs. An. Cotton's "An Account of our late Troubles in Virginia," in Force, *Tracts*, I, no. 9; "The History of Bacon's and Ingram's Rebellion," or Burwell MS., in Charles McLean Andrews, ed., *Narratives of the Insurrections, 1675-1690* (New York, 1915), pp. 45-98; and Berkeley's letter of Feb. 2, 1677, to Secretary Coventry, Longleat, LXXVII, foll. 350-355. Edward D. Neill, *Virginia Carolorum: The Colony under the Rule of Charles the First and Second, A.D. 1625-A.D. 1685* (Albany, 1886), pp. 373-378, lists the twenty-three executed. Neill's figure is probably correct, but one omission and one addition should be made to his list. Professor Frank Pierce Brent, in his paper "Some unpublished facts relating to Bacon's rebellion on the Eastern Shore of Virginia," in Virginia Historical Society, *Collections*, new ser., Vol. XI (Richmond, 1892), 185, quotes the petition of Mrs. Ione Occahone, whose husband " 'justly suffered death by the law' " for his rebellion. Berkeley granted her petition for relief from her husband's creditors on Jan. 11, 1677. He should be added to the list of those executed. On the other hand, one of those condemned by Berkeley and the commissioners, Robert Jones, was later pardoned by Berkeley at the request of Colonel Moryson (See later, p. 120).

20. Charles Campbell, *History of the Colony and Ancient Dominion of Virginia* (Philadelphia, 1860), p. 321.

21. For example, Sands Knowles, a rebel of Kingston Parish, Gloucester County, was captured Oct. 20, 1676, and his property confiscated for the use of the loyalist troops. Knowles was excepted from Governor

Berkeley's pardon of Feb. 10, 1677, and remained a prisoner until March 15, 1677. After he was released from jail in March, he "laid hold of his Majesty's most Gracious Pardon" and, with the help of the commissioners, demanded the return of his property (commissioners' "Exact Repertory of the General and Personal Grievances Presented to us," C. O. 5/1371, pp. 346, 352; proceedings of a civil court of March 15, 1677, Hening, *Statutes*, II, 552-553).

22. Commissioners to Berkeley, March 21, 1677, C. O. 5/1371, pp. 126-129; copy in Longleat, LXXVIII, fol. 12.

23. Berkeley to commissioners, March 7, 1677, C. O. 5/1371, pp. 123-124. The "Act of Attainder," prepared and passed by the assembly of February 1677 which was then still in session, specifically ordered that the estates of those attainted should only be inventoried until the King's pleasure was known (Hening, *Statutes*, II, 377). Colonel Edward Hill reported in his "Defense" against the Charles City County grievances that he was ordered by Governor Berkeley, following the publication of the proclamations of pardon on February 10, 1677, to "seiz Inventory, and secure" the estates of four named rebels, "which I accordingly did" (*Virginia Magazine*, 2 [1896], 343). Berkeley, as the King's governor, exercised control over the disposition of the seized estates. On March 31, 1677, for example, he authorized the York County court, "being at present destitute of a House to Keepe Court in...to keepe Court in the house lately belonging to Thomas Hansford, whose Estate for his rebellion and treason is forfeited to his sacred Majestie and the said Magistrates be thus permitted till further order" (York County Court MS volume, "Deeds, Orders, Wills, etc., No. 6, 1677 to 1684," p. 5).

24. C. O. 5/1371, p. 178.

25. C. O. 5/1371, pp. 180-181.

26. Grievances submitted by Isle of Wight, Nansemond, and Henrico counties, and commissioners' comments, in commissioners' "Exact Repertory of the General and Personal Grievances Presented to us," C. O. 5/1371, pp. 321, 329; McIlwaine, *Journals of the House of Burgesses, 1659/60-1693*, p. 102.

27. The sixty pounds of tobacco tax had been levied in the years immediately preceding the rebellion to send agents to London to fight Charles II's 1673 grant of all of Virginia's lands, rents, and powers of government to Henry, Earl of Arlington, and Thomas, Lord Culpeper, Baron of Thorsway. The grant is printed in Hening, *Statutes*, II, 569-578. It followed an earlier grant of the land lying between the Rap-

pahannock and Potomac rivers to other favorites. This grant had caused similar concern in Virginia, especially to those persons already living in the area. It must be said that many of the people seem to have been genuinely ignorant of the necessity for the tax to support the Virginia agents. The petitions from both Gloucester and Surry counties, for example, implied that the tax was a cheat and a fraud, the Gloucester petition even doubting the existence of the Arlington-Culpeper grant. The Gloucester County petition is in C. O. 1/39, no. 94. The commissioners' summary of it, with their answers to the grievances, is printed in *Virginia Magazine*, 2 (1894), 166-169. The Surry County petition is printed in *Virginia Magazine*, 2 (1894), 170-173. The commissioners' summary of it, with their answers to the grievances, is in C. O. 5/1371, p. 306.

28. Commissioners' "True and Faithful Account in what Condition we found Your Majesty's Colony," C. O. 5/1371, p. 427, printed in John Daly Burk, *The History of Virginia* (Petersburg, 1804-1805), II, 259.

29. "A Remonstrace [*sic*] of the Grand Assembly," April 1642, Hening, *Statutes*, I, 237; act of the assembly of November 1645, Hening, *Statutes*, I, 305-306; recommendation of Berkeley and council to house of burgesses, Sept. 16, 1663, McIlwaine, *Journals of the House of Burgesses, 1659/60-1693*, p. 24; Philip Alexander Bruce, *Institutional History of Virginia in the Seventeenth Century* (New York, 1910), II, 540-542.

30. Moryson's dedication of the laws of the assembly to Governor Berkeley, in *The Lawes of Virginia Now in Force* (London, 1662).

31. Hening, *Statutes*, II, 45.

32. *Ibid.*, p. 25.

33. Moryson and Berry to Williamson, Feb. 2, 1677, Longleat, LXXVII, fol. 364. See chap. vii, footnote 20.

34. Hening, *Statutes*, II, 23, 106, 398; Bruce, *Institutional History*, II, 435-449.

35. Commissioners' "Exact Repertory of the General and Personal Grievances Presented to us," C. O. 5/1371, pp. 305-306.

36. Act of assembly of March 1643, Hening, *Statutes*, I, 265-267. These regulations were reënacted in the 1662 revisal of the laws (Hening, *Statutes*, II, 143-146).

37. Commissioners' "Exact Repertory of the General and Personal Grievances Presented to us," C. O. 5/1371, p. 296.

38. Rappahannock County grievances, C. O. 5/1371, p. 297.

39. York County grievances and commissioners' answer thereto, C. O. 5/1371, p. 323.

40. C. O. 5/1371, p. 328.

41. Northampton County grievances, *Virginia Magazine*, 2 (1895), 291; also in C. O. 5/1371, p. 311.

42. Isle of Wight grievances and commissioners' answer thereto, C. O. 5/1371, pp. 316-319. The grievances have been printed in McIlwaine, *Journals of the House of Burgesses, 1659/60-1693*, pp. 101-104; in the *Virginia Magazine*, 2 (1895), 380-392; and in Merrill Jensen, ed., *American Colonial Documents to 1776* (New York, 1955), no. 94.

43. Isle of Wight County opposing grievances, Winder Transcripts, II, 175-179, Virginia State Library, Richmond.

44. McIlwaine, *Journals of the House of Burgesses, 1659/60-1693*, p. 88; county records quoted in John Bennett Boddie, *Seventeenth Century Isle of Wight County, Virginia* (Chicago, 1938), p. 164.

45. Winder Transcripts, II, 175-179 (opposing grievances), and 179-188 (grievances), Virginia State Library, Richmond. The *Virginia Magazine* also omits the opposing grievances, and Jensen, reprinting from that magazine, similarly overlooks them. Boddie, in his *Seventeenth Century Isle of Wight*, pp. 150-163, prints both petitions.

46. Personal grievances abstracted in *Virginia Magazine*, 22 (1914), 54-56, 140.

47. Commissioners' list of "Worthy Sufferers," C. O. 5/1371, p. 354.

48. McIlwaine, *Journals of the House of Burgesses, 1659/60-1693*, p. 79.

49. Sherwood to Williamson, April 13, 1677, C. O. 1/40, no. 43; copy in Winder Transcripts, II, 297-301, Virginia State Library, Richmond.

50. Thomas Jefferson Wertenbaker, *Virginia under the Stuarts* (Princeton, 1914), p. 205.

51. McIlwaine, *Journals of the House of Burgesses, 1659/60-1693*, p. 66; see earlier, p. 56.

52. Longleat, LXXVIII, fol. 19; copy in C. O. 5/1371, pp. 168-175.

53. Copy of Sarah Grindon's petition to the commissioners, unsigned, copied by Samuel Wiseman, clerk of the commissioners, "For my Lord Treasurers Inspection," Longleat, LXXVIII, fol. 6.

54. Berkeley to Thomas Ludwell, July 1, 1676, Longleat, LXXVII, fol. 144.

55. Sarah Grindon's petition, Longleat, LXXVIII, fol. 6.

56. Hening, *Statutes*, II, 371.

57. Commissioners to Thomas Watkins, March 27, 1677, Longleat, LXXVIII, fol. 19. The same assertion is made in the commissioners' letter to Secretary Coventry of same date, Longleat, LXXVIII, fol. 21; copy in C. O. 5/1371, pp. 133-147.

58. Commissioners to Coventry, March 27, 1677, Longleat, LXXVIII, foll. 21-22. My italics.

59. *Ibid.*, fol. 22.

60. Commissioners to Williamson, March 27, 1677, C. O. 1/39, no. 51, fol. 180.

61. Moryson and Berry to Coventry, April 5, 1677, Longleat, LXXVIII, fol. 32; copy in C. O. 5/1371, pp. 182-187.

62. Jeffreys and Moryson to Thomas Watkins, April 9, 1677, Winder Transcripts, II, 291, Virginia State Library, Richmond; paraphrase in *Cal. State Papers, Colonial, 1677-1680*, no. 173. The phrase "bring us to Cuddy Cuddy" means, in all probability, "make asses of us." See the *Oxford English Dictionary*, s.v. "Cuddy," (3), 1b.

63. Commissioners to Coventry, April 13, 1677, Longleat, LXXVIII, fol. 38.

64. Sherwood to Williamson, April 13, 1677, C. O. 1/40, no. 43, fol. 51.

65. Ludwell to Coventry, April 14, 1677, Longleat, LXXVIII, foll. 40-41; identical letter to Williamson, C. O. 1/40, no. 45.

66. C. O. 5/1371, pp. 208-211.

67. Commissioners to Berkeley, April 23, 1677, C. O. 1/40, no. 48.

68. Berkeley to commissioners, April 23, 1677, C. O. 1/40, no. 49; Lady Berkeley to commissioners, April 23, 1677, C. O. 1/40, no. 50; abstracts of these letters are printed in *Virginia Magazine*, 21 (1913), 369-370.

69. Commissioners to Thomas Watkins, May 4, 1677, C. O. 1/40, no. 66, fol. 131; copy in Winder Transcripts, II, 317-320, Virginia State Library, Richmond.

70. *Virginia Magazine*, 22 (1914), 44-45.

71. Berkeley to Jeffreys, April 28, 1677, Longleat, LXXVIII, fol. 34. The letter is dated April 7 in the Longleat copy but this is an obvious error. The correct date is April 28 as in the Public Record Office copy, C. O. 1/40, no. 54.

72. Jeffreys to Coventry, May 4, 1677, Longleat, LXXVIII, fol. 44. According to Governor Thomas Notley of Maryland, Berkeley left Vir-

ginia on May 5 (Notley to Charles, Lord Baltimore, May 22, 1677, *Cal. State Papers, Colonial, 1677-1680,* no. 263).

73. I have discussed Jeffreys' troubles after the departure of Berkeley in "Bacon's Rebellion, 1676-1677" (Harvard University doct. diss., 1955), chap. xii. Many of the documents concerning Philip Ludwell's denunciation of Jeffreys are printed in *Virginia Magazine,* 18 (1910), 4-18.

74. Berkeley's "Declaration and Remonstrance," May 29, 1676, Longleat, LXXVII, foll. 157-158. For examples of the about-face done by historians, see later, pp. 150-151.

75. Jeffreys to Coventry, May 4, 1677, Longleat, LXXVIII, fol. 44.

76. Jeffreys to "Right Honorable" [Coventry?], April 2, 1678, Longleat, LXXVIII, foll. 216-217.

77. Articles of Peace, May 29, 1677, *Virginia Magazine,* 14 (1907), 289-296; *cf.* especially Art. 4 of the treaty with the preamble to the act of 1662 in Hening, *Statutes,* II, 138-143.

78. Jeffreys to [Secretary Coventry?], June 11, 1677, Longleat, LXXVIII, foll. 64-65.

79. Articles of Peace, May 29, 1677, *Virginia Magazine,* 14 (1907), 291-292.

80. *Ibid.,* 293.

81. Commissioners' "Particular Account how wee ... have observed and Comply'd with our Instructions," C. O. 5/1371, p. 365.

82. Thomas Ludwell to Coventry, Jan. 30, 1678, Longleat, LXXVIII, foll. 202-203.

83. Thomas Ludwell to Coventry, June 28, 1678, Longleat, LXXVIII, fol. 264.

84. Thomas Ludwell to Coventry, Jan. 30, 1678, Longleat, LXXVIII, fol. 202; Thomas Ludwell to "Right Honorable" [Secretary Coventry?], Aug. 3, 1678, Longleat, LXXVIII, fol. 281. A letter of June 8, 1678, expressing sentiments similar to those of Ludwell in these letters, is printed in the *Virginia Magazine,* 5 (1897), 51-52, and described as "Probably from Governor Jeffreys to Sir Joseph Williamson, Secretary of State." The letter is more likely Thomas Ludwell's.

85. Council chamber proceedings, Oct. 19, 1677, McDonald Transcripts, V, 184-185, in Virginia State Library, Richmond.

86. By inference from the letters written following their receipt, the letters which arrived at this time were those written in the period February 1-14, 1677.

87. Pepys to Werden, April 18, 1677, and April 23, 1677, in J. R. Tanner, ed., *A Descriptive Catalogue of the Naval Manuscripts in the Pepysian Library at Magdalene College, Cambridge*, III [Publications of the Navy Records Society, XXXVI] (London, 1909), nos. 3879, 3892.

88. Coventry to Thynne, April 21, 1677, Longleat, V, fol. 151.

89. Letters of March 27, 1677, carried by Captain Grantham, as reported in Thomas Watkins to Secretary Coventry, May 7, 1677, Longleat, LXXVIII, fol. 48; see also Watkins to Coventry of same date, Longleat, LXXVIII, fol. 46, and Admiralty Journal of May 8, 1677, in Tanner, *Descriptive Catalogue*, IV, 417.

90. Undated notes in Coventry's hand, Longleat, LXXVII, fol. 449.

91. *Ibid.*, fol. 448.

92. C. O. 5/1371, pp. 542-544.

93. Abstract in *Virginia Magazine*, 22 (1914), 52.

94. Abstract in *Virginia Magazine*, 22 (1914), 54.

95. Charles II to Jeffreys, May 15, 1677, C. O. 389/6, pp. 202-203; printed in Hening, *Statutes*, II, 428-430, with incomplete date.

96. C. O. 389/6, pp. 194-198; abstract in *Virginia Magazine*, 22 (1914), 53.

Chapter 9

1. Secretary of State Henry Coventry to Berkeley, June 16, 1677, abstract in *Virginia Magazine*, 22 (1914), 142; undated petition of Berkeley to the King, in Colonial Office, Series 1, Vol. 40, no. 110, in Public Record Office, London (hereafter cited as C. O. 1/40, etc.). There is a full summary in W. Noel Sainsbury and J. W. Fortescue, eds., *Calendar of State Papers, Colonial Series, America and West Indies, 1677-1680* (London, 1896), no. 304 (hereafter cited as *Cal. State Papers, Colonial*).

2. *Dictionary of American Biography* and *Dictionary of National Biography*, s.v. "Berkeley, Sir William."

3. Coventry to Lieutenant Governor Jeffreys, Aug. 6, 1677, C. O. 389/6, p. 213; abstract in *Virginia Magazine*, 22 (1914), 232-233.

4. T. M. [Thomas Mathew], "The Beginning, Progress and Conclusion of Bacons Rebellion in Virginia in the Years 1675 and 1676" [1705], in Charles McLean Andrews, ed., *Narratives of the Insurrections, 1675-1690* (New York, 1915), p. 40. The expression about the King's remark may

have originated in Virginia from a comment of the commissioners when they were angered by Berkeley's intransigency. In a letter to their agent Thomas Watkins on February 10, 1677, the commissioners reported that Berkeley had hanged or intended to hang more persons than Charles II had for the death of his father (C. O. 1/39, no. 32, fol. 66). It is possible that the commissioners made the same remark to some of their Virginia acquaintances. After thirty years it would be easy to credit the expression directly to the King. It is a significant commentary on the assumptions historians carry to their work that almost all use Mathew's remark of 1705 while almost none use Robert Beverley's remark of the same year, in his *The History and Present State of Virginia*, ed. Louis B. Wright (Chapel Hill, 1947), p. 86 (Bk. I, chap. iv, sec. 114), that the King said he was well satisfied with Berkeley's conduct in Virginia.

5. See earlier, pp. 136-138.

6. See earlier, pp. 107-108.

7. Rough Journal of the Lords of Trade and Plantations, Aug. 2, 1677, pp. 145-146, Library of Congress, Washington; the rough journal supplements the formal entry-book journal in the Public Record Office, London, in this case, C. O. 391/2, pp. 100-101. The day before the meeting a merchantman arrived from Virginia with a letter from Colonel Jeffreys, dated June 11, 1677, recounting his troubles and enclosing Berkeley's blistering letter of April 28 to him denouncing his "irresistible desire to rule" (Thomas Watkins to Secretary Sir Joseph Williamson, Aug. 1, 1677, *Cal. State Papers, Colonial, 1677-1680*, no. 376). The significance of the personnel present and absent at the meetings held to discuss Virginia in this period is discussed in Wilcomb E. Washburn, "Bacon's Rebellion, 1676-1677," (Harvard University doct. diss., 1955), chap. xiii. In general, it can be said that Coventry, who might have been sympathetic to Berkeley, was forced by illness to be absent from most of the meetings at which decisions affecting the governor's reputation were made, while Williamson and Lord Treasurer Danby, who were probably inclined against Berkeley, were usually present at these meetings.

8. Berry and Moryson to Coventry, Aug. 22, 1677, in the Henry Coventry Papers at Longleat, estate of the Marquis of Bath (hereafter cited as Longleat), V, fol. 198; the King's orders not to return until authorization had been received are mentioned in Berry to Sir John Werden, secretary to the Duke of York, Feb. 2, 1677, C. O. 5/1371, p. 36. Berry's insubordination was not only allowed but commended by the King and the Lords of the Admiralty (Admiralty Journal, Aug. 25, 1677, in J. R.

Tanner, ed., *A Descriptive Catalogue of the Naval Manuscripts in the Pepysian Library at Magdalene College, Cambridge*, IV [Publications of the Navy Records Society, LVII] [London, 1923], 487).

9. See listing in *Cal. State Papers, Colonial, 1677-1680*, nos. 433-439.

10. Journal of the Lords of Trade and Plantations, Aug. 9, 1677, and Oct. 25, 1677, C. O. 391/2, pp. 105-106, 137-139; abstracts in *Cal. State Papers, Colonial, 1677-1680*, nos. 388, 457. See also the certificate of Lord Berkeley, Nov. 19, 1677, that he employed Mr. [Alexander] Culpeper to view the Virginia papers and take copies of such as most concerned his deceased brother, abstracted in *Virginia Magazine*, 23 (1915), 26.

11. For an extended treatment of her petition, see Wilcomb E. Washburn, "The Humble Petition of Sarah Drummond," *William and Mary Quarterly*, 3d ser., 13 (July 1956), 354-375.

12. Mrs. Drummond's second petition is discussed at length in Washburn, "Bacon's Rebellion, 1676-1677" (Harvard University doct. diss., 1955), chap. xii. Some of the source material is printed in the *Virginia Magazine*, 22 (1914), 239-243, and all of it is located in the Public Record Office in the following sources: C. O. 1/39, no. 51; C. O. 1/40, nos. 78, 79; C. O. 1/41, nos. 76, 96; C. O. 5/1355, pp. 192-197; C. O. 5/1371, pp. 149-159; C. O. 391/2, pp. 132-139.

13. Moryson to Thomas Ludwell, Nov. 2, 1677, in Manuscript No. 6, "Virginia. Miscellaneous Records, 1606-1692" ("The Bland Manuscript"), Jefferson Collection, Library of Congress, pp. 335-339. It is printed in John Daly Burk, *The History of Virginia* (Petersburg, 1804-1805), II, 265-269, with the date incorrectly transcribed as Nov. 28.

14. See earlier, pp. 77-78.

15. Berkeley to militia officers of Lower Norfolk County, Nov. 4, 1676; petition of militia officers of Lower Norfolk County to Berkeley, Jan. 17, 1677, and his answer, in *William and Mary Quarterly*, 1st ser., 3 (1895), 163-164.

16. *Virginia Magazine*, 23 (1915), 24-25.

17. Journal of the Lords of Trade and Plantations, Nov. 8, 1677, C. O. 391/2, pp. 146-148; abstract in *Virginia Magazine*, 23 (1915), 25.

18. Journal of the Lords of Trade and Plantations, Dec. 4, 1677, C. O. 391/2, pp. 170-172; abstract in *Virginia Magazine*, 23 (1915), 28.

19. Fairfax Harrison, "Proprietors of the Northern Neck," *Virginia Magazine*, 33 (1925), 354. Culpeper was sometimes designated "Captain" instead of "Colonel."

20. The original of the "Answer" is in C. O. 1/41, no. 119. There is a copy in C. O. 5/1355, pp. 230-239. The document is printed in Burk, *History of Virginia*, II, 259-264, and the *Virginia Magazine*, 6 (1898), 139-144. The Burk and *Virginia Magazine* copies show important variations from the Public Record Office documents.

21. Burk, II, 261-262; *Virginia Magazine*, 6 (1898), 142.

22. Burk, II, 263-264. This sentence is omitted in the original in C. O. 1/41, no. 119, and in the copy in C. O. 5/1355, pp. 230-239. How it came to be in the Randolph MS. (now in the Virginia Historical Society, Richmond) and in the Bland MS. (now in the Jefferson Collection, Library of Congress) from which the *Virginia Magazine* and Burk versions were taken is not known. On the day the "Answer" was presented, December 4, 1677, Culpeper asked permission to alter some expressions in the paper, "but their Lordships think fit that it be farther consider'd at the next meeting, whether after reading, in presence of the Commissioners (who are cheifly concerned) it bee proper to permit any alteration of it" (Rough Journal of the Lords of Trade and Plantations, Library of Congress). Culpeper may have added the sentence later.

23. Burk, II, 261.

24. Burk, II, 262-264.

25. Rough Journal of the Lords of Trade and Plantations, Dec. 4, 1677, p. 275, Library of Congress, Washington.

26. Memorandum on subject, C. O. 1/41, no. 122; abstract in *Virginia Magazine*, 23 (1915), 31.

27. Journal of the Lords of Trade and Plantations, Dec. 6, 1677, C. O. 391/2, pp. 173-179; abstract in *Virginia Magazine*, 23 (1915), 29-30.

28. List of the members of the council of Virginia prepared by Berry and Moryson for the Lords of Trade and Plantations, undated, C. O. 1/41, no. 121, foll. 278-279. The editors of *Cal. State Papers, Colonial, 1677-1680*, no. 510, think the marginal comments may be in the hand of William Blathwayt, secretary to the Lords of Trade and Plantations.

29. C. O. 1/41, no. 121, foll. 278-280. There seems little reason to doubt that Virginia's governors legally had the power to exercise martial law in time of rebellion. See Washburn, "The Humble Petition of Sarah Drummond," *William and Mary Quarterly*, 3d ser., 13 (July 1956), 366-367. If one condemns Berkeley's action in trying by court-martial and hanging those who tried to capture or kill him in their rebellion against the government, what must one say about Lord Culpeper, Berkeley's successor, who hanged two men for "treason" for demonstrating against ex-

cessive tobacco production by "plant-cutting"? See Culpeper's report on Virginia, Sept. 20, 1683, *Virginia Magazine*, 3 (1896), 226-231.

30. Journal of the Lords of Trade and Plantations, Dec. 11, 1677, C. O. 391/2, pp. 180-181; abstract in *Virginia Magazine*, 23 (1915), 31-32.

31. Order of the King in Council, Jan. 18, 1678, C. O. 5/1355, pp. 222-229; copy in McDonald Transcripts, V, 212-217, Virginia State Library, Richmond. See also the report of the Lords of Trade to the King in Council, Jan. 18, 1678, in W. L. Grant and James Munro, eds., *Acts of the Privy Council of England, Colonial Series*, Vol. I: *A.D. 1613-1680* (Hereford, England, 1908), no. 1198.

32. Lieutenant Governor Jeffreys, Culpeper's deputy after Berkeley's death, had died on December 18, 1678. (Sir Henry Chicheley to Secretary Coventry, Jan. 1, 1679, Longleat, LXXVIII, fol. 331.)

33. William W. Hening, *The Statutes at Large ... A Collection of All the Laws of Virginia* (Richmond, [etc.], 1819-1823), II, 458-464.

34. Robert Beverley, *History and Present State of Virginia*, ed. Louis B. Wright, p. 88 (Bk. I, chap. iv, sec. 118).

35. Hening, *Statutes*, II, 461.

36. Concerning the right to withhold the King's pardon, see earlier, pp. 107-110. The commissioners' stand on the right of the loyalists to sue the rebels is not entirely consistent. Sometimes they asserted that the loyalists might bring legal actions in the courts to recover goods stolen from them. However, when Philip Ludwell, in accordance with an act of the assembly of February 1677, attempted to sue Gregory Walklett, one of the rebels who had plundered his estate, Lieutenant Governor Jeffreys, on grounds which seem totally unconvincing, granted a protection to Walklett and prevented Ludwell from examining witnesses to prove the trespass. Ludwell thereupon denounced Jeffreys as "a pitiful Little Fellow with a perriwig" who had "broke more Laws in Six Months time than Sir William Berkeley Did in 35 Years Government...." If the courts allowed Jeffreys' protection to stand, said Ludwell, "they must allow and own the said Governor to rule by an Arbitrary power." Jeffreys not only prevented Ludwell from recovering his property, but ordered him tried for "scandalizing the Governor by saying that he was perjured and had broke several Laws." The details of this significant case are discussed in Washburn, "Bacon's Rebellion, 1676-1677" (Harvard University doct. diss., 1955), chap. xii. Many of the documents concerning the case are printed in the *Virginia Magazine*, 18 (1910), 5-24. Jeffreys, in a letter to Secretary of State Henry Coventry, admitted closing the courts of the colony for an

unspecified period of time in disgust at the assembly's act allowing loy-alists to sue rebels (see earlier, p. 134).

37. Journal of the Lords of Trade and Plantations, Feb. 6, 1679, C. O. 391/2, pp. 29-30; paraphrase in *Cal. State Papers, Colonial, 1677-1680*, no. 881.

38. See earlier, pp. 87-91, and Washburn, "The Humble Petition of Sarah Drummond," *William and Mary Quarterly*, 3d ser., 13 (July 1956), 364-365.

39. Commissioners' "Narrative," in Andrews, *Narratives*, p. 140.

40. See earlier, pp. 109-110, and footnote 21 of chap. viii.

41. Journal of the Lords of Trade and Plantations, Feb. 10, 1679, C. O. 391/2, pp. 305-306.

42. Hening, *Statutes*, II, 458-464.

43. Chicheley to "My Lord" [Thomas, Lord Culpeper], July 13, 1679, Longleat, LXXVIII, fol. 396. Nicholas Spencer, who succeeded Philip Ludwell as secretary of the council of state of Virginia, expressed himself in almost identical terms in a letter to Secretary Coventry, July 14, 1679, Longleat, LXXVIII, fol. 398.

44. Burk, *History of Virginia*, II, 222. Philip Alexander Bruce, in his *Institutional History of Virginia in the Seventeenth Century* (New York, 1910), II, 494-495, makes a similar about-face.

45. Lyon G. Tyler, "Virginia as a Royal Province, 1624-1763," Chap. ii of *The South in the Building of the Nation* [*The History of the Southern States*, I] (Richmond, 1909), p. 33.

46. *Virginia under the Stuarts* (Princeton, 1914), pp. 223-224.

47. Lyon G. Tyler, news article, printed in *Tyler's Quarterly Historical and Genealogical Magazine*, 23 (1941), 47.

48. Patricia Holbert Menk, "The Origins and Growth of Party Politics in Virginia, 1660-1705" (University of Virginia doct. diss., 1945), pp. 40-41.

49. Longleat, LXXVII, foll. 157-158.

Chapter 10

1. William Sherwood to Secretary of State Sir Joseph Williamson, June 28, 1676, in *Virginia Magazine*, 1 (1893), 171.

2. Morris Zucker, *The Philosophy of American History: Periods in American History* (New York, 1945), p. 211.

3. John Fiske, *Old Virginia and her Neighbours* (Boston, 1897), II, 104. Bernard Bailyn, in a paper entitled "Politics and Social Structure: Virginia in the Seventeenth Century" prepared for the Symposium on Seventeenth-Century Colonial History, Williamsburg, Virginia, April 8-12, 1957, makes a perceptive analysis of the class antagonisms existing at the time. He sees, on the one hand, the "numerically predominant ordinary planters" protesting against the "recently acquired superiority of the leading county families." On the other hand, Bailyn sees a parallel attack by "the dominant local leaders against the prerogatives recently acquired by the province elite, prerogatives linked to officialdom and centered in the Council." That these oppositions existed I have pointed out. That they express "deeper elements" than the more "immediate causes" of "race relations and settlement policy," as Bailyn believes, I deny.

4. Wesley Frank Craven, *The Southern Colonies in the Seventeenth Century, 1607-1689* (Baton Rouge, 1949), pp. 360-361.

5. This comment refers to Bacon and his friends.

6. See later, pp. 157-158.

7. Robert Beverley, *The History and Present State of Virginia* [1705], ed. Louis B. Wright (Chapel Hill, 1947), p. 74 (Bk. I, chap. iv, sec. 92).

8. *Ibid.*, p. 78 (Bk. I, chap. iv, sec. 96).

9. See earlier, p. 109.

10. Ludwell to Williamson, April 14, 1677, Colonial Office, Series 1, Vol. 40, no. 45, in Public Record Office, London (hereafter cited as C. O. 1/40, etc.).

11. *Ibid.*

12. Postscript of Richard Lee to letter of Isaac Allerton to Thomas Ludwell, Aug. 4, 1676, in the Henry Coventry Papers at Longleat, estate of the Marquis of Bath (hereafter cited as Longleat), LXXVII, fol. 161.

13. See later, p. 164.

14. Goode reported the dialogue to Governor Berkeley on January 30, 1677. There are two copies of this document, one in C. O. 5/1371, pp. 232-240, in the Public Record Office, London, and the other in Longleat, LXXVII, foll. 347-348, both in the hand of Samuel Wiseman, clerk of the commissioners. The document is printed in Fiske, *Old Virginia*, II, 83-86.

15. Craven, *Southern Colonies in the Seventeenth Century*, p. 389 n.

16. *William and Mary Quarterly*, 3d ser., 14 (July, 1957), 406.

17. H. R. McIlwaine, *Journals of the House of Burgesses of Virginia, 1619-1658/59* (Richmond, 1915), p. 76; also in *Virginia Magazine*, 1 (1893), 77.

18. McIlwaine, *Journals of the House of Burgesses, 1619-1658/59*, pp. 76-78.

19. The documents bearing on Berkeley's acceptance are in the MS. volume entitled "Virginia. Instructions, Commicions, Letters of Advice and Admonitions..." [1606-1680], pp. 142-160, in the Jefferson Collection, Library of Congress, Washington. They were transcribed by Peter Force, sent to the editor of the *Southern Literary Messenger*, and printed in that publication, 11 (January 1845), 1-5. A small amount of additional information on the election of Governor Berkeley is contained in William W. Hening, *The Statutes at Large ... A Collection of All the Laws of Virginia* (Richmond, [etc.], 1819-1823), I, 5, 530-531, 544-545. For secondary interpretations of this much disputed episode, see Craven, *Southern Colonies in the Seventeenth Century*, pp. 264-265, and Thomas Jefferson Wertenbaker, *Virginia under the Stuarts* (Princeton, 1914), pp. 109-113.

20. Thomas Ludwell to Henry Bennet, Lord Arlington, Sept. 16, 1666, *Virginia Magazine*, 21 (1913), 37.

21. Virginia council to the King, received Oct. 11, 1673, *Virginia Magazine*, 20 (1912), 236-237.

22. Francis Moryson, "Virginia Heads to be presented to the Ministers of State and to the Right Honorable the Lords the Commity for forraine plantations," undated, Longleat, LXXVII, fol. 48. Printed with slight differences in Hening, *Statutes*, II, 527.

23. Thomas Jefferson Wertenbaker, *Patrician and Plebeian in Virginia, or the Origin and Development of Social Classes in the Old Dominion* (Charlottesville, 1910), p. 144, cites the years 1660-1676 as "a period of oppression." Most writers see Berkeley gradually becoming oppressive in this period.

24. C. O. 1/36, no. 64, fol. 137. See earlier, pp. 41-42.

25. Longleat, LXXVII, foll. 157-158. See earlier, p. 47.

26. McIlwaine, *Journals of the House of Burgesses, 1659/60-1693*, p. 66. See earlier, p. 56.

27. Thomas Jefferson Wertenbaker, *Torchbearer of the Revolution: The Story of Bacon's Rebellion and Its Leader* (Princeton, 1940), pp. v-vi.

28. Charles Campbell, *History of the Colony and Ancient Dominion of Virginia* (Philadelphia, 1860), p. 298.

29. Fiske, *Old Virginia*, II, 107.

30. Armistead C. Gordon, "The Laws of Bacon's Assembly. An address delivered before the Beta of Virginia Chapter of the Phi Beta Kappa Society at the University of Virginia, June 17, 1914," University of Virginia, *Alumni Bulletin*, 3d ser., 8 (1914), 573.

31. John Daly Burk, *The History of Virginia* (Petersburg, 1804-1805), II, 193.

32. In my doctoral dissertation entitled "Bacon's Rebellion, 1676-1677," Harvard University, 1955, chap. xiv, I have attempted to prove these assertions by a detailed examination of the land records and court records as they pertain to the leaders on both sides. Rebels who possessed large estates include William Drummond, Richard Lawrence, Charles Scarborough, William Kendall, William Byrd I, Giles Brent, Thomas Goodrich, and Giles Bland.

33. Thomas Ludwell to Secretary Coventry, Jan. 30, 1678, Longleat, LXXVIII, fol. 204. See also Wilcomb E. Washburn, *Virginia under Charles I and Cromwell* [Jamestown 350th Anniversary Historical Booklet, Number 7] (Williamsburg, 1957).

34. Fairfax Harrison, *Virginia Land Grants: A Study in Conveyancing in Relation to Colonial Politics* (Richmond, 1925), pp. 31-32, 139 n., 141 n. See also Berkeley to Secretary Williamson, April 1, 1676, C. O. 1/36, no. 36, fol. 66.

35. Manning C. Voorhis, "Crown versus Council in the Virginia Land Policy," *William and Mary Quarterly*, 3d ser., 3 (1946), 502.

36. Harrison, *Virginia Land Grants*, pp. 42-59.

37. Thomas Ludwell to Secretary Coventry, Jan. 30, 1678, Longleat, LXXVIII, fol. 202. My italics.

38. C. O. 5/1371, p. 425.

39. *Virginia Magazine*, 14 (1907), 291.

40. Moryson to Coventry, Sept. 6, 1676, Longleat, LXXVII, fol. 205.

41. Commissioners' "Exact Repertory of the General and Personal Grievances Presented to us," C. O. 5/1371, p. 321.

42. Richard Hildreth, *The History of the United States of America from the Discovery of the Continent to the Organization of Government under the Federal Constitution* (New York, 1849), I, 556.

43. Roy Harvey Pearce, *The Savage of America: A Study of the Indian and the Idea of Civilization* (Baltimore, 1953), *passim*.

44. Thomas Perkins Abernethy, *Three Virginia Frontiers* (University, La., 1940), p. 24.

45. McIlwaine, *Journals of the House of Burgesses, 1659/60-1693*, p. 65.

46. *Ibid.*, pp. 73-74.

47. *Ibid.* The Burwell MS. states that Bacon, on his deathbed, called for Mr. James Wadding, the minister who had previously, at Gloucester courthouse in September 1676, urged others not to take Bacon's oath. Bacon had at that time committed him to the guard, telling him he might say what he pleased in church, but could say no more in camp than what pleased him (Bacon), unless he could fight better than he could preach (Charles McLean Andrews, ed., *Narratives of the Insurrections, 1675-1690* [New York, 1915], p. 74).

48. C. O. 5/1371, p. 322.

49. Winder Transcripts, II, 177-178, Virginia State Library, Richmond.

Essay on the Sources

1. I expect to discuss the matter in my introduction to the collection of documents on Bacon's Rebellion which I am preparing for the Virginia Historical Society. See also earlier, pp. viii-ix.

2. Sherwood to Secretary Williamson, April 13, 1677, C. O. 1/40, no. 43, fol. 51.

3. *Ibid.* For Sherwood's criminal record, see his letters to Williamson, June 17, 1671, and April 10, 1672, in *Virginia Magazine*, 20 (1912), 18-19, 128.

4. See earlier, footnote 24 to chap. vi.

Index

Index